We Are
Not
Dreamers

We Are Not Dreamers

Undocumented Scholars Theorize
Undocumented Life in the United States

Edited by
LEISY J. ABREGO AND GENEVIEVE NEGRÓN-GONZALES

Duke University Press   *Durham and London*   2020

© 2020 DUKE UNIVERSITY PRESS. All rights reserved.
Designed by Courtney Leigh Baker
Typeset in Whitman by Westchester Publishing Services
Printed and bound by CPI Group (UK) Ltd, Croydon, CR0 4YY

Library of Congress Cataloging-in-Publication Data
Names: Abrego, Leisy J., editor. | Negrón-Gonzales, Genevieve, editor.
Title: We are not dreamers : undocumented scholars theorize undocumented life in the United States / Leisy J. Abrego, Genevieve Negrón-Gonzales.
Description: Durham : Duke University Press, 2020. | Includes bibliographical references and index.
Identifiers: LCCN 2019047967 (print)
LCCN 2019047968 (ebook)
ISBN 9781478009795 (hardcover)
ISBN 9781478010838 (paperback)
ISBN 9781478012382 (ebook)
Subjects: LCSH: Illegal aliens—Education (Higher)—California. | Children of immigrants—Education—California. | Illegal aliens—California—Social conditions. | Deportation—California. | Adult children of immigrants—California. | Emigration and immigration law—United States. | United States—Emigration and immigration—Social aspects.
Classification: LCC LC3746.5. C2 W44 2020 (print)
LCC LC3746.5.C2 (ebook)
DDC 371.826/91209794—dc23
LC record available at https://lccn.loc.gov/2019047967
LC ebook record available at https://lccn.loc.gov/2019047968

COVER ART: Julio Salgado, *Bigger Than Any Border*. © Julio Salgado.

To the 11 million undocumented immigrants in the United States and to all those who have been displaced from their homes by wars, foreign intervention, and the consequences of neoliberal policies around the world.

Contents

Acknowledgments ix

Introduction 1
LEISY J. ABREGO AND GENEVIEVE NEGRÓN-GONZALES

1
"Other" Borders: The Illegal as Normative Metaphor 23
JOEL SATI

2
"I felt like an embarrassment to the undocumented community":
Undocumented Students Navigating Academic
Probation and Unrealistic Expectations 45
GRECIA MONDRAGÓN

3
Disrupting Diversity: Undocumented Students
in the Neoliberal University 66
GABRIELLE CABRERA

4
American't: Redefining Citizenship in the
U.S. Undocumented Immigrant Youth Movement 87
GABRIELA MONICO

5
Contesting "Citizenship": The Testimonies of Undocumented
Immigrant Activist Women 110
GABRIELA GARCIA CRUZ

6
Undocumented Young Adults' Heightened
Vulnerability in the Trump Era 127
CAROLINA VALDIVIA

7
Beyond Identity: Coming Out as UndocuQueer 146
MARIA LILIANA RAMIREZ

8
Me Vestí De Reina: Trans and Queer Sonic Spatial Entitlement 168
AUDREY SILVESTRE

9
Legalization through Marriage: When Love and Papers Converge 190
LUCÍA LEÓN

10
Undocumented Queer Parenting: Navigating External
and Internal Threats to Family 211
KATY JOSELINE MALDONADO DOMINGUEZ

Appendix: Keywords 235
KATY JOSELINE MALDONADO DOMINGUEZ

Contributors 241

Index 245

Acknowledgments

We would like to thank all the authors who contributed to this volume. We appreciate their insightful research, as well as the trust and patience they gifted us through this process. Each author came to this project with an initial draft of their work, having already benefited from feedback from professors, mentors, and community advisors. We would like to acknowledge the labor of those who supported the authors in earlier versions of the chapters.

Abrego: Thank you, Genevieve, for your friendship and dedication. I remember fondly the morning in 2016 when we met up for breakfast in Oakland to catch up. I shared my idea for a future dream project and without saying anything else, you enthusiastically announced, "I'm in!" And so it became our project. Your brilliance, energy, and vision provide clarity and inspiration that seep through every page of this book. Working with you made this truly a beautiful labor of love. Gracias.

Negrón-Gonzales: I want to thank Leisy for what is now years of professional and personal sisterhood. This book came to fruition through equal parts hard work, visionary imagination, and political clarity. Your ability to hold these in balance, not just in the process of writing this book but in the way you live your life, has made working with you a joy and an honor. Thank you, hermana, for all you do.

We also appreciate the patience and support of our families who made it possible to dedicate time to completing the volume. Jason, Carlos, Mateo, Amado, Mayari, Diego, you make life beautiful and justice worth fighting for.

During her time as an undergraduate student at UCLA, along with contributing an important chapter, Katy Maldonado provided invaluable research assistance for the book. At Duke University Press we feel so fortunate to have worked with Gisela Fosado and Alejandra Mejía. Gisela's warm and enthusiastic support of this project was palpable from our first conversation and at every turn.

LEISY J. ABREGO AND GENEVIEVE NEGRÓN-GONZALES

Introduction

Undocumented students' access to higher education has taken many turns over the last thirty years. A series of legislative and policy fights in California stretch back to the *Leticia A* case in 1985 and culminate, in many ways, in the passage of the California Dream Act in 2011.[1] These wins—secured through the daring activism of undocumented young people and their allies—have not only made possible undocumented students' greater access to higher education, but have also remade the political landscape of the state as a whole (Negrón-Gonzales 2015). And in this remaking, there is another transformation underway that is perhaps less visible, but nonetheless deeply meaningful. As undocumented students enter and graduate from college, and in some cases even pursue an advanced degree, they have begun to speak back to the burgeoning body of literature that has grown alongside this process of increased access. The undocumented young people who have been the "objects" of study are increasingly present in the places, sites, and spaces within which this knowledge is produced. Their work theorizing illegality, citizenship, education, and belonging has the potential to grow the field, shift understandings, and remake the bodies of literature that speak to their experiences. This intervention is profound—both deeply personal and intimately political.

As two Latina professors in California—Salvadoreña and Chicana—we have witnessed these developments and had the honor of working with many of these students. This book emerged from our shared experiences not only of mentoring undocumented students in their research investigating and theorizing different aspects of undocumented life in this country, but also through a shared insight into how uniquely challenging this process can be for them. These are often students we know not just because of their academic lives, but because we have encountered them at protests, rallies, and meetings; they are the leaders who motivate others to fight for change. We have listened to their political analysis and strategic vision from behind the megaphone and recognized their quiet courage in acts of civil disobedience when they make our news feeds. In their everyday lives, they refuse to be defined by the arbitrary and unjust immigration policies of the United States, motivated by an understanding of the global forces that pushed them and their families out of their countries of birth and the knowledge that the United States benefits from their labor and civic contributions. They are, in short, uniquely positioned during a specific historical moment, to think and write about the complexities and nuances of what it means to be undocumented in this country right now.

When they seek our guidance through the research process, it is clear that they envision this research as their chance to talk back to all of the scholarship that has been produced *about* their experiences. Familiar with the discourses and fields of inquiry that theorize their lives and experiences, they demand to be knowledge-producers in that sphere. Many are not only tired of being what they describe at times as the guinea pigs of academia, but are ready to intervene in these scholarly conversations. As undocumented students embark on the process of designing research projects, however, they often hit a roadblock.

We have experienced a dynamic whereby undocumented students begin the writing process—to capture the complexity and complication of the undocumented experience—and find themselves paralyzed when they realize through their writing that they must name the things they work so hard to resist; the laws they deemphasize to be able to navigate and create paths for themselves in higher education stand powerfully on the page, too difficult to ignore. In and through writing, they must come face to face with the institutionalized, legal challenges that have the very real potential to derail them. They are forced to confront the fear that punctuates undocumented life, oftentimes a fear they struggle to quiet.

A 2013 interview Abrego conducted with a college graduate named Sam (pseudonym) exemplifies this dynamic:

> I remember first being depressed [at various moments] and then again in my last year [in college] when I was graduating and thinking about my senior research and then just thinking about being undocumented

every single day. Like, what should I write? What is relevant? . . . I think I was really hard on myself as well, because I felt like there weren't a lot of undocumented folks producing work about undocumented people and so I felt like it had to be right. I got myself in this frame of thinking of like, right or wrong, or like, how would I combat arguments that go against this, and things like that. But that last year thinking about being undocumented every day—which is something that if you're undocumented you know you're undocumented and it impacts all aspects of your life in one way or another—but it's also the thing you try to not think about the most or try to have it not hinder you as much, so you kind of ignore it. But intentionally and actively thinking about it was very heavy . . . just thinking about it every day was a lot.

Of course, there are other barriers. The structural barriers they face may force undocumented students to spend their days working long hours, or commuting long distances daily on inefficient public transportation. Some deal with the emotional weight of the consequences of immigration enforcement in their communities, or are left to pick up the pieces after the deportation of a loved one. They may be unable to focus due to financial worries, or absent from school while searching for care options for ailing parents without health insurance. The structural inequalities created by immigration policies affect all aspects of their lives. In the face of poverty and legal violence (Menjívar and Abrego 2012), many undocumented students come to consider research and writing as luxuries that are out of their reach. Once again, Sam was able to capture these challenges as they affected the research process during the final year of college.

You're thinking, what's going to happen after college? Because being in school does offer a level of security for undocumented folks . . . I know if I'm going to go into work, it's going to be minimum wage . . . I'm going to be exploited on various levels, and there are things that you have to accept in one way or another, or that are at least more difficult to challenge and advocate for [outside of the context of school]. And so there's just so much uncertainty.

As mentors and advisors, we work to support these students through the writing process—a navigation that inevitably involves grappling with their own legal status. Many have published brilliant research. Some, though, even with exceptional research projects, have struggled with putting their work and their words out into the world, deeply hindered by the emotional challenges required by the process to document the complicated web of (il)legality, educational opportunity, the carceral state, and the deportation regime.

Understanding these unique challenges, we have recruited ten undocumented, DACAmented, or recently formerly undocumented students in California, to build this volume that clearly demonstrates that not only is their scholarship not a luxury, but also that it is incredibly important for the continued growth of this academic field. This project grew out of a set of relationships built through the academy and the activist/advocacy work on the ground. The final product is a collection of chapters by a cross-section of authors—some of whom we have long-standing relationships with, and some who we met through this process. We solicited contributions by reaching out to current and former students, scholars whose work we came into contact with online, and scholars whose advisors we know. As curators and editors of the volume, we solicited contributions from these authors, and built the volume around the themes and issues their research prioritized. This work is their own. Each chapter was solo-authored and born of the authors' scholarly engagement with the topic of illegality and undocumented status within and outside of the academy. It is important to note that some authors regularized their status during the production of this volume. Thus, while there are some variations in terms of the precise status of the contributors, each author shares the experience of living as an undocumented immigrant in the United States for many years into their young adult lives and draws on this experience in intimate ways to theorize citizenship, illegality, and undocumented life more broadly. This, we believe, is a profoundly important contribution.

How We Came to This Work

Our own political and academic work as scholars and allies of and advocates for undocumented young people began at a time when undocumented youth had very little access to higher education. Most of those we met through community organizations were only barely coming to understand that they were undocumented, and felt great shame and fear to disclose their status (Abrego 2006; Negrón-Gonzales 2014). Educators, mostly not yet aware that some of their students may be undocumented, were often unhelpful, even when the students gathered the courage to share their status with them. In such a context, undocumented young people often gave up hope of attending college. Those who were unaware of their status or who ignored it to earn college admission found that they were ineligible for any kind of financial aid. Most often, this meant that the best they could do was attend the least expensive option of community college, despite having been admitted to prestigious universities. As more people became aware of these structural barriers and missed opportunities for students, supportive educators, grassroots organizations, and young organizers worked together to change the educational policies that impeded their chances. In California, this took place in the late 1990s and early 2000s.

It was during this period that, driven by a commitment to young people, education, and immigrant rights, we each began to research and write about undocumented students, the structural barriers that thwarted their educational aspirations, and their political consciousness. As part of our attempt to accompany them in their advocacy work, our own research theorized their experiences. Very limited scholarship existed on undocumented students because it was a phenomenon that scholars were only beginning to notice. The last mass legalization program in the United States took place in 1986 through the Immigration Reform and Control Act (IRCA). As De Genova (2004) reminds us, however, every legalization is also an illegalization and just as IRCA moved to incorporate a large group of migrants, it also further reinforced the marginalization and subjugation of those who did not meet the policy's stringent criteria: migrants young and old who arrived after the dates of eligibility faced much stricter policies and blocked access to legalization.

In the early 2000s, therefore, those who arrived as children were starting to come of age and beginning to learn that their undocumented status had potentially devastating consequences for their lives. They had grown up in a country that, thanks to the Supreme Court decision of *Plyler v. Doe* in 1982, legally allowed them to attend public school from kindergarten through high school graduation. But, as they approached the end of high school and were required to supply a social security number to apply for jobs or to college, many were forced to confront the reality of what the lack of a social security number meant for their future. This stark contradiction between full participation in school on the one hand, but inability to be legally present in the country, on the other hand, framed their lives and their uneven access to institutions that determined their life chances. It was the deep unfairness of this transition that compelled students to collectively demand changes to the system.

Access to higher education, however, is only one notable facet in a greater landscape of inequality and injustice. Indeed, this book emerged from our shared experience of teaching, mentoring, and supporting incredible undocumented students who were making nuanced, thoughtful, original arguments that speak to the field, but who were also continually stymied in the process of writing. Given the legal challenges and exclusions that undocumented students and their families face, they often grow up in limited socioeconomic conditions with unsatisfactory training to attend college (Abrego and Gonzales 2010). Those who are admitted to four-year universities often struggle financially to cover tuition and other related costs. Even when they manage to gather the necessary resources, the opportunity to reflect on their experiences can be painful because they have had to overcome countless barriers to simply be present in a college classroom. Significantly, during a historical moment of heightened policing of immigrants and record numbers of deportations, even when they attend school, they worry constantly about their safety and the safety of their family members (Menjívar and Abrego 2012). Being an undocumented scholar, therefore, raises empirical, methodological, and theoretical challenges that these scholars are navigating in unique and meaningful ways.

As practices and policies have changed nationally, and especially in California, thanks in large part to these youths' activism, almost two decades after we embarked on this research we have been heartened to see increasing numbers of undocumented and Deferred Action for Childhood Arrivals (DACA) recipient students thriving in undergraduate and graduate programs. Many have been theorizing experiences within their community, yet have struggled with the research process. We have witnessed the pain that frequently accompanies the process of writing in an analytical way about the indignities and suffering of undocumented life in a racist, cruel system. We have witnessed undocumented scholars develop skillful analyses and we feel strongly that they have unique contributions to make. This book was born from the frustration of seeing these bright young people in distress about getting their work out into the world, and from our strong belief that they have an important role to play as leaders in the growing research field of undocumented immigrant youth within and beyond education.

This, we hope, is a transformative project: budding scholars transform into full-fledged knowledge-producers and authors while also transforming the field through their theorizing of the undocumented experience. In the following sections, we provide a broad overview of the existing academic literature in these areas as well, noting the gaps in knowledge.

What We Already Know and Still Need to Learn about Undocumented Young People

Since the last mass legalization program over thirty years ago—the Immigration Reform and Control Act of 1986—hundreds of thousands of children who arrived without lawful permission in the United States have faced an unyielding and unforgiving legislative environment, which has strictly limited their opportunities to legalize their status. Neither their long-term residence, nor their acquisition of the English language, nor their participation in their communities allows them to become legal permanent residents or naturalized citizens. In many cases, despite educational excellence and notable civic participation, and even when they have met with lawyers to explore their options, they find that they are not eligible for legalization through any existing means.

Their predicament is especially taxing because these young people have come of age in a contradictory educational context: though they are not legally permitted to reside in the United States, they do have legal access to public education. The 1982 Supreme Court ruling *Plyler v. Doe* affirms that it is unconstitutional to deny children access to K–12 public schooling due to their immigration status. Undocumented children, therefore, may legally attend school and expect not to be asked about their status. In 2019, it is estimated that out of 125,000 undocumented youth across the nation who are graduation age, 98,000 graduate from high school every year (Zong and Batalova 2019) and because their educational protections end at that point, they are likely to face stringent barriers to continued education. Categorized as international students in states that do not offer them in-state tuition, they are charged exorbitant rates. In most states, they also continue to be blocked from access to financial aid. In those instances, the select few who manage to attend college struggle to finance and navigate their education. Nationally, students and allies have organized for greater college access since the late 1990s.

In academia, we know much of their experience through the rigorous work of scholars from a variety of disciplines. Indeed, research on undocumented students has grown tremendously over the last decade, documenting the experiences (Gonzales 2011; Perez et al. 2009), challenges (Abrego 2006), strategies (Heredia 2015; Negrón-Gonzales 2014, 2015; Nicholls 2013), and policy changes across states (Flores 2010; Olivas 2005, 2010). Scholars have followed closely, providing analysis of the educational (Abrego 2006; Nájera 2015; Pérez Huber et al. 2006; Perez Huber and Malagon 2007; Perez et al. 2009; Soltis 2015; Teranishi et al. 2015), social (Abrego 2011; Gonzales 2016), psychological (Gonzales and Chavez 2012; Gonzales et al. 2013), political (Heredia 2015; Negrón-Gonzales 2014, 2015; Nicholls 2013; Schwiertz 2016; Seif 2004; Terriquez 2015; Zimmerman 2012), economic (Cho 2017; de Graauw and Gleeson 2016), and legal contexts (Abrams 2014; Abrego 2008; Buenavista 2012, 2018; Olivas 2005; Silver 2018) as students go through transitions, benefit from new laws, and attain higher education. Today, under the harsh anti-immigrant policies of the Trump administration, the field is ripe for expansion.

The vast majority of published researchers are not themselves undocumented immigrants (for exceptions, see Aguilar 2018 and Chang 2018). As we have learned from the work of Black and Chicana feminist scholars (see Anzaldúa 2012; Hull 1980; Collins 2000; Pérez 1999; Sandoval 2013; Taylor 2018), ways of knowing and knowledge production are situated and partial. Positionality is an integral part of the research process (cf. Rosaldo [1989] 1993). We occupy structural locations from which we observe with a particular angle of vision (Dillard 2000; Milner IV 2007; Takacs 2003; Zavella 1989). Scholars in the fields of Women's Studies, Black Studies, and Chicana/o Studies have convincingly argued that we need to make space for cultural, class, ethnic, and gender diversity among researchers, and welcome their unique analytical insights (Blauner and Wellman 1973; Gilligan 1982; Gordon et al. 1990; Zinn 1979). As scholars in the field of undocumented youth studies, we also now acknowledge the need to include insights of scholars from diverse legal status positions.

While many in the field of undocumented youth identify as scholars of color, the lived experiences of being undocumented inevitably make visible particular kinds of understandings that should be centered in the field. Although much of the research on undocumented youth is qualitative in nature and includes the voices of undocumented student interviewees as data, missing are the analytical voices of the undocumented students themselves. Following in the tradition of Black and Chicana feminist scholars whose work underscores the transformative possibilities of centering experiential knowledge in the research process, this book includes the original analyses of scholars who are currently or have recently been undocumented.

This volume reveals the urgent need for greater inclusion of undocumented scholars as knowledge producers and central leaders in the field. The voices of researchers whose lives are shaped by the contemporary production of "illegality" are critical in understanding the varied and complex ways that citizenship status shapes lived experiences. Their contributions have the potential to transform our understanding of undocumented youth and more broadly of how immigration policies play out in the lives of individuals and targeted communities at different life stages and in various social contexts.

The DREAMer Narrative

As educators, school staff, and university officials became increasingly familiar with the struggles of undocumented students, a discourse began to emerge to illuminate this conundrum among the mainstream. The extensive barriers undocumented students face in their pursuit of education require them to be resourceful and build strong networks to succeed. Their stories of incredible sacrifice to attain an education that permanent legal resident and citizen students often take for granted, as well as the inherent unfairness embedded in an educational system that proclaims a meritocratic ethos, caught the attention and garnered the support of dedicated educators and university staff. The stories that became the most salient, as emblematic of this inherent unfairness, were of students who had earned college admission but were unable to matriculate due to their status. Allies—nonprofit leaders and educators—began using this powerful narrative to advocate for the educational rights of these promising students and increasingly, many undocumented students took up these narratives to make a strategic and compelling appeal for their rights (Abrams 2014; Nicholls 2013). This came to be known as the "DREAMer narrative" because it argues for citizenship for those who stood to benefit from the federal DREAM Act were it ever to pass—undocumented, but young and educated. The nonprofit industrial complex, DC lobbying groups, journalists, and researchers also played a role in the narrative's solidification.

In this now well-known portrayal, undocumented young people are presented as those who, by no choice of their own, were brought to the United States unlawfully as innocent children. Though their parents are to blame for the decision, the narrative affirms, the children did their best to attain the American Dream by working hard in school and making great sacrifices to complete a college education. Even without financial aid and despite various barriers produced by poverty, these students do not complain; rather, they put their heads down, work hard, and earn stellar grades. Their behavior is seen as evidence of their superior work ethic manifested in a determination to not let structural barriers thwart achievement. The DREAMer narrative has good intentions—it was deployed as a way to win the hearts and minds of the broader populace to build popular support for the educational rights of undocumented young people; it insists that undocumented students are being punished for a decision they did not make and for which they should therefore not be held responsible. Their potential for great productivity, as model neoliberal subjects (Pallares 2014), seeks to make the case that they have earned a chance to live in the United States.

Their proximity to Americanism is critical in this formulation. The DREAMer narrative not only celebrates these young people for their accomplishments and success, but also implicitly and explicitly celebrates their affinity with "American" values: "Their parents brought them to this country when they were infants in most cases, and for many of them this is the only home they know.

They have grown up "American" in every way possible; their dominant language is English, they proclaim an American identity, and they live an American lifestyle. In various ways, their community service participation and activities reinforce their affinity toward American society" (Perez 2009, xii). This "affinity" for Americanness is important to recognize as central to the DREAMer narrative because it is intricately wrapped up with notions of deservingness (Negrón-Gonzales, Abrego, and Coll 2015). Indeed, claims to an "Americanness" situate the right to belong in this country as the domain only of those who abandon a non-American identity, or who do not question the basic mainstream tenets of what the United States represents. In particular, such a notion upholds a myth of meritocracy that suggests that all immigrants have the ability to pull themselves up by their bootstraps without demanding inclusion or structural changes (Abrego 2008).

This narrative has powerfully captured the attention and sympathy of a large swath of the U.S. polity (Nicholls 2013). Along with dedicated organizing, in 2012 it led to President Obama's signing of the DACA program. Under the Trump administration, DACA is under threat to end (though court injunctions permit renewal applications), but the added protections from deportation along with permission to work and to drive legally have allowed beneficiaries to make great educational and occupational strides (Abrego 2018). It is important to point out that both nationally and regionally, the kinds of policy advances we have seen have not come about as a result of the goodwill of politicians but because undocumented young people, their families, and their allies have pushed the boundaries of these restrictive laws, advocating for institutional and policy change through bold acts of civil disobedience and grassroots organizing.

It is within this context in which we see the flourishing of more critical perspectives regarding the political narratives that frame undocumented youth's experiences. Readers of this volume will note that almost all the authors, from different situated experiences and through various analytical approaches, explicitly resist the DREAMer narrative. This is a theme we had not anticipated would end up being a framing analytical structure, but when it emerged as such, we tailored the volume accordingly.

The California Context

The state of California is uniquely important as a site to understand these experiences. Home to the largest population of undocumented students, California's evolving policies amply reveal the fruits of the advocacy and organizing of undocumented activist young people. In 2001, following Texas's lead, California passed Assembly Bill 540, which allowed undocumented students to qualify as in-state residents for tuition purposes. AB 540 significantly brought down the cost of college and permitted growing numbers of youth to enter community colleges and four-year colleges and universities. The result of further organizing and political pressure, California passed two pieces of legislation together known as the California Dream Act in 2011, which gave undocumented students access to private and state-based financial aid. Paired with the federal executive action of DACA, these policies have greatly transformed the possibilities in higher education and professional pathways for undocumented students in California.

Though we did not set out to write a book about undocumented life in California, the location of the authors and the place California has occupied in the national undocumented youth movement have created an undeniable bias toward California experiences and processes in the book. Though unintended, all of the authors have lived in California at some point, even when they are not from the state or even if they do not currently reside there. Importantly, their empirical and theoretical work in this volume was conducted in California and readers should be mindful of the unique policy and associated social contexts that inform the chapters. The Undocumented Youth Movement, however, is national and there are vast networks across states and regions that also contextualize the work. For this reason and because legal and social contexts throughout the country are constantly in flux, we believe the volume has theoretical and analytical resonance for a broader national audience.

A Methodological Intervention

This is a unique volume. There is currently no other collection of empirical and theoretical work by undocumented or recently undocumented scholars. As editors of this volume, this was certainly an empirical and analytical matter, but also a methodological one. Each author details their own methodological approach in the chapters, but there are broader methodological interventions that must also be named. These involve explicitly positioning undocumented scholars as theorists of the undocumented experience while being mindful of the ethics involved in doing this work.

At the outset of this project, we were clear that we did not want this to be a collection of testimonies, narrative reflections, or first-person essays; this is not to say that there is not value in such endeavors, but rather to be clear that such a project is politically, analytically, and methodologically distinct from our aims here. This volume is an intentional effort to position this work as critical to the field in that it pushes our understanding of undocumented life in the United States at this time. Thus, the positioning of the undocumented immigrant as scholar is a direct departure from the treatment of the undocumented immigrant as subject or object. This positioning is not only pragmatic or practical, it is also methodological.

Part of our politic and analytic around this is that this process of undocumentation (Negrón-Gonzales 2018), while it is discussed in public discourse as a clear-cut matter, is a social, legal, and political construction. There is nothing inherent in people that makes them undocumented. There is nothing unchangeable in society that determines that undocumented people are criminals. On the contrary, people move in and out of undocumented status and legal, political, and social treatment of undocumented people changes across different historical moments (Ngai 2004). Methodologically, then, it made sense to us to capture these experiences by including people who have direct experience with being undocumented and scholars, whether they are currently undocumented, DACA recipients, or formerly undocumented for a notable part of their lives as students. We feel strongly that the authors in this volume have an important role to play in shaping the field.

The other methodological dimension worth illuminating concerns research ethics. Many theorists of undocumented migration have aimed to be thoughtful in how they approach research ethically (Hernández et al. 2013; Suárez-Orozco and Yoshikawa 2013). Some have written about the ethics of cocreating theory with undocumented students who are the focus of analysis (Pérez Huber 2010), while others provide undocumented students with research training and writing support (Clark-Ibáñez 2015; Mena Robles and Gomberg-Muñoz 2016; Unzueta Carrasco and Seif 2014). There is, however, a persistent disconnection in the field more broadly. Undocumented young people note that there is a pattern of researchers entering spaces of organizing—sometimes without permission—only to gather information for their studies, never to be seen again. Those researchers have failed to reciprocate with undocumented immigrant communities, rarely using their skills to support the advocacy work that they document. And in most of those cases, people who participated in the study were not informed of the findings. Authors in this volume have had conversations about how to address these concerns regarding immigration scholars who are not themselves undocumented. One response, in particular, thoughtfully details the problems and suggests best practices for scholars to follow when conducting research with undocumented communities.

Gabrielle Cabrera, one of the authors featured in this volume, along with Ines Garcia and an anonymous student at their undergraduate institution in California, got together shortly after the election of Donald Trump. In an attempt to be proactive in this new political context and rooted in what they saw as the nonreciprocal pattern of engagement described above, they developed a brief guide on research ethics for scholars and researchers who were turning to write about undocumented youth in the midst of heightened political threats.

November 30, 2016

Dear Researchers,

We'd like to emphasize that Undocumented students are not research subjects. We respectfully, but adamantly ask faculty members who are conducting research on and with Undocumented people to please conduct ethical research. By ethical research, we mean:

1. the questions asked to participants should not attempt to uplift the "progressive" efforts of the university;
2. sharing the research and findings with our community through relevant and accessible means; and
3. researchers should not treat Undocumented students as a "trendy" research topic.

We'd also like to take this moment to express the need for critical research on and with Undocumented students. We believe the efforts of faculty are grounded in good intentions and understand the importance of it. We also want to name that research causes harm to our community as it has been known to exploit and commodify our bodies and experiences.

Researchers should not collect data about our lives and publish the knowledge solely for their own benefit. Researchers should intentionally disseminate findings into our communities in meaningful and relevant ways. "Policy Recommendations" at the end of articles are not enough. Researchers should not claim to give us "voice" when current research on Undocumented students perpetuate the violent "DREAMer" narrative.

A change in the ways in which Undocumented students are researched needs to occur. We are scholars. We are community members. We are collaborators in the research process. Researchers should not speak on our behalf. Rather, researchers should give us the platform to speak for ourselves. Faculty members have the ability to do this by conducting ethical research that engages our community throughout the process.

As is true of many scholars we have worked with, Cabrera, Garcia, and their peers highlight the need to push back on the DREAMer narrative, not only identifying its limitations but also highlighting how it reifies and sanctifies a certain kind of "good" immigrant. This pushback is a persistent theme across the chapters in this book, and the analytical contributions of these young scholars remind us that a key part of decolonizing research methodologies involves disrupting the assumed unmovable distinction between the researcher and the researched. Part of that process involves marginalized people theorizing and producing scholarship about the experiences of their communities.

"We Are Not DREAMers" as Analytical and Empirical Interjection

The subtitle of this collection is "Undocumented Scholars Theorize Undocumented Life in the United States." One way to curate such a volume would have been to identify the key spheres of undocumented life and solicit chapters on each of those—perhaps one chapter on schools, one on work, one on family, and so forth. However, in our conversations with the authors, a much more nuanced conception of undocumented life emerged, which ultimately served as the organizing logic of the book. The first half of the book engages in the connection between identity, illegality, and resistance as a way to critically analyze how undocumented migrants have been "made" through these processes. The second half of the book centers quotidian life as a medium for the exploration of what an intersectional analysis of undocumented status looks like by grappling with the structures of relationships, family, and identity. These two halves, then, constitute a recasting of how we think about undocumented life in the United States; not simply as a collection of institutional interactions or a constellation of spheres of engagement, but rather as an examination of the ways undocumented actors move through the spaces of daily life and in doing so, remake those spaces in fundamental ways.

Although much of the initial research on the undocumented 1.5 generation focuses on their educational success and the support they received from institutions of higher education, the authors in this book challenge that narrative. Many highlight the role that scholars, along with journalists, political pundits, and the mainstream immigrant rights organizations played in creating and inflating a good immigrant narrative to support the notion of a perfect "DREAMer." Joel Sati's chapter is a theoretical formulation which draws the lines between discourse and policy to interrogate race, naturalization, the state, and the DREAMer identity in the immigrant rights movement. The work of Grecia Mondragón exposes the pressures and expectations that students are forced to navigate within higher education while carrying the weight of the DREAMer narrative, which often adds stress to their lives and makes it difficult to focus on their education. Gabrielle Cabrera analyzes the political and moral economy of the undocumented DREAMer narrative within the institution of higher education. Gabriela Monico examines how young activists left out of the DREAM Act discourse navigate the arguments for market citizenship often embedded in immigrant legislation and activism. Gabriela Garcia Cruz deliberately thinks more broadly about undocumented activism and turns away from young people specifically to focus on the political engagement of older undocumented women activists and how this activism reshapes lived experiences of citizenship and dignity.

Turning most intentionally toward the quotidian, the second half of the book highlights the need to examine identity and day-to-day life, often through an intersectional lens. Carolina Valdivia's work examines the daily manifestations of undocumented life, with a particular focus on immigrants' mental health under the Trump administration. Maria Liliana Ramirez employs intersectionality as a theoretical tool to underscore the point that undocumented status is not always the only or the most important identity for queer immigrants, particularly as they navigate relationships with family. Audrey Silvestre, meanwhile, urges readers to center joy and the quotidian in the lives of all undocumented immigrants, but especially for Trans undocumented immigrants who are often made the most vulnerable through immigration, detention, and other policies. The research on immigrant families has highlighted the ways in which deportability weighs heavily on undocumented and other members of their families. Lucía León extends this line of research by emphasizing the insidious effects of immigration policy that determine even how people must represent their love to one another and to the state in the most mundane ways. In her chapter, Katy Maldonado calls us to think more deeply about the day-to-day processes of families that are more powerfully impacted by other aspects of their lives. In the case of queer families, this means a fear of separation that is lived internally due to homophobia and externally due to immigration policy.

The work of these young scholars contributes to the field broadly, not only as critical and thoughtful empirical and theoretical work being done by undocumented scholars but also because this work brings out the nuances and complications of undocumented life in the United States, which as a field we have not fully considered in all its dimensions. Four important themes emerge from these chapters. First, authors point to the ways in which access to education and the space of the college/university has both opened tremendous opportunity yet also requires certain kinds of sacrifice while complicating already difficult dynamics involved in undocumented life and relationships. Second, authors point to the diversity within the 1.5-generation undocumented immigrant experience. This critique rests both on complicating the conception that being undocumented is a monolithic experience, and also articulates the dangers of exclusion that are embedded in perpetuating this conception. Third, authors stress the importance of understanding different life stages in the undocumented experience and examining how undocumented status is experienced differently within and through the life course. Last, and most prominently, there is deep resistance to the DREAMer narrative and a call for a nuanced understanding of how this critique aims to shift conceptions not just of deservingness but also of how undocumented subjectivities are negotiated and created through this process.

The Shifting Terrain of Immigration Policies and "Illegality" Studies

Following 9/11, immigration has increasingly been treated as a national security issue (Abrego et al. 2017; Menjívar and Kanstroom 2013). This is evidenced by the development of the dissolution of the Immigration and Naturalization Service and the creation of Immigration and Customs Enforcement, which was then brought under the jurisdiction of the newly-developed Department of Homeland Security. In the wake of the War on Terror, and an increased hostility toward immigrants, migrants, refugees, and asylum-seekers, undocumented young people waged a movement that shifted the political terrain around access to education for undocumented youth in this country. The policies and laws born as a result of the impressive movement built by undocumented young people and their allies have meaningfully reframed questions of access on the ground, yet the fundamental policing of illegality and criminalization of migrants persists (Gonzales 2013). The Obama administration, while credited with the passage of DACA, also oversaw a period of mass deportations that both rivaled those of previous administrations and created the institutional infrastructure that laid the groundwork for Trump's immigration enforcement machine.

Today, we are living in a deeply consequential period regarding immigration policy and immigrant communities in the United States. This moment is both crucial and noteworthy—not only because of the particular policies that are being legislated, arbitrated, debated, and enacted, but also because of the long-lasting impacts they will have on family formation and immigration pathways, as well as conceptions of belonging, illegality, and citizenship for future decades. Since taking office in January 2017, Trump has ushered in a number of policies and programs that aim to increase deportations and family separations (Abrego et al. 2017). Among these are Executive Order 13768, passed in January 2017, which increased border enforcement; drastic expansion of the parameters for who the government considers a priority for deportation; threats to remove funding from sanctuary cities; and an expansion of categories that make migrants deportable without due process. In September 2017, Trump ordered the end of the DACA program, which gave some measure of protection to eligible undocumented young people who had grown up in the United States, including protection from deportation and a legal work permit. At the time of this writing, the Supreme Court is set to decide the fate of DACA in the coming months.

The Trump administration's April 2018 Zero Tolerance Border Policy ushered in the practice of criminally prosecuting every adult apprehended entering the United States. When parents and children are apprehended together, this policy has the effect of separating minors from their parents because once charged with a crime, adults are routed for criminal prosecution mandating placement in adult-only jails and detention centers. Children are processed separately through the Office of Refugee Resettlement. All of this takes place without a central plan to identify or track these families. Although Trump officially retracted this policy just months after its official initiation, thousands of children were and continue to be separated from their families; too many remain separated today.

At the end of 2017 and in early 2018, Trump also ended Temporary Protected Status (TPS) for over 300,000 people from Haiti, Nicaragua, El Salvador, Syria, Nepal, and Honduras. TPS—itself a response to organized protest against the U.S. government's discrimination against Central American asylum-seekers in the 1980s—was developed in 1990 as a humanitarian program to provide refuge for migrants from countries destabilized through war, natural disaster, or catastrophe (Hallett and Abrego 2017). Trump's attempt to end the program seeks to push these migrants, many of whom have lived in the United States for decades, out of legal status; to force them either to leave or risk being deported. At the time of this writing, TPS holders have organized their resistance on multiple fronts, including litigation that has temporarily halted the program's termination.

Many of Trump's policies and executive orders, along with his attempts to end legal protections for immigrants, are not generally identified as specifically targeting young people. However, together they profoundly shape the lives of many undocumented young people and their families. This is the historical moment these young scholars are navigating personally, professionally, and emotionally; and this is the sociopolitical context their work engages.

The undocumented scholars who have contributed to this book are impacted by these policies. They are members of family units who are weathering these changes. They are activists and advocates who have played leading roles in fighting for the rights of immigrants in various sectors and spheres. Also, importantly, they have been educated within this shifting political terrain—these fights have resulted in increased access to higher education for many, particularly in places like California—and thus, are now positioned to be active and insightful participants as writers, scholars, and theorists of the undocumented experience in the United States. This volume is dedicated to illuminating this work and elevating these voices, not simply out of the belief that their voices are important, or merely due to ethics or toward building more inclusive practices within the academy, but also because we deeply believe that the work they are producing has the potential to transform the field and help bring about new and critical understandings of undocumented life in the United States.

NOTE

1. The California Dream Act is composed of two bills passed in 2011. Assembly Bill 130 was implemented in 2012 and made undocumented students in California public colleges and universities who qualify for in-state tuition also eligible to access private sources of financial aid (see https://leginfo.legislature.ca.gov/faces/billNavClient.xhtml?bill_id=201120120AB130). Assembly Bill 131 was implemented in 2013 and made undocumented college students in California public colleges and universities who qualify for in-state tuition also eligible for California state sources of aid, such as Cal Grants (see https://leginfo.legislature.ca.gov/faces/billCompareClient.xhtml?bill_id=201120120AB131).

REFERENCES

Abrams, Kathryn R. 2014. "Performative Citizenship in the Civil Rights and Immigrant Rights Movements." UC *Berkeley Public Law Research Paper No. 2409971*.

Abrego, Leisy J. 2006. "'I Can't Go to College Because I Don't Have Papers': Incorporation Patterns of Latino Undocumented Youth." *Latino Studies* 4(3): 212–31.

Abrego, Leisy J. 2008. "Legitimacy, Social Identity, and the Mobilization of Law: The Effects of Assembly Bill 540 on Undocumented Students in California." *Law and Social Inquiry* 33(3): 709–34.

Abrego, Leisy J. 2011. "Legal Consciousness of Undocumented Latinos: Fear and Stigma as Barriers to Claims Making for First and 1.5 Generation Immigrants." *Law and Society Review* 45(2): 337–70.

Abrego, Leisy J. 2018. "Renewed Optimism and Spatial Mobility: Legal Consciousness of Latino Deferred Action for Childhood Arrivals Recipients and Their Families in Los Angeles." *Ethnicities* 18(2): 192–207. https://doi.org.10.1177/1468796817752563.

Abrego, Leisy, Mat Coleman, Daniel E. Martínez, Cecilia Menjívar, and Jeremy Slack. 2017. "Making Immigrants into Criminals: Legal Processes of Criminalization in the Post-IIRIRA Era." *Journal on Migration and Human Security* 5(3): 694–715.

Abrego, Leisy J., and Roberto Gonzales. 2010. "Blocked Paths, Uncertain Futures: The Postsecondary Education and Labor Market Prospects of Undocumented Latino Youth." *Journal of Education of Students Placed at Risk (JESPAR)* 15(1): 144–57.

Aguilar, Carlos. 2018. "Undocumented Critical Theory." *Cultural Studies ←→ Critical Methodologies* 19(3): 152–60. https://doi.org.10.1177/1532708618817911.

Anzaldúa, Gloria. 2012. *Borderlands/La Frontera: The New Mestiza*. San Francisco: Aunt Lute Books.

Blauner, Robert, and David Wellman. 1973. "Toward the Decolonization of Social Research." In *The Death of White Sociology*, edited by Joyce Ladner. New York: Vintage.

Buenavista, Tracy. 2012. "Citizenship at a Cost: Undocumented Asian Youth Perceptions and the Militarization of Immigration." *Asian American and Pacific Islander Nexus* 10(1): 101–24.

Buenavista, Tracy. 2018. "Model (Undocumented) Minorities and 'Illegal' Immigrants: Centering Asian Americans and US Carcerality in Undocumented Student Discourse." *Race, Ethnicity, and Education* 21(1): 78–91. https://doi.org.10.1080/13613324.2016.1248823.

Chang, Aurora. 2018. *The Struggles of Identity, Education, and Agency in the Lives of Undocumented Students: The Burden of Hyperdocumentation*. Switzerland: Palgrave Macmillan.

Cho, Esther Yoona. 2017. "Revisiting Ethnic Niches: A Comparative Analysis of the Labor Market Experiences of Asian and Latino Undocumented Young Adults." *RSF: The Russell Sage Foundation Journal of the Social Sciences* 3(4): 97–115. https://doi.org.10.7758/RSF.2017.3.4.06.

Clark-Ibáñez, Marisol. 2015. *Undocumented Latino Youth: Navigating Their Worlds*. Boulder, CO: Lynne Rienner.

Collins, Patricia Hill 2000. *Black Feminist Thought: Knowledge, Consciousness, and the Politics of Empowerment*. New York: Routledge.

De Genova, Nicholas P. 2004. "The Legal Production of Mexican/Migrant 'Illegality.'" *Latino Studies* 2(2): 160–85.

de Graauw, Els, and Shannon Gleeson. 2016. "An Institutional Examination of the Local Implementation of the DACA Program." Center for Nonprofit Strategy and Management Working Paper Series. New York: Baruch College, City University of New York, School of Public Affairs. https://digitalcommons.ilr.cornell.edu/cgi/viewcontent.cgi?article=1186&context=workingpapers.

Dillard, Cynthia B. 2000. "The Substance of Things Hoped For, The Evidence of Things Not Seen: Examining an Endarkened Feminist Epistemology in Educational Research and Leadership." *International Journal of Qualitative Studies in Education* 13(6): 661–81. https://doi.org.10.1080/09518390050211565.

Flores, Stella M. 2010. "State Dream Acts: The Effect of In-State Resident Tuition Policies on the College Enrollment of Undocumented Latino Students in the United States." *Review of Higher Education* 33(2): 239–83.

Gilligan, Carol. 1982. *In a Different Voice: Psychological Theory and Women's Development*. Cambridge, MA: Harvard University Press.

Gonzales, Alfonso. 2013. *Reform without Justice: Latino Migrant Politics and the Homeland Security State*. Oxford: Oxford University Press.

Gonzales, Roberto. 2016. *Lives in Limbo: Undocumented and Coming of Age in America*. Berkeley: University of California Press.

Gonzales, Roberto G. 2011. "Learning to Be Illegal: Undocumented Youth and Shifting Legal Contexts in the Transition to Adulthood." *American Sociological Review* 76(4): 602–19.

Gonzales, Roberto G., and Leo R. Chavez. 2012. "'Awakening to a Nightmare': Abjectivity and Illegality in the Lives of Undocumented 1.5 Generation Latino Immigrants in the United States." *Current Anthropology* 53(3): 255–81.

Gonzales, Roberto G., Carola Suárez-Orozco, and Maria Cecilia Dedios-Sanguineti. 2013. "No Place to Belong: Contextualizing Concepts of Mental Health among Undocumented Immigrant Youth in the United States." *American Behavioral Scientist* 57(8): 1174–99. https://doi.org.10.1177/0002764213487349.

Gordon, Edmund W., Fayneese Miller, and David Rollock. 1990. "Coping with Communicentric Bias in Knowledge Production in the Social Sciences." *Educational Researcher* 19(3): 14–19. https://doi.org.10.3102/0013189X019003014.

Hallett, Miranda Cady, and Leisy J. Abrego. 2017. "Seeking a Permanent Protected Status." In NACLA *Report on the Americas*. Washington, DC.

Heredia, Luisa Laura. 2015. "Of Radicals and DREAMers: Harnessing Exceptionality to Challenge Immigration Control." *Association of Mexican American Educators Journal* 9(3): 74–58.

Hernández, María G., Jacqueline Nguyen, Saskias Casanova, Carola Suárez-Orozco, and Carrie L. Saetermoe. 2013. "Doing No Harm and Getting It Right: Guidelines for Ethical Research with Immigrant Communities." *New Directions for Child and Adolescent Development* 2013(141): 43–60. https://doi.org.10.1002/cad.20042.

Hull, Gloria T. 1980. "Researching Alice Dunbar-Nelson: A Personal and Literary Perspective." *Feminist Studies* 6(2): 314–20.

Mena Robles, Jorge, and Ruth Gomberg-Muñoz. 2016. "Activism after DACA: Lessons from Chicago's Immigrant Youth Justice League." *North American Dialogue* 19(1): 46–54. https://doi.org.10.1002/cad.2004210.1111/nad.12036.

Menjívar, Cecilia, and Leisy Abrego. 2012. "Legal Violence: Immigration Law and the Lives of Central American Immigrants." *American Journal of Sociology* 117(5): 1380–424.

Menjívar, Cecilia, and Daniel Kanstroom, eds. 2013. *Constructing Immigrant "Illegality": Critiques, Experiences, and Resistance*. Cambridge: Cambridge University Press.

Milner, H. Richard, IV. 2007. "Race, Culture, and Researcher Positionality: Working through Dangers Seen, Unseen, and Unforeseen." *Educational Researcher* 36(7): 388–400. https://doi.org/10.3102/0013189X07309471.

Nájera, Jennifer R. 2015. "Unauthorized Education: Challenging Borders between Good and Bad Immigrants." *Association of Mexican American Educators Journal* 9(3): 35–46.

Negrón-Gonzales, Genevieve. 2014. "Undocumented, Unafraid and Unapologetic: Re-articulatory Practices and Migrant Youth 'Illegality.'" *Latino Studies* 12(2) :259–78.

Negrón-Gonzales, Genevieve. 2015. "Undocumented Youth Activism as Counter-Spectacle: Civil Disobedience and Testimonio in the Battle around Immigration Reform." *Aztlán: A Journal of Chicano Studies* 40(1): 87–112.

Negrón-Gonzales, Genevieve. 2018. Presentation at the Migrant Illegality across Uneven Legal Geographies Conference. University of Colorado, Denver. April 6.

Negrón-Gonzales, Genevieve, Leisy J. Abrego, and Kathleen Coll. 2015. "Immigrant Latina/o Youth and Illegality: Challenging the Politics of Deservingness." *Association of Mexican American Educators Journal* 9(3): 7–10.

Ngai, Mae. 2004. *Impossible Subjects: Illegal Aliens and the Making of Modern America*. Princeton, NJ: Princeton University Press.

Nicholls, Walter J. 2013. *The DREAMers: How the Undocumented Youth Movement Transformed the Immigrant Rights Debate*. Palo Alto, CA: Stanford University Press.

Olivas, Michael. 2005. "The Story of Plyler v. Doe, the Education of Undocumented Children, and the Polity." In *Immigration Stories*, edited by David A. Martin and Peter H. Schuck, 197–220. New York: Foundation Press.

Olivas, Michael. 2010. "The Political Economy of the DREAM Act and the Legislative Process: A Case Study of Comprehensive Immigration Reform." *Wayne Law Review; University of Houston Law Center No. 2010-A-6*.

Pallares, Amalia. 2014. *Family Activism: Immigrant Struggles and the Politics of Noncitizenship*. New Brunswick, NJ: Rutgers University Press.

Pérez, Emma. 1999. *The Decolonial Imaginary: Writing Chicanas into History*. Bloomington: Indiana University Press.

Pérez Huber, Lindsay. 2010. "Using Latina/o Critical Race Theory (LatCrit) and Racist Nativism to Explore Intersectionality in the Educational Experiences of Undocumented Chicana College Students." *Educational Foundations* 24: 77–96.

Pérez Huber, Lindsay, Ofelia Huidor, Maria C. Malagón, Gloria Sánchez, and Daniel G. Solórzano. 2006. "Falling through the Cracks: Critical Transitions in the Latina/o Educational Pipeline." Report published by UCLA Chicano Studies Research Center.

Perez Huber, Lindsay, and Maria C. Malagon. 2007. "Silenced Struggles: The Experiences of Latina and Latino Undocumented College Students in California." *Nevada Law Journal* 7: 841–61.

Perez, William. 2009. *We ARE Americans: Undocumented Students Pursuing the American Dream*. Sterling, VA: Stylus.

Perez, William, Roberta Espinoza, Karina Ramos, Heidi M. Coronado, and Richard Cortes. 2009. "Academic Resilience among Undocumented Latino Students." *Hispanic Journal of Behavioral Sciences* 31(2): 149–81.

Rosaldo, Renato. [1989] 1993. *Culture and Truth: The Remaking of Social Analysis.* Boston, MA: Beacon Press.

Sandoval, Chela. 2013. *Methodology of the Oppressed.* Minneapolis: University of Minnesota Press.

Schwiertz, Helge. 2016. "Transformation of the Undocumented Youth Movement and Radical Egalitarian Citizenship." *Citizenship Studies* 20(5): 610–28. https://doi.org.10.1080/13621025.2016.1182680.

Seif, Hinda. 2004. "'Wise Up!' Undocumented Latino Youth, Mexican-American Legislators, and the Struggle for Higher Education Access." *Latino Studies* 2(2): 210–30.

Silver, Alexis M. 2018. *Shifting Boundaries: Immigrant Youth Negotiating National, State, and Small-Town Politics.* Stanford, CA: Stanford University Press.

Soltis, Laura Emiko. 2015. "From Freedom Schools to Freedom University: Liberatory Education, Interracial and Intergenerational Dialogue, and the Undocumented Student Movement in the U.S. South." *Souls* 17(1–2): 20–53. https://doi.org.10.1080/10999949.2015.998578.

Suárez-Orozco, Carola, and Hirokazu Yoshikawa. 2013. "Undocumented Status: Implications for Child Development, Policy, and Ethical Research." *Frameworks and Ethics for Research with Immigrants: New Directions for Child and Adolescent Development* 141: 61–78.

Takacs, David. 2003. "How Does Your Positionality Bias Your Epistemology?" *Thought and Action* 27(summer): 27–38.

Taylor, Keila D. 2018. "Rejecting Objectivity: Reflections of a Black Feminist Researcher Interviewing Black Women." *a/b: Auto/Biography Studies* 33(3): 721–26. https://doi.org.10.1080/08989575.2018.1499505.

Teranishi, Robert T., Carola Suárez-Orozco, and Marcelo Suárez-Orozco. 2015. "In the Shadows of the Ivory Tower: Undocumented Undergraduates and the Liminal State of Immigration Reform." Report published by the Institute for Immigration, Globalization, & Education at UCLA, Los Angeles, CA.

Terriquez, Veronica. 2015. "Intersectional Mobilization, Social Movement Spillover, and Queer Youth Leadership in the Immigrant Rights Movement." *Social Problems* 62(3): 343–62. https://doi.org.10.1093/socpro/spv010.

Unzueta Carrasco, Tania A., and Hinda Seif. 2014. "Disrupting the Dream: Undocumented Youth Reframe Citizenship and Deportability through Anti-Deportation Activism." *Latino Studies* 12(2): 279–99.

Zavella, Patricia. 1989. "The Problematic Relationship of Feminism and Chicana Studies." *Women's Studies* 17(1–2): 25–36.

Zimmerman, Arely M. 2012. "Documenting DREAMs: New Media, Undocumented Youth and the Immigrant Rights Movement." Report published by University of Southern California, Los Angeles, CA.

Zinn, Maxine Baca. 1979. "Insider Field Research in Minority Communities." *Social Problems* 27(2): 209–19.

Zong, Jie, and Jeanne Batalova. 2019. "How Many Unauthorized Immigrants Graduate from U.S. High Schools Annually?" Factsheet published by Migration Policy Institute. Washington, DC.

JOEL SATI

1

"Other" Borders
The Illegal as Normative Metaphor

The American debate on whether to grant undocumented immigrants legal status raises, at its heart, questions about the procedural fairness of the American immigration apparatus and how public perceptions of that apparatus manifest themselves in discourse. Procedural fairness, according to Tom Tyler, queries the "manner in which authorities [exercise] their authority—on the fairness of processes rather than the fairness of outcomes" (Tyler 2004, 440). In creating an immigration apparatus that aims to be procedurally fair, there are numerous interests that must be accounted for: administrative efficiency bound up in the state's need to control its borders, residents and citizens' sense of a national identity, and the humanitarian interests of immigrants, among others. Emily Ryo describes immigration law as occupying "a unique position in our legal system as the only domestic law that is largely directed at regulating the behavior of noncitizens" (Ryo 2013, 575). The way we marshal those competing interests, both as a political and, more centrally for the purposes of this chapter, as a *linguistic* maneuver, reveals how prima facie procedurally just immigration policy makes exclusion invisible to the bodies it excludes.

This chapter investigates metaphor as it relates to the law, the theory, and the politics of immigration, with a focus on the deliberative space in which immigrant and anti-immigrant rights groups negotiate immigration reform. I take "immigration reform" to mean any significant piece of legislation passed at the federal level that directly responds to the presence of over eleven million undocumented persons in the United States. Though immigration reform has been synonymous with granting residency and citizenship to undocumented immigrants—a term I call "regularization," this chapter does not directly contend with this view; rather, my primary interest here is the political and epistemic climate in which such a debate takes place, and the role that metaphor plays in constructing the debate.

That said, I argue that when it comes to discussions of procedural fairness, undocumented persons are at a disadvantage when perceptions of procedural fairness are applied to deliberations on immigration policy. Said differently, the metaphors used against undocumented immigrants are an important dimension in making certain anti-immigrant measures salient in political discourse.[1] An example would be the metaphor of "illegals" as an indiscernible mass (are they asylum seekers or ISIS fighters?) undergirding policies such as building a wall and other draconian measures. In addition to imbalances related to the availability of resources and lack of legal status, undocumented immigrant groups suffer from a more dangerous disadvantage: the metaphors that carry weight in policy discussions have the ability to warp the very narratives necessary for immigration relief. In other words, it is not only the issue of the presence of metaphor and narrative, but it is also the perspective of the people and entities creating them; this constitutes much of the disadvantage undocumented immigrants and other marginalized groups must contend with.

In making this argument, I remark on the political climate that makes it difficult for undocumented immigrants to advocate for their interests. I am interested in how metaphor affects conceptions of procedural fairness, which I define as the extent to which American legal procedures of including and excluding immigrants are seen as legitimate. The central questions I contend with are: how do legal institutions—in particular, the courts—and the public political discussion figure into how undocumented immigrants make their claims for immigration reform? More centrally, how do the *metaphors we live by* in discussing immigration reform shape and constitute the responses that we devise for dealing with concerns of immigration reform? I respond by maintaining that procedural fairness plays a role in immigration discourse because either undocumented immigrants are accused of having seemingly flouted it (in, say, entering without authorization or overstaying their visa) or immigration reform that benefits undocumented immigrants is assumed to negatively impact considerations of procedural fairness vis-à-vis other groups (say, undocumented immigrants seemingly cutting in line for benefits legal residents have waited years for). Metaphor not only frames the issue; it does so in ways that maximize rhetorical value based on a group's desired ends.

In her paper, "Deciding to Cross: The Norms and Economics of Unauthorized Migration," Emily Ryo concludes that "insofar as deterrence is an important goal in U.S. immigration policy, fostering greater *perceptions of legitimacy* (e.g., through promotion of greater procedural fairness) ought to be an urgent priority for U.S. policymakers" (Ryo 2013, 592). I am particularly interested in what she means by the phrase "fostering greater perceptions of legitimacy." *To whom is this procedural fairness accountable?* Ryo appears to suggest that it is the *appearance*, not the *existence* of legitimacy that would make immigration policy more procedurally just. There exists a loose metaphorical relationship between appearance and reliability; in other words, if we see things as legitimate, then they are in fact legitimate—seeing is believing, the relationship would proceed.[2] Recognizing how we can move from the appearance of legitimacy to actual legitimacy is critically important for those in immigrant rights. Examining immigrant rights campaigns and their appeals to legitimacy (for example, Clean Development, Relief and Education for Alien Minors [DREAM] Act legislation as aligning with core American values),[3] without a substantive analysis of whether the legislation that results will actually help immigrants, will put an already-compromised community into further, unconscionable harm (United We Dream 2017). That is not to say that appearance of legitimacy is bad per se; however, it is dangerous to take the state's self-assessment as legitimate as the only word on the matter. Language is important, metaphors matter, and both can efface the distinction between mere appearance of legitimacy, stifling critique from at-risk groups before it has a chance to begin.

This chapter proceeds in three parts. In the first section, I explain that metaphors are much more than linguistic flourishes; they structure our thinking at a fundamental level (Lakoff and Johnson 1980). Indeed, we do not think about metaphor; rather, we think in metaphor. In addition, metaphors also shape how we think about policy. Thus, through highlighting some aspects and eliding others, metaphors make certain policies palatable in political discourse. Given this power, I focus on the pragmatics of metaphors rather than their truth-value.

In the second section, I explore some of the most influential metaphors in the American immigration context, with particular focus on the "Illegal Immigrant as Alien" conceptual metaphor. Further, I use the metaphor of the "Immigrant as Dreamer" to argue that immigration reform politics is not an example of an egalitarian meaning-making contest. In making appeals for relief, immigrant rights activists are constricted in the kinds of appeals they can make due to more powerful anti-immigrant interests having their cognitive structures legitimated by the state. In addition, the narratives deployed by immigrant rights activists serve to undermine undocumented immigrants' push toward immigration reform.

Let us take "Illegal Immigrant as Alien" as an example of the above. Since the late eighteenth century, the legal term "alien" refers to a foreign individual. However, in the mid-twentieth century, science fiction writers appropriated the term to discuss extraterrestrial, nonhuman beings (think green monsters with tentacles). Given the interchange of law and culture in this example, the term "alien" not only carries the legitimacy reinforced by case law, but also the valences attached to it by the prevailing culture.[4] Thus, it makes it easier to conceive of immigrants as foreign and nonhuman, contributing to their place outside the polity. Then-Justice Rehnquist, in his dissent in *Sugarman v. Dougal* (1973), writes that aliens are unlike naturalized citizens who have assimilated "to our patterns of living and attitudes, and have demonstrated a basic understanding of our institutions, system of government, history, and traditions."[5] Undocumented immigrants become alien not only as a matter of phenotype, but also as a matter of understanding—citizenship is impossible for illegal aliens because they do not operate in the same cognitive, moral, or political space as citizens do.[6] The urgency that derives from this characterization and its implications is that because common understanding is incommensurable, the American way of life is under existential threat.

Law professor Kenneth Cunningham-Parmeter examines the normative policy consequences of the "Illegal Immigrant as Alien" conceptual metaphor and resulting cognitive structure: "if immigrants are viewed as *illegal alien criminals*, then they should be captured and deported. If immigration is an *invasion* from the south, then the government should construct a virtual fence across the border to resist the Mexican offensive. These 'common sense' responses are made possible by selective metaphoric framing" (Cunningham-Parmeter 2011, 1550). The interchange of the unfamiliar and familiar within the two valences of the term "alien" is particularly interesting for this reason: the unfamiliar alien as nonhuman, foreign being is placed in terms of the legalized familiar, the alien as foreigner. Those who advocate for the expulsion of immigrants can draw on the legal import of the term alien while also drawing on its cultural import as green-monster-with-tentacles bent on destroying those considered humans—in this case, those who are citizens. Alienage and the term "alien" have proven a unique ability to conceptualize foreignness in both the legal and cultural consciousness. In utilizing metaphor to convey an existential threat, the state can manipulate the cultural valence and legal import of alienage to push a protectionist policy agenda vis-à-vis immigration.

In the third section, I gesture toward an account of oppositional meaning-making through conceptual metaphor. My goal is to expose and dismiss the pernicious metaphors used to frame the immigration debate. I argue that the metaphors and frames used in the DREAMer narrative pacified the immigrant rights movement and made it much more difficult to push for more comprehensive immigration reform. In other words, undocumented immigrants were made to grovel for a humanity that ought to be presupposed (Sati 2017). This is important because, if we assume that procedural fairness is valuable in itself and only needs to be reworked, immigrant rights activism's push for more humanizing metaphors is likely to contribute to positive changes to immigration law, as well as changes in attitudes toward immigrants that also take into account other displaced and marginalized peoples. This chapter's implications, I argue, are as follows: how we think about immigrants shapes how immigrants are viewed, how immigrants view the world, and ultimately, what policies become all too real in the lives of undocumented immigrants.

Metaphor, Cognitive Structures, and Policy Deliberation
In *Metaphors We Live By*, linguist George Lakoff and philosopher Mark Johnson argue that metaphor is not just a flourish of language; it is human cognition, and the interpretations and actions derived from it are structured through metaphors. Lakoff and Johnson develop what they call the "experiential" account of metaphor; because the mind "operates in conjunction with a physical body that dwells in the physical world. Physical and spatial perceptions largely determine our metaphoric understandings" (Lakoff and Johnson 1980). Thus, when Lakoff and Johnson speak of metaphor, they move past the general definition of metaphor as a linguistic term and instead speak of "conceptual metaphor," which emphasizes the cognitive potentialities of the concept (Lakoff and Johnson 1980, 6). As Lakoff and Johnson note, we humans "typically conceptualize the nonphysical in terms of the physical—that is, we conceptualize the less clearly delineated in terms of the more clearly delineated" (Lakoff and Johnson 1980, 59). A conceptual metaphor's power lies in its ability to emphasize aspects of the unfamiliar and intangible in terms of the familiar in such a way as to shape the target of the metaphor (i.e., the unfamiliar). In that process, the very systematic nature that allows humans to understand one aspect of a concept in terms of another necessarily emphasizes one aspect while eliding others (Lakoff and Johnson 1980, 10).

Metaphors, therefore, exert influence by instantiating frame-consistent cognitive structures—that means that a particular metaphor can manifest itself in a variety of contexts, a phenomenon that becomes all too clear in our speech. As an example of what I mean by "cognitive structure," consider the conceptual metaphor "Time is a Valuable Commodity." From this metaphor, we can speak of *wasting* time, *spending* time, *budgeting* time, making things *worth one's time*, living on *borrowed* time, *investing* time, and so forth (Lakoff and Johnson 1980, 10). The cognitive structure molds our conception of time to that of a limited, zero-sum commodity that must be invested well; this happens in various contexts, each one consistent with the larger frame the metaphor instantiates. Thus, the ways in which we speak of time comprise the cognitive structure that the conceptual metaphor underpins. The best way to appreciate the importance of these cognitive structures is that they do not structure our thoughts about time; rather they structure our conception of what time actually is.

As I apply the time example to matters of law and politics, I want to note Lakoff and Johnson's point that metaphors possess a self-fulfilling quality. That is, because metaphors serve as a guide for future actions that fit the metaphor, this will, in turn, reinforce the metaphor's ability to give coherence to one's experience. In this sense, "metaphors can [have] self-fulfilling properties" (Lakoff and Johnson 1980, 156). The suggestion that the powerful and privileged can easily create and impose metaphors underlies the integral role of metaphors in creating the public discursive space. Metaphors, as conceptual schema, thus structure how we view certain issues as salient; that is, metaphors not only define an issue for us, but they also inform us how much we should care about it and how we should approach it through policy.

Legal scholars have explored how metaphors and their resulting cognitive structures are employed in policing and crime control. In their paper, "Metaphors We Think With: The Role of Metaphor in Reasoning," cognitive scientists Thibodeau and Boroditsky (2011) reveal that linguistic framing shapes reasoning and that systems of power (i.e., the legal system and the political process) consolidate meaning instantiated by metaphor. These authors argue that the cognitive structure inherent in a metaphorical system may undergo what they call analogical transfer. Analogical transfer "can license the transfer of inferences from one domain to the other, and the most striking or stable structural similarities can be highlighted and stored in memory" (Lakoff and Johnson 1980, 9). Repeated analogical transfer from the source domain to the target domain reifies structural similarity between them. In other words, the transfer from the familiar to the unfamiliar becomes seamless such that we cease to think of one thing in terms of another and think of *one thing as another*.

Thus, I argue that metaphors not only determine how we make sense of issues, but how we seek out information in constructing possible policy responses. Before delving into that further, I should note the following: metaphors about immigration rarely stand up to scrutiny. As a test case, consider the metaphorical frame "The Immigration System is a Line One Waits In." Part of why that metaphor sticks is its simplicity; think of how angry you would be if you were cut in line for something. However, on the other hand, the metaphor is pernicious in its simplicity. The processes of immigration and naturalization cannot be conceptualized in terms of a line, and even if it could be, it would be a slow-moving one that leaves those waiting for naturalization for up to two decades. Lastly, the line metaphor gives too much credence to the procedure and the institution that operationalizes it. The immigration regime, which many activists rightly rail against, is given a prima facie legitimacy that forestalls critiques of detention, family separation, and restrictionist policy and rhetoric.

Another aspect that affects the salience of metaphor is whether the public will use a certain cognitive structure if experts reinforce its meaning. "Experts" here refers to legal officials: judges, lawyers, politicians, bureaucrats, and so on.[7] Experts are in a unique position to manipulate metaphors and cognitive structures in one of two, non-mutually exclusive ways: (1) experts do not know all the metaphors they use, but they can still deliberately pick which ones to use at times, or (2) experts may not be aware of the metaphors they use, but they still unconsciously select and use metaphors that are advantageous to themselves due to their position as experts (for more information, see Putnam 1973). And, as I will argue later, the products of such manipulation—cognitive structures finding their way into judicial decisions, legislation, or the administrative state's modus operandi—provide the underwriting necessary for the polity at large to structure their normative policy goals according to the promulgations of the state.

That said, what is most important about these metaphors is not about whether they are accurate, *but why they exist*. In this sense, the metaphor's importance moves from the meanings metaphors instantiate to their pragmatic value. Finn Makela, epistemologist of law, characterizes this as "refocus[ing] the analysis of law from what metaphors *mean* to what metaphors *do*" (Makela 2011, 407).[8] The importance of understanding metaphors and the cognitive structures they instantiate only ratchets up in a society such as ours, where the myth of objectivity has such controlling power. In a culture where the myth of objectivism is a constitutive part of Western culture "and truth is always absolute truth, the people who get to impose their metaphors on the culture get to define what we consider to be true—absolutely and objectively true" (Lakoff and Johnson 1980, 160). All of this suggests that the importance of metaphors for policy discussions hinges on their ability to galvanize public and institutional support for certain policy positions.

The resulting influence of cognitive structures in politics not only shapes how we view policy, but how we *think we should* view policy. A critically important consequence of metaphors and the cognitive structures they instantiate is that they influence our conception of what truth is. According to Lakoff and Johnson, what matters is not "[the] truth or falsity of a metaphor but the perceptions and inferences that follow from it and the actions that are sanctioned by it" (Lakoff and Johnson 1980, 158). Cunningham-Parmeter also comes to the conclusion that "the more we repeat, circulate, and repackage certain metaphors, the more our conceptual domains become tied to a limited set of associations" (Cunningham-Parmeter 2011, 1548). And the more that the law sanctions these limited sets of associations, metaphors and their resulting cognitive structures cease to be ways we view law and *instead become the law*.

I use this example to contend that given metaphor's unique ability to corrupt notions of procedural fairness, we can assess the utility of procedural fairness in two ways: either procedural fairness is problematic insofar as it serves as an ideological frame that legitimates the unfair implementation of state authority (so notions of procedural fairness are a kind of dominance framework), or procedural fairness is corrupted in a particular political context because it does not account for the input of noncitizens. The former possibility suggests that procedural fairness is itself a suspect idea, while the latter case suggests that oppositional movements can potentially reconstitute procedural fairness and popular understandings of it to make good on the promise that public discussion on political issues claims it holds. Therefore, for this chapter I will work on the latter possibility and analyze its use in the immigration reform context.

Immigration Metaphors and Cognitive Structures

In the face of competing ideas of the ideal society, and the differing opinions among people as to how immigrants figure into conceptions of the ideal society, immigration policy debates become meaning-making competitions among interest groups. "Metaphors play a critical role in making meanings for the groups that use them; those who oppose immigration have an interest in propagating metaphors that emphasize the undesirable aspects of immigrants and hide other aspects. The metaphor 'immigration as a wave' will emphasize the destructive force of migration while hiding the fact that migrants are human beings" (Santa Ana, 2002). It also makes a certain policy proposal—that of a physical bulwark (i.e., a wall)—appear to be a reasonable goal. Just like it would be absurd to deal with a wave at the molecular level, the metaphor of "Immigration as a Wave" makes it absurd to look at immigration at the level of the immigrant (see Santa Ana 2002 for more on the "immigration as a wave" metaphor). The metaphor characterizes the problem in a way that implies, or makes necessary, a certain solution. Voters and policymakers who strongly support immigration restrictions might view procedural fairness as summary deportation and use the metaphor to achieve their policy aim.

If we take political and legal disputes to be meaning-making competitions, those competing in the political process seek the state's legitimacy for their policy proposals in line with a group's interests. Metaphor plays a critical role in this process; a particular metaphor's endorsement through its use in establishing precedent and grounding legislative discussion gives the metaphor a kind of "legitimacy-at-first-glance" and, through its constant framing of a certain issue, *actually* becomes socially desirable. It is safe to assume that in conversations about immigration reform, the political interests of residents and citizens will outweigh those of undocumented immigrants.[9] From this assumption, I argue that undocumented immigrants do not have as much access to the political process as is necessary to ensure an outcome they would view as procedurally fair. This is because the metaphors that the courts and politicians use to refer to undocumented immigrants normalize a particular way of speaking to and about those without status, and the inability of undocumented migrants to contend with this discourse politically exists in large part because of such metaphors. Metaphors become a tool of exclusion that, by the time deliberation occurs on undocumented immigration, renders their exclusion as given. In answering how political institutions consolidate the instantiation of meaning in the political context, my contention is that legal and political institutions (i.e., the courts and the legislature) not only imbue the meanings of *political metaphors* but, due to their position, play a unique role in accelerating the salience of certain metaphors—I focus on immigration metaphors—as tools of political exclusion.[10]

Cunningham-Parmeter provides a convincing account of the staying power of metaphors and their ability to warp, irreversibly, lay views on immigrants. He finds that "the more we repeat, circulate, and repackage certain metaphors, the more our conceptual domains become tied to a limited set of associations"(Cunningham-Parmeter 2011, 1548). Placed in the immigration context, the constant propagations of the "Nation as Body" or the "Illegal Alien as Pathogen" metaphors by the courts, the legislature, and interest groups (i.e., those with the power to determine and influence law and policy) become the best way to characterize the political situation that unauthorized immigration presents, thus fueling their continued use. Assuming that deliberations about procedural fairness between proponents and opponents of regularizing undocumented immigrants require that they have equal access to the tools of political participation, there exists an unfairness in deliberation whereby undocumented immigrants and the groups that work in their interest have fewer opportunities to deliberate about immigration reform than legal residents and citizens. And, say, if a candidate for political office who supports immigration restrictions thinks it procedurally fair to build a wall, that might carry more weight in discourse relative to the policy ideas of undocumented immigrants and their interest groups.

Conversely, undocumented immigrant interest groups, who have to first fight to be recognized as human, have a difficult time erasing their association with aliens and alienage. For example, suppose undocumented immigrant groups wage a campaign against the term "alien" because it is dehumanizing; immigrants are not extraterrestrial monsters with green skin and tentacles (drawing on the cultural valence of the term). However, the legal tradition the term "alien" carries makes that difficult. This is a prime example of the reifying power inherent in political metaphors. Thus, in its interaction with systems of power, metaphor plays a critical role in establishing the normativity of cognitive structures, which in turn influence the salience and the perceived normativity of certain policy positions. Here, "perceived normativity" is equivalent to what Ryo and the procedural justice literature label as "perceptions of greater procedural fairness." Grounding this view is the assumption that the appearance of fairness in an immigration system is sufficient for the policy to be desired. Lakoff and Johnson (1980) note as much; they argue, "Metaphors may thus be a guide for future action. Such actions will, of course, fit the metaphor. This will, in turn, reinforce the power of the metaphor to make experience coherent," harkening back to the invidious cycle that Lakoff and Johnson note (156). Metaphor is integral in constructing what law promulgates as procedurally fair, which, in turn, shapes the polity's conception of procedural fairness.

Take, for example, the metaphor of the "Nation as Body." In the cognitive structure this metaphor creates, undocumented immigrants are a foreign invasion that pose an existential threat to the health of the nation qua body (Chavez 2013). When a pathogen is detected, the body unleashes a swift, fatal response to what it perceives as a threat. Further, given how much weight this metaphor carries in political discourse, swift responses to remove the invasive force that is undocumented immigration appear to be a fair response. People with significant political clout can employ this metaphor in rhetoric aimed at residents as well as in the written law, such that metaphor is indistinguishable from legal terms. If immigrants are metaphorically characterized as a pathogen, the policy idea of swift action—that is, summary deportation—fits the conceptual structure the metaphor creates. The metaphor characterizes the unfamiliar (undocumented immigrants) in terms of the familiar (a pathogen), and the prefigured response to immigrants as pathogens is tantamount to a swift, targeted, and decisive bodily reaction to an existential threat— think of penicillin responding to bacterial agents. Such a conception of dealing with the expulsion of noncitizens thus justifies and makes normative the characterization of undocumented immigrants as pathogens, and the invidious cycle continues.

Thus, there is one more powerful party imposing its metaphors at play here; it is those who have the status and goods of citizenship who control the terms of the debate on procedural fairness surrounding immigration. The deliberative unfairness manifesting itself in the politics of immigration reform will lead to either no reform, piecemeal policies that fracture and pacify immigrant subgroups, or, worse yet, predatory policies against undocumented immigrants. As I have argued, it is not merely enough to expose these metaphors as inaccurate or unjust; the metaphors, given the power held by who is imposing them, receive the state's legitimacy, making them a normal part of immigration discussions.

The discussion of metaphors in the American political space is, therefore, of critical contemporary importance. Those with access to the political and legal arms of the state can more easily impose their cognitive structures, influencing how members of the polity metaphorically reason through, and thus normatively conceive of, policy. A prime example of this is "Naturalization as a Line/Queue." Through this metaphor, American policymakers and laypeople conceive of the naturalization process (and, as a corollary, the entire immigration apparatus) as procedurally fair. One of the most common retorts in opposition to undocumented immigrants' residency claims is to demand that they "go to the back of the line." Policymakers deploy the "line" metaphor to describe the order in which noncitizens should arrange themselves according to their anticipated enjoyment of state benefits. Some people come to consider unauthorized immigration as not only illegal but *unjust* because migrants are portrayed as looking for easy access to benefits and jumping the queue. According to Bergeron (2013), lawmakers' admonition that undocumented immigrants "go to the back of the line" is one they adopt ostensibly "to convey the intent to grant legal status to unauthorized immigrants only after existing backlogs have been cleared." Absent in this metaphor and its presentation is the fact that there are statutory limits to the number of visas that the United States Citizenship and Immigration Services (USCIS) can grant in any given year. In addition, it takes years—even decades in some instances—to receive permanent residency. Thus, the conceptual metaphor "Naturalization as a Line/Queue" emphasizes the normativity of order—that is, those who are first in line have a stronger claim—and hides other aspects such as the excessive demand for visas relative to the actual number USCIS allocates annually.

Immigrants who migrated to the United States and were able to be regularized can take the high ground and proclaim that they did things the right way. In political discourse, the line becomes a device that citizens use to enable a hierarchy, in which we order those noncitizens more deserving of benefits ahead of those noncitizens who are less deserving. For the most part, citizens would not imagine *themselves* to even need to be in the line. They circumvent that line altogether. *The line doesn't apply to citizens.* Even more consequential is that undocumented immigrants themselves are unable to gain residency and citizenship due to bars that prevent those who have accrued unlawful presence from adjusting their status. These bars, and the fact that the line metaphor conceals them, are important to note. Even if adjustment of status were an option for many undocumented immigrants, they must leave the country to obtain their visas from consular outposts abroad. Depending on the amount of unlawful status an immigrant has accrued, there exists an immigration provision[11] that bars them from entering the United States for either three or ten years. Employing the line metaphor in that way adds a normativity to the metaphor that further adds to the marginalization of undocumented immigrants in that they are now taken to not have an understanding of law or morality, which are (rhetorically) considered lynchpins of the American nation-state.

Oppositional Cognitive Structures and Undocumented Immigrant Movements

Perhaps the most pernicious effect of the power imbalance indicated in the acceptance of certain cognitive structures at the expense of undocumented immigrants is that, in contending against an anti-immigrant political environment, anti-immigrant metaphors and cognitive structures restrict undocumented immigrants' ability to construct humanizing narratives as well as concrete policy proposals. Such proposals become so restricted that the most successful ones almost always must receive the approval of the very political establishment they aim to critique. Thus, these "oppositional cognitive structures," as I label them, are either made in response to, or in light of, the cognitive structures of those with power. Regarding metaphor and the cognitive structures they instantiate, I contend that in making claims in the political sphere, undocumented immigrant groups are all but forced to operate under the establishments' framings—in this case, anti-immigrant interests as well as the national myth that places them outside the polity.

In this section of the chapter, I develop an account of the importance of building an oppositional cognitive structure and making it the new norm in contemporary American immigration discourse. By this I mean that, given metaphor's role in highlighting certain aspects of a target domain and eliding others, an important part of narrative-building strategy must include an analysis of metaphors that anti-immigrant interests use and courts legitimate. The oppositional cognitive structures immigrants' rights movements must expose should engage, but not align with, politically dominant cognitive structures. The goal should be to expose these cognitive structures' specious claims to normativity, which with sustained activism will hopefully lead to their disuse by legal institutions.

In developing this basic account, I do not argue for the normative value of legal institutions as currently constructed. Rather, I recognize that policy must go through legislative deliberation and judicial review and strategizing in light of them will have a real effect on the daily lives of undocumented immigrants and their capacity for political action. Political engagement for undocumented immigrants and other marginalized groups is critical to surviving in an environment that presupposes their lack of humanity and puts into practice their dehumanization through deportation, stigma, and denial of necessary services. I take as given the assumption that the aims of oppositional cognitive structures are better policy. If oppositional cognitive structures are not sufficiently differentiated from powerful cognitive structures, this serves to undermine not only the oppositional cognitive structure's policy aims, but the normative value of good policy.

As a cautionary example, consider the "DREAMer." The DREAMer, in discourse on immigration, denotes someone who entered this country at a young age, achieves impeccable grades or is otherwise high-achieving professionally, has unaccented speech or otherwise accepts various aspects of American culture, and wholeheartedly believes in the American Dream and its attendant myth of meritocracy. Despite their undocumented status, DREAMers consider themselves part of the American community in every relevant way, save papers. In making a claim for immigration reform or for a more piecemeal policy, DREAMers mark themselves as deserving of residency and citizenship. For example, consider when high-profile DREAMers endorsed candidates in the 2016 democratic presidential primaries. DREAMers garnered influence within their communities, and used the resulting clout to back a candidate who would be a fierce advocate for immigrant interests. Here are how the major endorsements shook out: Erika Andiola and Cesar Vargas endorsed Bernie Sanders, Astrid Silva endorsed Hillary Clinton, and Jonathan Jayes-Green endorsed Martin O'Malley (Carrascillo 2015; Silva 2016; Hernández 2015).

For the purposes of my argument, I will introduce what I call "meta-endorsement." Meta-endorsement as a concept is cognizant of the ways in which power shapes resistance and those who carry it out. What is especially pernicious about meta-endorsement is that, though undocumented immigrants may have access to the political system and have some political power, they are still subject to the political system and are nevertheless answerable to it. How does meta-endorsement operate in this example? The candidate can gain the support of the community that the DREAMer represents. However, the candidate—many orders of magnitude more influential than the DREAMers—retains the ability to determine who can endorse them. In partnering with high-achieving undocumented immigrants with spotless records, strong community ties, and a robust belief in the American political system, the candidates reify the caricature of the DREAMer as the subgroup within the larger cohort of undocumented immigrants that most deserves to benefit from immigration reform.

This example shows how meta-endorsement, in exposing the inner workings of the political system, relegates—or exposes—endorsement as a mere tool of politics. This caricature of the DREAMer as the most deserving immigrant allows for only some undocumented immigrants to benefit from rights-protecting policies, such as Deferred Action for Childhood Arrivals (DACA). There exists the argument that young immigrants have the time and can present themselves as more sympathetic, placing themselves at the forefront of immigration activism. In other words, DREAMers have a comparatively extensive ability, relative to their influence, to shape the narrative in contrast to their parents, unmarried undocumented adults (mostly men), and undocumented immigrants with criminal records. To the extent that the trope of the young, high-achieving immigrant who believes in the American Dream holds sway, they are able to shape the narrative for all undocumented immigrants, placing themselves at the forefront. Within this particular metaphor there are numerous controlling assumptions: that there is a clearly delineable process for prospective migrants to follow, that those who do not take part in this process choose not to do so, and further, that the choice not to do so is a violation that demands criminal sanction; offenders should be punished with deportation (Murdock 2018).

At this juncture, it is critical to note two things. The first is that it is easy for me to conduct the foregoing analysis after the fact. Though the DREAMer narrative is one that is accepted by significant constituencies within the immigrant rights movement as being dangerous, there is much to be said for the argument that such a narrative represented the most pragmatic argument possible at the time in which it became salient. The second is that there is an ongoing dialectic between the piecemeal and the comprehensive. This dialectic compels those within the immigrant rights movement to be conscious of framing claims-making in such a way as to secure the proximate avenues of relief while not sacrificing the movement's more comprehensive political objectives.

In her paper "Legal Consciousness of Undocumented Latinos," sociologist Leisy Abrego (2011) contests the idea that undocumented immigrants' integration processes are monolithic. She argues that examining differences in claims-making behaviors among undocumented immigrants "reveal[s] an interplay between legal status . . . as well as experiences with migration and social institutions that differentially affect their sense of belonging and incorporation experiences" (Abrego 2011, 339). She begins by introducing Adela, a mother whose child plays a prominent role in DREAM Act activism. Though her child can play a prominent role due to possessing the prototypical "DREAMer" narrative, Adela herself is much more removed; her status as the stereotypical undocumented immigrant makes her not only less sympathetic a figure, but also a target. Though Abrego seeks to examine how positionality determines the types of claims undocumented immigrant subgroups make and does so in a way seldom done in the literature, she does not consider the effects of race in her analysis.

Granted, work on undocumented Black immigrants, though ongoing at the margins for years, faced significant barriers to inclusion in the larger immigrant rights movement until the Black Lives Matter movement became the touchstone of social justice activism. To wit, there was little to no treatment of the plight of Black undocumented folks until the Black Alliance for Just Immigration published their "State of Black Immigrants" Report in 2016, in conjunction with New York University School of Law. Still, the lack of a deep race analysis within the immigration movement at the time of the DREAMer's creation facilitated the adoption of a model-minority narrative that marginalized both non-DREAMers as well as Black people, immigrants or otherwise.

Though I cannot conduct a deeper dive into how race plays a part in political analysis, I want to note its general relevance especially given recent, grave developments in American politics. On November 5, 2016 Donald Trump—who holds unabashedly anti-immigrant views—was elected President of the United States. In a *60 Minutes* interview, he promised to prioritize the deportation of three million so-called criminal immigrants (Davis and Preston 2016). The three million figure is a red herring (Abrego et al. 2017). Of note is the "criminal" label: by leaving the term undefined yet still allowing it to fester in the public consciousness, I contend that there will be an expanded notion of criminality such that all immigrants will be regarded as criminals without necessarily having a criminal record. There is an interplay between the two cognitive structures that is metaphorical in nature—the unfamiliar immigrant is referred to in terms of the familiar criminal/illegal cognitive structure (Stumpf 2006). In not separating the criminal from the immigrant, and in not delineating what a noncriminal immigrant would look like, such rhetoric seeks to conflate the two. Further, policies such as mass deportation and the increase in incarceration of criminal others—Black and Brown bodies—will continue to reify the conceptual metaphor as the normative framework for dealing with the immigrant as well as the criminal.

The Trump administration is, in ways both public and private, attempting to fracture the immigrant rights movement by separating the wheat from the chaff, metaphorically speaking. President-elect Trump indicated amenability toward helping DREAMers; nevertheless, he made good on his promise to rescind DACA by instructing Acting Department of Homeland Security Secretary Elaine Duke to wind down the program (Foley 2016; Department of Homeland Security 2017). However, at the time of writing, Judge William Haskell Alsup of the U.S. Court of Appeals for the Ninth Circuit ruled that, while cases against the Trump administration are ongoing, USCIS will accept DACA renewal applications (McCallister 2018). Concurrently, Democrats in Congress are attempting to strike a compromise with the Trump administration on a permanent fix for DACA, which would go above and beyond its predecessor in providing a path to citizenship for undocumented immigrants who arrived as children (Manchester 2018). The critical impasse is whether protections for these immigrants will be at the cost of increased immigration enforcement, the absence of which immigrant rights advocates maintain is a necessary condition of a "Clean DREAM Act" (National Immigration Law Center 2017).

I have made the point that DACA, as a political tool, served to pacify DREAMers. Relative to other undocumented immigrant subgroups, they have the time, the zeal, and the support to make claims against the state. But as

I showed, their strategies further marginalized undocumented immigrants who do not fit the mold, such as adults and those with criminal records. Moving back to the undefined Trumpian notion of the "criminal," there is little indication that DREAMers will be shielded from the presumption of criminality that now receives state approval. Further, the "Immigrant as DREAMer" conceptual metaphor and resulting cognitive structures elide the intersections of race and criminality. Just as Abrego argues that various undocumented immigrant subgroups occupy different positionalities as a function of their age at entry and socialization, others differ based on race.

The construction of oppositional cognitive structures is important for undocumented immigrants as people who deserve recognition. In discussing the rights consciousness of undocumented immigrants, Abrego (2011) reports on a 2008 immigration raid in Postville, Iowa, in which although the employers provided the workers with false documents, it was the workers who were detained and punished (355). As an explanation for why the undocumented workers did not defend themselves, an interpreter describes what one worker told them: "No matter how many times his attorney explained it, he kept saying 'I'm illegal, I have no rights. I'm nobody in this country. Just do whatever you want with me'" (Preston 2008). The cognitive structures "Illegal Immigrant as Alien" and "Illegal Immigrant as Criminal" work together such that the undocumented immigrant does the work of dehumanization for the state, which propagates these cognitive structures. Regarding the former cognitive structure, the undocumented worker does not deserve rights because only humans have rights, whereas the latter cognitive structure decrees that he does not have rights because criminals by definition give up their rights. The legitimation of these cognitive structures through legislation and judicial decisions means that undocumented immigrants develop conceptions of self that are deeply imbricated within these cognitive structures.

Moving further along this line of thought, Tamara Nopper has done helpful and important work in exposing the cognitive structures that mold existing conceptions of the undocumented immigrant worker. Indeed, discourses centering on undocumented workers draw upon "managerial and capitalist perspectives of labor as well as antiblack rhetoric regarding African Americans as lacking a work ethic, being militant, xenophobic, and costly to society" (Nopper 2011, 2). Conceptions of undocumented immigrant productivity—in this case, Nopper focuses on Latinos—is amplified at the expense of African Americans; the immigrant cares about and needs work whereas African Americans are lazy due to benefiting from welfare. In further contrast to undocumented workers, who are actively positioning themselves as valuable human capital despite hardship, African Americans are considered physically imposing and threatening, indicating that they do not "know their place" in the American racial hierarchy (Nopper 2011, 8).

Perhaps the most important aspect of Nopper's work is her conclusion that despite the existing discourse situating itself in a discussion of neoliberal globalization, it does not—in fact, it cannot—be antagonistic to capital because its central thrusts are firmly within the cognitive structures that place capitalism as both instrumental to citizenship and normatively desirable (Nopper 2011, 17). With this conclusion in mind, I turn to Cunningham-Parmeter's proposition of the conceptual metaphor *economic sanctuary* (his italics) as foundational to an immigrant counternarrative. He writes that the *economic sanctuary* metaphor "emphasizes the connections shared by migrants and displaced American workers; just as Americans become unemployed when their jobs are shipped overseas, migrants feel the consequences of international trade from the other side of the border" (Cunningham-Parmeter 2011, 1596). I am intrigued by the possibilities of the metaphor, though I would add that given where I think Cunningham-Parmeter wants to go with the metaphor, the word "economic" is subject to an anticapitalist critique.

Despite the foundational flaws of the DREAMer metaphorical framework, it has nevertheless secured important victories at the federal and state levels, thus providing a safer academic and political environment for undocumented scholars like myself to begin developing the kinds of cognitive structures that will replace the moribund DREAMer framework. In an op-ed published by the *Washington Post*, I argue that DACA, despite all its benefits, did significant harm due to its roots in the DREAMer framework (Sati 2017). Using myself as an example, though I have the opportunity to secure advanced degrees at two elite universities because of DACA, my achievements do not make me any more deserving than those without them. Still, I can use my position to argue for undocumented immigrants in a more precarious position. Thus, in protecting and, more importantly, building on DACA, I implore the immigrant rights movement to begin adopting alternative frameworks.

Despite the necessity of creating oppositional frameworks, I do acknowledge Cunningham-Parmeter's effort and agree that conceptual metaphors will fail to capture everything. It might be the case that the immigrant rights movement will develop cognitive structures that rely on some notion of respectability, especially when it comes to converting those in the immigration debate who are unconvinced by our position. Nevertheless, it is important that undocumented immigrants understand the role of metaphor in creating cognitive structures that exist outside notions of capital and criminality, as well as the notions of deservingness inherent in both. Thus, undocumented immigrants are better able to utilize new frameworks and fight back against what Cunningham-Parmeter labels the "jurisprudence of otherness" present in metaphorical frameworks such as "Illegal Immigrant as Alien," "Immigration is a Flood," and "Immigration is an Invasion." Therefore, it is critical that undocumented scholars take the forefront in developing oppositional analysis that contends with the problem of noncitizenship in our time.

Conclusion

In this essay, I argue that examining conceptual metaphors and the cognitive structures they instantiate sheds important light on the political discourse in which undocumented immigrant activism takes place. Analyzing the entities that normalize metaphors and the cognitive structures that spring from them reveals not only something about the power of such entities, but also illumines how these metaphors can become significant such that we not only think about them, but think on their terms. Regarding undocumented immigrant activism, I argue that the creation of oppositional cognitive structures that are completely cleaved from dominant ones will help create policy that is more inclusive of the various identities that intersect with undocumented status—such as race, gender, and criminal record, among others. Furthermore, such oppositional structures are more attentive to undocumented immigrants' policy aims. In addition, differentiated oppositional cognitive structures result in normatively better policy debates and, in turn, normatively better policy *for everyone*. In all, a push for greater procedural fairness rings hollow without a thorough discussion of the role that noncitizens play in the deliberative framework.

NOTES

I would like to thank K. T. Albiston in the Jurisprudence and Social Policy PhD program, Sunmin Kim and the Immigration Working Group in UC Berkeley's Sociology Department, and the editors of this volume for their constructive feedback. Lastly, I would like to thank my partner Bianca Waked and my pet cats Langshaw and Marlo, all of whom keep me sane.

1. This essay focuses on metaphors about immigrants. Though immigrants do use metaphors about citizens, this dimension of the debate is not the focus of this chapter if only for the reason that I want to make clear the link between metaphor and policy. Focusing on metaphors about immigrants presents the link in stark relief, though I want to emphasize that metaphors about immigrants are not the totality of metaphors in the immigrant rights debate.

2. This sentence reminds me of the cliché phrase "seeing is believing." The cognitive framework that the phrase instantiates had a significant influence in my reading of Ryo's paper. As a further avenue of research, I am interested in how empiricism or

empirical-like considerations structure our conception of truth and the many ways such a conception manifests itself in the law.

3. "Passing a Clean DREAM Act is the Top Political Priority of This Year." In this article, billionaire and Democratic donor Tom Steyer is quoted as saying "When we stand up for Dreamers and the whole immigrant community, what we are really standing up for is justice in America and the rights of Americans everywhere. The triumph of America is when we move our laws to line up with our values—and that's what we're asking for today. *So let's live up to our true American values and pass a Clean DREAM Act*" (emphasis added). For more information on the Clean DREAM Act, see this guide by the National Immigration Law Center: https://www.nilc.org/wp-content/uploads/2017/10/Clean-Dream-Act-1pg-2017.pdf.

4. Given the importance of immigration as an issue, much more work needs to be done on how narratives are constructed vis-à-vis the conceptual structure of IMMIGRANT AS ALIEN.

5. *Sugarman v. Dougall*, 413 U.S. 634, 662 (1973) (Rehnquist, J., dissenting).

6. Another thing that occurs to me about the term "alien" is the movement back and forth between cultural and legal contexts. What is the law to do? At first glance, the law's almost-apotheosis of precedent means that the law should not be counted on to disuse the term "illegal alien." Further yet, I conjecture that any attempt by the law to disuse the term is, to use an idiom, locking the barn door well after the horse has bolted. Though an investigation of the ILLEGAL AS ALIEN metaphor is a fruitful endeavor and pushing for its use in legal contexts a worthwhile exercise, the cultural valence attached to the terms makes any effort an extremely difficult one.

7. It is important to define what an expert is. For the purposes of this discussion, experts (1) have esoteric knowledge about a certain discipline, and (2) engage in foundational debates about things that they have esoteric knowledge of. I will call (1) the *esoteric* condition and (2) the *positionality* condition. For example, a professor in the philosophy of language is an expert because (1) she has esoteric knowledge of a philosophical subdiscipline, and (2) she holds a professorship and engages in academic discourse about esoteric subjects within said subdiscipline. Consider another example: it is neither necessary nor efficient that every person who wears a gold ring engage in buying and selling gold or in determining the authenticity of gold, since there are experts to fill both niches.

8. Emphasis in original.

9. Admittedly, this is a very U.S.-specific assumption. That is, though true in the American context, it is not a given in other countries. For example, in the late 1800s and early 1900s, several Latin American countries aimed to attract Europeans to become citizens. They viewed this as a whitening process that would dilute African and Indigenous races through miscegenation. In that racist process, they prioritized the rights and the humanity of white immigrants above those of other populations. Many thanks to Leisy Abrego for this insight.

10. I am not trying to conflate equality of opportunity with equality of influence. I argue that metaphors and accompanying cognitive structures manipulate the very notion of opportunity operant in political discourse. If undocumented immigrants are

metaphorically constructed as the nonhuman alien and undeserving of rights, arguing for equal influence seems pointless. What is more important is that undocumented immigrants do not have the opportunity to influence, and it is this knowledge that undocumented immigrant groups must be aware of when constructing opposition.

11. INA § 212(a)(9)(B).

REFERENCES

Abrego, Leisy J. 2011. "Legal Consciousness of Undocumented Latinos: Fear and Stigma as Barriers to Claims-Making for First- and 1.5-Generation Immigrants." *Law and Society Review* 45: 337–370. https://www.jstor.org/stable/23012045.

Abrego, Leisy, Mat Coleman, Daniel E. Martínez, Cecilia Menjívar, and Jeremy Slack. 2017. "Making Immigrants into Criminals: Legal Processes of Criminalization in the Post-IIRIRA Era." *Journal on Migration and Human Security* 5(3) :694–715. https://doi.org/10.14240/jmhs.v5i3.105.

Bergeron, Claire. 2013. "Going to the Back of the Line: A Primer on Lines, Visa Categories, and Wait Times." *Migration Policy Institute*, March 2013. https://www.migrationpolicy.org/research/going-back-line-primer-lines-visa-categories-and-wait-times.

Black Alliance for Just Immigration. 2016. "State of Black Immigrants." *Black Alliance for Just Immigration.* http://www.stateofblackimmigrants.com/.

Carrascillo, Adrian. 2015. "Bernie Sanders Just Hired the Best Known Immigration Activist in the Country." *BuzzFeed News*, October 30, 2015. https://www.buzzfeednews.com/article/adriancarrasquillo/bernie-sanders-just-hired-the-best-known-immigration-activis.

Chavez, Leo. 2013. *The Latino Threat: Constructing Immigrants, Citizens, and the Nation.* Palo Alto, CA: Stanford University Press.

Cunningham-Parmeter, Keith. 2011. "Alien Language: Immigration Metaphors and the Jurisprudence of Otherness." *Fordham Law Review* 79: 1545–98. https://heinonline.org/HOL/P?h=hein.journals/inlr32&i=627.

Davis, Julie Hirschfeld, and Julia Preston. 2016. "What Donald Trump's Vow to Deport up to 3 Million Immigrants Would Mean." *New York Times*, November 14, 2016. http://www.nytimes.com/2016/11/15/us/politics/donald-trump-deport-immigrants.html?_r=0.

Department of Homeland Security. 2017. "Rescission of Deferred Action for Childhood Arrivals (DACA)." *Department of Homeland Security*, September 5, 2017. https://www.dhs.gov/news/2017/09/05/rescission-deferred-action-childhood-arrivals-daca.

Foley, Elise. 2016. "Trump Says, without Specifics, He'll 'Work Something Out' for Dreamers." *Huffington Post Politics*, December 7, 2016. http://www.huffingtonpost.com/entry/donald-trump-daca-dreamers_us_58481963e4b0d0df18372021.

Hernández, Arelis R. 2015. "Martin O'Malley Is Targeting Latino Voters." *Washington Post*, June 1, 2015. https://www.washingtonpost.com/news/post-politics/wp/2015/06/01/martin-omalley-is-targeting-latino-voters/.

Lakoff, George, and Mark Johnson. 1980. *Metaphors We Live By*. Chicago: University of Chicago Press.

Makela, Finn. 2011. "Metaphors and Models in Legal Theory." *Les Cahiers de Droit* 52(3–4): 397–415. https://doi.org/10.7202/1006668ar.

Manchester, Julia. 2018. "Warren: 'Glad We Are Moving Forward on Getting a Clean DREAM Act.'" *The Hill*, January 10, 2018. http://thehill.com/homenews/senate/368261-warren-glad-we-are-moving-forward-on-getting-a-clean-dream-act.

McCallister, Doreen. 2018. "Federal Judge Temporarily Blocks Trump's Decision to End DACA." *NPR*, January 10, 2018. https://www.npr.org/sections/thetwo-way/2018/01/10/576963434/federal-judge-temporarily-blocks-trumps-decision-to-end-daca.

Murdock, Deroy. 2018. "Fence-Climbing Illegal Aliens Cut in Line as Legal Immigrants Wait in Obscurity." *National Review*, May 4, 2018. https://www.nationalreview.com/2018/05/legal-immigrants-vs-illegal-immigrants-cutting-line/.

National Immigration Law Center. 2017. "What is the DREAM Act." *National Immigration Law Center*. https://www.nilc.org/wp-content/uploads/2017/10/Clean-Dream-Act-1pg-2017.pdf.

Nopper, Tamara K. 2011. "The Wages of Non-Blackness: Contemporary Immigrant Rights and Discourses of Character, Productivity, and Value." *InTensions Journal* 5: 1–25. http://www.yorku.ca/intent/issue5/articles/pdfs/tamaraknopperarticle.pdf.

Preston, Julia. 2008. "An Interpreter Speaking Up for Migrants." *New York Times*, July 11, 2008. http://www.nytimes.com/2008/07/ll/us/llimmig.html.

Putnam, Hilary. 1973. "Meaning and Reference." *Journal of Philosophy* 70(19): 699–711.

Ryo, Emily. 2013. "Deciding to Cross: Norms and Economics of Unauthorized Migration." *American Sociological Review* 78(4): 574–603. https://doi.org/10.1177/0003122413487904.

Santa Ana, Otto. 2002. *Brown Tide Rising: Metaphors of Latinos in Contemporary American Public Discourse*. Austin: University of Texas Press.

Sati, Joel. 2017. "How DACA Pits 'Good Immigrants' against Millions of Others." *Washington Post*, September 7, 2017. https://www.washingtonpost.com/news/posteverything/wp/2017/09/07/how-daca-pits-good-immigrants-against-millions-of-others/?noredirect=on&utm_term=.785fbd34950e.

Silva, Astrid. 2016. "Astrid Silva: I Stand with Hillary Because She Stands with Immigrant Families." *Univision Noticias*, February 3, 2016. http://www.univision.com/noticias/opinion/astrid-silva-i-stand-with-hillary-because-she-stands-with-immigrant-families.

Stumpf, Juliet. 2006. "The Crimmigration Crisis: Immigrants, Crime, and Sovereign Power." *American University Law Review* 56(2): 367–420. https://heinonline.org/HOL/P?h=hein.journals/aulr56&i=379.

Thibodeau, Paul H., and Lera Boroditsky. 2011. "Metaphors We Think With: The Role of Metaphor in Reasoning." *PLoS ONE* 6(2): 1–11. https://doi.org/10.1371/journal.pone.0016782.

Tyler, Tom. 2004. "Procedural Justice." In *The Blackwell Companion to Law and Society*, edited by Austin Sarat, 435–52. London: Blackwell Publishing.

United We Dream. 2017. "Passing a Clean DREAM Act Is the Top Political Priority of This Year." *United We Dream*, October 5, 2017. https://unitedwedream.org/2017/10/passing-a-clean-dream-act-is-the-top-political-priority-of-this-year/.

2

"I felt like an embarrassment to the undocumented community"

Undocumented Students Navigating Academic Probation and Unrealistic Expectations

In the last few years, undocumented students have received national attention and support for their compelling stories of academic resilience despite financial burdens and lack of legal status (Abrego 2006; Borjian 2018; Gabrovsky 2009; Goffard 2012; Jones 2010; Madera 2008; Mirseyedi 2010; Pérez et al. 2009; Wong 2012). Through organizing and advocacy efforts, undocumented immigrant youth in California have pushed for policies that alleviate their financial burden, such as in-state tuition (Assembly Bill 540) and state-based financial aid (Assembly Bills 130 and 131 of the California Dream Act), thereby permitting them access to higher education in larger numbers. However, the dominant discourse—also known as the "DREAMer" narrative, defined as an undocumented student with "good grades and appealing as cultural Americans" (Schwiertz 2015, 2)—tends to center on only these students' academic excellence. While it is important to highlight the academic achievements and contributions of undocumented youth, it is also necessary to recognize that there are diverse experiences, many of which do not fit into this stereotype of high performance. The emphasis on stellar students has problematically overlooked the academic struggles of undocumented students, especially the experiences of those students with a history of academic probation during their undergraduate education.

In this chapter, I analyze the experiences of undocumented students who have been placed on academic probation and subject to dismissal from the University of California. Being on probationary status is a stigmatizing and isolating process for students in general, but for undocumented students, it also disrupts the dominant narrative about them, thereby leading to unique challenges. The mainstream narrative that depicts undocumented students as high achievers and valedictorians equates their worthiness and humanity solely with their academic excellence. I argue that these unrealistic standards set by the DREAMer narrative are especially difficult to meet given the structural realities shaped by college students' legal status and the associated complexities of their real lives. The findings show that depression, financial burdens, family health, and family separation stemming from their own or their loved ones' undocumented status weigh heavily on students, who then struggle with the added pressure of meeting unrealistic academic expectations.

Academic Probation

Universities across the United States often place students on academic probation when their grade point average drops below a certain GPA threshold—usually a 2.0. Academic probationary status can consist of various stages and procedures such as academic probation (Tovar and Simon 2006), academic dismissal, appealing dismissal, and readmission (Dozier 2001; Brost and Payne 2011). In many cases, however, placing a student on academic probation often discourages the student from returning to school, leading them to withdraw or "drop out" from college (Lindo, Sanders, and Oreopoulos 2010; Fletcher and Tokmouline 2010). As a result, it directly affects graduation rates and retention in higher education (Lindo, Sanders, and Oreopoulos 2010; Barefoot 2004).

The scholarship in this area often focuses on individual-level factors associated with academic probation. For example, scholars cite unpreparedness, lack of focus, insufficient motivation, personality, health, self-perception, values, and time management as problems (Tovar and Simon 2006; Kelley 1996). They focus on students' characteristics and capabilities, suggesting that often the issue is merely procrastination and laziness (Barefoot 2004; Brost and Payne 2011; Tovar and Simon 2006). Others point to personal factors such as family and financial issues, and the lack of awareness pertaining to academic probation policies at the university as culprits leading to academic probation (James and Graham 2010). A few cite a combination of internal and external factors that contribute to a student's academic performance (Kelley 1996).

Latinxs and other underrepresented minorities are overrepresented in academic probation (Brost and Payne 2011; Nance 2007). There is a correlation between psychological distress and poor academic performance

(Nance 2007), and historically marginalized groups experience academic difficulty in higher numbers. Being on academic probation often leads to stigma as students are ashamed to tell friends and family (Brost and Payne 2011). The stigma of academic probation can often serve as an additional push-out factor for students if they cannot access adequate supportive services (Tovar and Simon 2006). In this chapter, I call for us to think further and to understand the complexities of academic probation experiences for undocumented youth.

Setting Unrealistic Expectations

Scholarship on academic probation has not yet centered the experiences of undocumented students who face unique legal, social, and financial challenges. On the contrary, over and over, scholars have uplifted the stories of undocumented students graduating from high school with GPAs above a 4.0 (Madera 2008) while managing to work long hours (Pérez et al. 2009) and creating the immigrant youth movement (Madera 2008; Wong 2012; Schwiertz 2015). Teachers, counselors, parents, peers, and academic outreach programs can all influence an undocumented student's academic trajectory (Pérez and Cortés 2011). When these factors line up favorably, academic success is evident through a student's high GPA, receipt of academic awards, and list of rigorous courses taken (Pérez et al. 2009). However, as an immigrant organizer explains, the DREAMer narrative created an expectation "to complete a four-year degree in communities where the system historically has been set up for just a few to succeed" (Perez 2015). Given the economic, social, legal, and educational circumstances of immigrant youth of color in the United States, this narrative is likely to produce a damaging effect in the lives of those who could not meet the expectations and were therefore excluded (Schwiertz 2015). In fact, an undocumented student's legal status is not only an additional stressor (Pérez 2012), but it often may require students to work long hours, which leaves less time for their studies (Dozier 2001). Also, factors such as fear of deportation, loneliness, and depression affect the academic accomplishment of undocumented students (Dozier 2001).

The undocumented student population is diverse, and as we aim to build a stronger movement in the face of new political challenges, it is crucial to expand our understanding of this community. I contribute here to that goal by uncovering the various academic experiences of these students that do not fit the DREAMer narrative and are overlooked within the academic probation literature.

Methods and Data

This chapter draws on seven in-depth semi-structured interviews with former and current UCLA undocumented (and DACA recipient) students who experienced academic probation and subject to dismissal. Given the sensitive nature of the topic, it was difficult to recruit participants. I found two participants through my personal networks and the other five through a recruitment email sent to the listserv of Improving Dreams, Equality, Access and Success (IDEAS), the undocumented student-led support and advocacy organization for undocumented students at UCLA. This population is hard to reach, but because I was part of the undocumented student organization, our shared experiences created a sense of trust and safe space. The small sample size allowed me to connect deeply with each participant and conduct follow-up interviews and check-ins throughout the analysis and writing process. It was important to me to ensure that they were comfortable with the way their story was presented in the chapter. To that end, I had multiple conversations with each of them: first to explain the project and answer their questions, and then to conduct the interview. Also, I have been able to keep in contact by sharing a draft of the chapter and encouraging feedback.

Participants were between the ages of 20 and 26 at the time of the interview and dates of attendance ranged between 2007 and 2016. To protect their identity, I have omitted any identifying information and assigned participants a pseudonym.[1] Participants were Mexican, Central American, and South American. The interviews took place at either coffee shops in Los Angeles or the UCLA campus. Each lasted between one to two hours. The interview questions focused on three themes: participant background, experiences while attending UCLA, and experiences of academic probation. Each participant was able to contextualize their experiences through responses to open-ended questions. I recorded and transcribed all interviews with the consent of each participant.

Positionality

My own experience as an undocumented student who was placed on subject to dismissal inspired this project. I started at UCLA in 2010, before the passage of the California Dream Act and Deferred Action for Childhood Arrivals (DACA). Without any access to financial aid, I had to commute and work informally for low wages away from campus. During my first year, I only attended two terms as a part-time student and then declared nonattendance for the next four consecutive terms because I could not afford tuition. Coming from a neighborhood and high school with few resources, and as the first person in my family to go to college, the transition was difficult. I did not do well during my first term back in school; my GPA fell below a 1.5 for the term and I was placed on subject to dismissal.

Being on subject to dismissal was scary and confusing and I was not sure how to seek help. I was ashamed of disclosing this information to anyone because it made me doubt my potential. Also, my counselor recommended that I change my major so I could graduate on time and insisted that I not attempt to retake the courses because it could lead to my dismissal. I felt overwhelmed and worried and decided to change my major. Although I was able to return to "good" academic standing after an entire year, I regretted changing my major and often felt like a failure because I was not studying what I enjoyed. This, in turn, affected my motivation.

Additionally, I was faced with the contradiction of being heavily involved with the support and advocacy group for undocumented students and not being the perfect undocumented student. I organized and attended rallies and events that upheld the image of an idealized undocumented student that did not represent my situation. As I reflect back, I realize now that I was struggling to come to terms with the fact that while I was working hard to get DACA and the California Dream Act passed, it felt like our experiences as undocumented students were reduced to these policies and financial burdens. This made me very angry at educational and legal institutions that determined the course of our lives because we were expected to be grateful and stoic, to merely move on after the implementation of these policies, as though we were not deeply affected by our fight to secure these rights.

Beyond my personal experience, this project developed from conversations with close friends who also struggled academically and experienced academic probation or subject to dismissal while attending UCLA. Interestingly, we were only sharing our experiences years later, after having gone through this process alone. It was through these conversations that I found validation. It was redeeming to explore together how the university had failed us and how it further marginalized us when we found ourselves in this situation. Recently, Rosemary (participant) shared, "I am glad someone took the time to research on academic probation and our stories are being told by someone who went through the experience and not from an outside point of view. You were very respectful of our history and used language that was appropriate." Through these interviews, I wanted to learn about the differences and similarities between our experiences and to highlight the importance of contextualizing our own stories.

Factors Leading to Academic Probation

The seven interviews reveal critical themes about undocumented students who experience academic probation. First, students' ability to perform well academically is influenced by various circumstances, many of which are directly related to immigration status. Second, placing students on academic probation serves as an additional stressor that feels isolating and lonely for most students. Third, students seek two primary resources: academic counseling and mental health services. In general, study participants reveal that placing students on academic probation can have a long-term adverse effect on students' educational careers.

All participants identified specific stressors that directly interfered with their academic performance. These include the reappearance of previous trauma like child abuse and cancer, or current stressors such as family separation and family health issues. Importantly, most stressors were produced or exacerbated by immigration status and presented in the form of financial burdens and depression. In fact, due to lack of legal status, many students worked informally and were paid under the table for long hours at minimum wage jobs which inevitably impacted the time they were able to devote to their studies. Also, they lacked access to culturally sensitive health care, especially mental health services. Because undocumented students are portrayed in scholarship, mainstream media, and in the immigrant rights movement as individuals who despite all the challenges and institutional barriers, prevail and succeed, these students felt uniquely high levels of shame.

TRAUMA

Two study participants were dealing with the untreated trauma that drastically influenced their mental and emotional health while blocking their ability to perform at the minimum university academic standards. Isabela was coping with the trauma that she experienced in high school when she was diagnosed with cancer and underwent chemotherapy treatment. Although she is a cancer survivor, she stayed busy with school and work, not allowing herself to really think about those struggles. It was not until her second year at UCLA that she began to process this and fear the possibility of a relapse. Isabela describes how she lived this experience:

> I started getting more emotional about it . . . so that took away a full part of my college experience because I started getting depressed. I stopped seeing my friends for a long time, so I started being lonely a lot . . . it was depressing alone, and then I couldn't concentrate in class, I couldn't concentrate in my readings.

Unable to focus on school, it was also stressful for Isabela to know that as an undocumented immigrant, she would have more limited access to healthcare outside of the university.

In Carmen's case, academic probation and subject to dismissal were directly connected to the reappearance of unaddressed child abuse trauma. Although she had experienced a brief reemergence of this trauma during her high school years, it was while attending UCLA that this distress began to affect her mental health profoundly. In addition, she learned during college that her younger sister had also experienced child abuse by the same perpetrator. She shares how this situation pushed her to seek psychological assistance:

> I could not get out of the mental low I was in . . . I was going to CAPS [Counseling and Psychological Services] during the monthly allocated amount for the quarter. I was maxing them out just to deal with some of the root issues . . . my parents found out about the child abuse that happened to me and my older sister, and we found out that it happened to my little sister.

In Carmen's case, the child abuse experienced was not only affecting her mental health, but also the well-being of her entire family. Although she sought out available mental health resources on campus, her healing process could not be limited to a single quarter as implicitly expected under university practices, and she was forced to withdraw during two consecutive terms. According to university policy, if a student withdraws from the university for two consecutive quarters, the student is automatically placed on subject to dismissal. Carmen's counselor recommended that she take time off from school to deal with mental health and seek outside psychological services, but her undocumented status only placed her in a more precarious status as a nonstudent. Without health insurance or a reliable source of employment, she was unable to cover the high costs of therapy, preventing her from seeing a therapist for an entire year. Being forced out of school, therefore, prolonged Carmen's untreated trauma for years when her immigration status blocked her from accessing mental health care.

FAMILIES

Family-related stressors also impacted students' academic performance. Specifically, study participants dealt with family health complications and physical family separation, issues that were exacerbated by immigration status and the immigration system that powerfully shapes undocumented students and their mixed-status families (Menjívar, Abrego, and Schmalzbauer 2016).

Marcos, for example, identified the health of his father, and the lawsuit his father filed against his employer as an issue that shifted his priorities and inevitably affected his academic performance. During the last term of his second year, Marcos's father had a nearly fatal job-related accident, leaving him unable to work. Due to this unfortunate occurrence, Marcos and his family were struggling economically. His father was forced to file a lawsuit against his employer as they refused to provide any medical or financial assistance. However, during the legal battle, his father's undocumented status was exposed, thereby adding extra anxiety and stress to the entire family because they were uncertain of how this could affect his father and the lawsuit. Especially worrisome was the fact that the exposure of his father's status could have led to his deportation. Marcos initiated his junior year at UCLA with this concern, haunted by the fear of its possible implications:

> His health was always on my mind. I would go home more than I should have because I wanted to check-up on his health. I was worried about everything because he stopped working [and] we didn't know how [to] pay their [parents] rent and I still had to pay for my rent. I took on two jobs, and I realized I didn't know what was going on in my life science class . . . I need[ed] to work first, I need[ed] to make sure that I could pay my bills and then I'll study [for] my final.

Marcos was not only experiencing distress due to his father's accident and interaction with the legal system, but he also was forced to shift priorities to aid his family emotionally and financially. Unable to prioritize his courses, Marcos was placed on academic probation, and later on subject to dismissal.

Students in the study were also afflicted by the stress and pain due to physical family separation. In Marta's case, her aunt was going through the process of legalizing her immigration status and was required to return to her country of birth for two months. However, there was a complication with her case that unexpectedly delayed her aunt's return to the United States for almost two years. Fearing that she may never be allowed to return to the United States, Marta's uncle suffered health complications that landed him in the hospital multiple times during the separation. Marta's aunt was the only family member from her maternal side living in the United States. This separation, therefore, especially affected her mother and, in turn, affected Marta:

> So before starting winter quarter, I also had to go through that, just having to be there for my family and having to be there for my mom too because that's her sister and I know my mom was having a hard time

> with it . . . I know she [was] going through depression because she was separated from her sister. They are pretty close . . . I was going home every weekend so I feel like going through all of that affected me too.

Family separation has an emotional toll on the entire family and often the student provides emotional support to their relatives. In fact, Marta was going home every weekend to be physically present with her family, and that took time from her studies. In this case, Marta's emotional distress was not only due to her aunt's prolonged delayed return to the United States but also to the associated issues of her uncle's deteriorating health and her mother's suffering. Furthermore, it is important to note that there is a sense of powerlessness that students go through when their immediate family members are undocumented and cannot travel or access resources. Marta was placed on subject to dismissal at the time she was dealing with this family situation; she could not confide in her family regarding this academic experience because she did not want to burden them any further.

Esperanza also experienced family separation during her second year at UCLA; her father took the tough decision to go back to his country of birth to care for his ill mother. Although this was a voluntary decision, due to his undocumented status, he was unable to come back to the United States. Her father's departure caused emotional distress among the entire family. This affected Esperanza's mental health as she shares how difficult it was for her to cope with this situation, "So I had to process the thought that I wasn't going to be able to see my dad for the next ten years and that was too much for me and it was mentally draining." Although Esperanza was devastated by the separation and the uncertainty of reunification, there was no time to process because she became one of the main financial providers for the household. The weight of new responsibilities and challenges forced her to balance school and work, putting her in a somewhat difficult and almost ironic situation:

> So if I had to miss a class to work to come up with the money to pay for tuition, I would worry about going to my shift. So I started to have lower standards. When you're worn out, and you're stressed out, then you just take what you can get to pass and to move on, and you hope that the finish line is closer and closer.

To afford school and be able to provide for her family financially, Esperanza had to miss class time, and this took a toll on her grades. During our interview, she recalls how this affected her physically: "my body started to just shut down, like if it was tired. I would fall asleep wherever I was at and it reflected on my grades." She was working close to forty hours a week while suffering the absence of her father and serving as a board member of IDEAS. At the time, she did not have DACA, and the California Dream Act had not yet passed, so she was working at a low-wage job, late hours, and commuting a long distance to and from school. Inevitably, Esperanza's and her family's immigration status profoundly shaped the factors that led to her poor academic performance, and she was placed on academic probation.

INTERSECTING STRESSORS

Other participants were also experiencing multiple stressors that intersect with immigration status. Carlos, for example, was facing several stressors simultaneously throughout college that impeded his ability to excel academically:

> So it was a mixture of having insomnia, anxiety, depression, and alcoholism all at once and still having to do homework, so it didn't matter you know. At the time, I knew it was a bad decision, and I knew there would be consequences, but I think where I was at too in terms of depression, I was like, well, I don't care.

The multiple stressors pushed Carlos to neglect academics when his mental and physical well-being were suffering intensely. During the interview, he conveyed a sense of anger and disappointment as a consequence of realizing the limitations his undocumented status placed on his everyday life, especially during his senior year in high school when he was unable to attend his dream school because it was financially impossible. Also, he shared how his status was very much on his mind since the transition to college, in ways that were different than in high school:

> At the time I started at UCLA, it was more of a constant reminder that my undocumented status would be a challenge. Something that I did not really think about in high school. Now it was centered, a constant reminder that I wasn't really welcomed.

Although Carlos qualified for in-state tuition under AB 540, without financial aid or the ability to work legally, he was forced to look for other alternatives to cover tuition costs. Priced out of living on campus, he worked as a part-time tutor while commuting to UCLA from downtown every day. Furthermore, Carlos defines his decision to not care about his academics and not turn in assignments as a way of "complaining to a system" that did not care about him. In fact, during his interview, he noted that his classes were not speaking about his lived experiences. Intriguingly, he reveals that in a way his poor academic performance was also a "cry for help." It was a combination of alcohol abuse, the institutional barriers that came with being undocumented, and depression which all affected his academic performance because he did not receive psychological services until his last year. Throughout his undergraduate career, he was placed in subject to dismissal and academic probation a few times.

Likewise, Rosemary shares how her daily efforts to attend UCLA often left her drained and overwhelmed: "I was so stressed because not only I had to worry about my education, I had to worry about going to work, getting up for class, and transporting myself to school." At the time she only benefited from AB 540 (meaning that she was allowed to pay in-state, rather than international, tuition and fees) and worked part-time as a babysitter. Rosemary was also adjusting to the quarter system as a first-year transfer student while encountering a hostile environment in her classrooms. For example, during an immigration class, the professor used the term "illegal aliens" when speaking about undocumented individuals. When she let the professor know that she was uncomfortable with the use of such language, his response was "that's how it's referred as in our research studies." Rosemary was not only dealing with a transition in her education, working, and commuting, but she also had to deal with faculty who were not necessarily aware or sensitive to undocumented students' needs. This type of unwelcoming environment was extra stressful, even while attending class. It is no surprise that these factors and her undocumented status sometimes made her feel discouraged to turn in assignments because of the uncertainty of the future. She sums up her frustration with the question she asked herself often, "what am I going through all this trouble for if when I graduate, I'm not going to [legally qualify to] get a job?"

SHAME AND ISOLATION

As these experiences reveal, all students were already dealing with different stressors that directly influenced their academic performance and being placed on academic probation served as an additional stressor in a student's life. Institutions can make students' well-being more central to their mission by better understanding how to support, rather than to further isolate, students on academic probation. Academic probation can be a lonely process for a student, and it comes with shame, isolation, emotional distress, and anxiety. In fact, the interviews reveal that most students did not discuss their academic probation with other peers, friends, or family. Students highlighted a shared feeling of shame due to academic probation. For example, Esperanza shares:

> Personally, I felt very ashamed, I was very ashamed, and I felt like I couldn't live up to these standards and I was taking in the feeling of being a failure. I was really believing it . . . I was scared that the school was just going to decide to kick me out.

Being placed on academic probation negatively affected Esperanza's self-perception and caused a constant fear of being dismissed from the university. Her case makes visible how setting unrealistic expectations serves as an additional layer of shame for an undocumented student. As Esperanza explains:

> I had to juggle so many things that I didn't have such a high GPA, that I started not to fit into that perceived Dreamer, perfect student thing. And little by little I started to feel less identified as a Dreamer and more as a failed undocumented student because I couldn't hold the image.

She felt an extra sense of shame because she was not meeting the expectations upheld by the DREAMer narrative for undocumented students. At the same time, she began to feel less identified with this narrative that no longer represented her.

Likewise, there was a shared sense of confusion among participants about the implications of being placed on academic probation. In fact, students like Marcos noted that they did not know what academic probation was, nor what options they had in this situation. Marcos shares how he felt when he found out that he was placed on academic probation:

> I don't know what this means, I don't know how to feel. I don't know how I'm going to tell my parents, *if* I'm going to tell my parents. They sacrificed their entire lives to come here and here I am failing college. It just made me feel very insecure, very vulnerable because I didn't know whom to turn to.

Marcos experienced uncertainty and stress because in his mind, his bad grades translated into failure not only for himself but also for his family, and Marcos did not want to disappoint his parents. In the same way, Carmen admits that she has never disclosed her academic status to her parents because bad grades were never acceptable; she felt like a failure for herself and her family. Unable to meet her parent's expectations, she describes how she felt about falling into academic probation and subject to dismissal: " so it was scary, it's scary being out on academic probation cause if I fail again I could be dismissed from the school, and I would have to reapply again and how was I going to explain that to my parents?" There is a real feeling of shame at being placed on academic probation and the consequences it may lead to. During this time, Carmen's parents were supporting her financially to attend UCLA as the California Dream Act and DACA were not in effect yet.

Placing a student on academic probation, moreover, can have a long-term effect on the rest of the student's academic career, leading to a decreased level of motivation to perform well. Rosemary shares how experiencing academic probation and subject to dismissal affected her in the long term:

> I was so tired and stressed and sometimes before midterms and finals, I would get much anxiety because I was like; I'm going to fail, I'm going to fail. It [academic probation] just traumatized me so much that every time I took an exam, I used to get panic attacks too because I was so stressed.

Common aspects in her education turned more stressful than usual as a result of being placed on academic probation. She felt the added pressure to prove herself on every assignment and exam, living college in constant tension. Also, Rosemary immediately realized how her academic standing now was also a barrier to apply for scholarships, a primary funding source for her education. She shares her frustration, "I couldn't apply for scholarships because I didn't have the grade point average so that's when I decided, I can't afford it and then I took two years off from school." In this case, her academic probation status served as an obstacle to isolate her further because now she could not seek financial support from scholarships due to her grades and she was forced, instead, to take time off from her academics.

Resources: Academic Counseling and Mental Health Services

Students expressed that the university did not provide the support needed prior, during, or after academic probation. However, all participants did use two resources when placed on academic probation: academic counseling and mental health services. These services were pivotal in either aiding students in getting back in good academic standing or in further isolating some of them. In the following section, I provide examples from the interviews about how staff delivery of these services influenced students' receptivity to such services and their academic pathways post probation.

When students are placed on academic probation, they are required to meet with a full-time academic counselor. In fact, a hold is placed on the student's account until they see a counselor. Consequently, all participants met with a counselor, and these one-on-one meetings with the counselors proved vital to how they understood their situation and what other resources they sought. In fact, counselors were the first people participants talked to when placed on academic probation. On the one hand, some students found the meeting positive and helpful, while other students felt that the counselors did not provide adequate support. For example, Esperanza shares the negative encounter she had with her counselor:

> When I got to the counselor's office, they pull out your record and they see your grades and they place the blame on you. I mean they are your grades. But when they would be like what did you do wrong? It was the way they would say it [like] what did you do wrong? you know. I had to work and to be honest, because I told this to a counselor once, I don't care about my grades as much as I care about making rent, or making money to pay for tuition, but I did not want to be kicked out either. And then they were like, "everyone works, that's not an excuse." The moment that he said that, I really wanted to just sit there and cry and I was shocked and the whole meeting after that I just shook my head, because I didn't know how to make him understand that it wasn't just work, that my dad had left. They make it sound like you're putting all these excuses out without trying to be very understanding and stuff.

In Esperanza's case, she felt judged and misunderstood by the counselor, and it influenced her decision not to continue seeking academic counseling. She was frustrated because she felt that the counselor was blaming her, so she did not feel comfortable enough to disclose that her father had gone back to their birth country. Although most counselors can see your records and know that you are an undocumented student, this counselor did not take the time to try to find out what other factors might have led this student to this situation.

On the other hand, other students expressed their gratitude and appreciation for the counselors that helped them when they found themselves in this situation. For these students, meeting with their counselor played a crucial role in efficiently dealing with their academic probation. In essence, it was the first step toward moving forward. Carlos shares his positive and helpful experience with the counselor:

> The counselor really understood where I was coming from, and I could tell that the person wasn't judging me. They were just like, "hey, I really acknowledge what you're going through," and that went a long way. I think that's what I wanted since the beginning. I got it like four years

after when I was already on academic probation, but that's really all I wanted at the end.

Contrary to Esperanza's experience, it was during this meeting with the counselor that Carlos found validation and finally understood that he was not being judged. Carlos's experience shows that a counselor can make a positive impact on a student by acknowledging their struggles and situations. This can be a source of motivation for students to move forward despite going through academic probation. This validation opened the doors for Carlos to access mental health services, as recommended by his counselor during this meeting.

Another resource that students sought while on academic probation was Counseling and Psychological Services (CAPS) at UCLA. Five out of the seven participants sought this support on campus. The majority of participants who did seek CAPS services were recommended to do so by their academic counselors during their visits when already placed on academic probation. However, unlike academic counseling, which was required, seeking mental health services was voluntary. As their stories reveal, all participants were already dealing with multiple stressors that led to academic probation. Therefore, CAPS was crucial in helping some students cope with all the different things happening in their lives. After being placed on academic probation, Marcos realized that he needed to deal with his emotional well-being. He recalls how seeking support through CAPS was affirming in various ways:

> My therapist really helped me figure out how to feel good about myself and how to not label myself according to academics, how to not think of myself as just a student because I am all these things . . . and it's not my fault that I have been getting C's in my class and it just made me feel good about myself, and I realized, I can solve this, and it's not my fault.

Marcos's self-perception shifted entirely to a positive and self-affirming one; psychological services provided emotional support while on academic probation. The therapy sessions provided Marcos the space to talk about his feelings and explore the factors that led him to this situation; but more importantly, it motivated him to move forward.

While therapy helped some students deal with the intellectual insecurities brought up by their academic probation, in Carmen's case, receiving mental health services helped her cope with the resurfacing of childhood trauma. As she describes, these services prevented her from harming herself:

> It [therapy] helped me patch it . . . like emergency care at that point, making sure I wasn't going to kill myself and making sure I wasn't going

to fail during this quarter. So that's what those sessions were there for. We kind of talked about some of the root issues, but it was never about treating the root issues . . . at least for those sessions, it was patching things up so I was functional again.

Mental health services provided Carmen the opportunity to see a therapist to help her establish a basic level of stability so she could at least complete the academic term. Carmen benefited significantly from these sessions, but many root issues were left unaddressed when she took time off from school. Since she was not enrolled, she was ineligible to continue receiving therapy, and access to mental health was limited and costly without health insurance.

Advocacy

Six of the seven participants were members of IDEAS. In fact, Carmen was a member, and Carlos, Esperanza, Marcos, Marta, and Isabela held board positions at least once during their dates of attendance. As I have shared, I was also involved in the organization and served as a board member for three years. During our meetings and events, academic difficulty was not a topic we openly discussed in the organization although we later realized that many of us were struggling. However, we did share many of our worries, pains, hardships, frustrations, and challenges that affected our lives—many of which were related to immigration status.

Although the organization was not directly addressing academic probation, it did serve as a supportive space. Marta and Esperanza found validation in interactions with other IDEAS members. Through the organization's retention program, Marta was paired up with a mentor with whom she developed a strong relationship and who was also aware of her aunt's immigration situation. Additionally, Marta revealed her subject to dismissal status to her mentor, who played a crucial role in the coping process and provided Marta with emotional support. After disclosing this information, her mentor revealed she had also been on academic probation. Marta expressed that knowing that her mentor had experienced academic probation helped reduce the anxiety and uncertainty that she felt after she found out about her subject to dismissal status.

Similarly, Esperanza disclosed her academic probation status in a conversation with an IDEAS member, Carlos—another participant in this project. One day, as Carlos drove Esperanza home, he asked her how she was doing, and Esperanza shared with him what was going on with her academics. During this conversation, he told her not to be ashamed and that this situation did not define who she was. Reflecting on this encounter, Esperanza states, "honestly that is probably the only thing I wanted to hear from somebody else." In other words, Esperanza found validation and emotional support in a fellow undocumented student who also discussed with her the importance of taking care of her mental health. In both cases, there was an already established relationship and trust that made these students comfortable enough to disclose this sensitive information. Interestingly, the other two IDEAS members they chose to reveal their status to had also previously been on academic probation.

IDEAS provided an important and necessary space for these students. In fact, Carlos and Esperanza both expressed that they found more value in student activism than in their classes because it spoke to their experiences. Their activities there felt more relevant to addressing some of their immediate needs as undocumented students. Also, Isabela shares that she would spend more time taking care of her board duties than in her classes. In my interview with Carlos, he points out that being involved in IDEAS made him feel better about his grades because despite a low GPA, he was advocating for change and social justice. Indeed, one of the focal points in research on undocumented students is their celebrated civic engagement. This is true for my study, as although some of these students were having academic difficulty, six out of seven were involved in student activism. I was involved in IDEAS for five years, and I know the organization was not openly addressing academic probation. Nonetheless, there were intimate and personal conversations happening among students who were experiencing academic difficulty. Later, there were efforts to develop a retention program for undocumented students. It is my understanding that this has recently been officially established.

Though Rosemary was not involved in IDEAS, during the time that she took two years off, she was working to save money and was involved in an undocumented student organization and advocating for social change. Like Marcos and Sofia, Rosemary shared a feeling of hope. She goes on to share "I think that's what kept me motivated that a lot of us wanted to continue in higher education so then the [CA] DREAM Act passed, and I went back in 2013."

Recommendations

Universities and colleges have implemented various programs to intervene when students are placed on academic probation. There are two main types of intervention programs that are generally adopted: "intrusive" (mandatory) and "nonintrusive" (voluntary), but with the same goal to help students improve their GPA and overall academic performance (Damashek 2003). While some universities make the program credit-bearing (McGrath and Burd 2012), other programs are more flexible and provide online academic support (Seirup and Rose 2010). Some programs also require students to meet with advisors multiple times throughout a term and participate in structured activities (Kamphoff et al. 2007).

The literature reveals that there is not a "one size fits all" intervention approach and institutions should carefully analyze the student population when designing and implementing a program. For instance, in the case of undocumented students, institutions should take into consideration how their immigration status and external, but associated factors such as depression, financial burdens, family health, and family separation affect students' performance. I highly encourage institutions to take the time and use input from students previously placed on academic probation because they can provide unique insight and advice to develop a supportive system. Additionally, because mental health was a recurring theme in this chapter, universities should improve the way they refer students to counseling services. Often, students only meet with a counselor when they are placed on academic probation, but there is no follow-up; checking in with students consistently is important to ensure progress. Also, as one participant suggested, universities should be attentive to red flags, such as when a student fails a midterm and a final, or when they miss multiple assignments. This could be a crucial time to intervene and check up on the student and refer the student to adequate resources. There are various reasons why a student might not be performing well and changing how we approach these students is key. Intervention should be presented as an opportunity for the student to receive support and move forward, thereby destigmatizing academic probation.

Conclusion

Academic probation among undocumented students is a multifaceted issue and needs to be explored within various contexts to support the different needs of the diverse undocumented student population. Undocumented students carry the burden of being undocumented, and often they are students of color, low-income and first-generation college students. The narratives of the seven students in this study reveal that academic probation is not an individual failure. Rather, it is often a result of familial, prior trauma, and immigration status stressors influencing the lives of these students. These stressors, in turn, impact the emotional and psychological well-being of students and therefore affect their ability to focus on academics. Most participants, moreover, were not aware of their options such as withdrawing from courses, withdrawing from a term, being a part-time student or merely declaring nonattendance until they were already on academic probation. While on academic probation, many students felt isolated and stigmatized because academic performance—especially for undocumented students—is so often equated to intelligence and deservingness. As a result, they rarely shared their situation with anyone.

Additionally, undocumented students must navigate the powerful model minority myth that idealizes "DREAMers" and overlooks the deeply rooted institutional barriers that affect their lives and their families. These stories provide a counternarrative to this narrative and reveal how intersecting factors such as family separation, access to health care, and legal status play a crucial role in their academic performance.

In the case of the seven students in my study, mental health services proved to be pivotal in ensuring that they could continue their education while addressing some of the causes of their poor academic performance, which in most cases were not related to their academic abilities. Under current practices, the university often creates a hostile environment where students do not feel comfortable reaching out or seeking resources. Based on these findings, I urge universities to find ways to better support students when they are struggling academically in a larger context of legal and economic uncertainty.

NOTE

1. At the outset of the project, most participants were comfortable using their real names and identifiable information. As the political context has become more harshly anti-immigrant, I followed up with them to suggest that we use pseudonyms and better protect their identity. These are the kinds of ongoing conversations that I, as an undocumented researcher, felt compelled to pursue in the project. It is the type of conversation that does not always happen when research is conducted by people who are not undocumented.

REFERENCES

Abrego, Leisy J. 2006. "'I Can't Go to College Because I Don't Have Papers': Incorporation Patterns of Latino Undocumented Youth." *Latino Studies* 4(3): 212–31. https://doi.org/10.1057/palgrave.lst.8600200.

Barefoot, Betsy O. 2004. "Higher Education's Revolving Door: Confronting the Problem of Student Drop Out in US Colleges and Universities." *Open Learning: The Journal of Open, Distance and e-Learning* 19(1): 9–18. https://doi.org/10.1080/0268051042000177818.

Borjian, Ali. 2018. "Academically Successful Latino Undocumented Students in College: Resilience and Civic Engagement." *Hispanic Journal of Behavioral Sciences* 40(1): 22–36. https://doi.org/10.1177/0739986317754299.

Brost, Jennifer, and Kelly Payne. 2011. "First-Generation Issues: Learning Outcomes of the Dismissal Testimonial for Academically Dismissed Students in the Arts and Sciences." *New Directions for Teaching and Learning* 127: 69–79. https://doi.org/10.1002/tl.458.

Damashek, Richard. 2003. "Support Programs for Students on Academic Probation." *ERIC* ED475734 1–18. https://eric.ed.gov/?id=ED475734.

Dozier, Sandra Bygrave. 2001. "Undocumented and Documented International Students: A Comparative Study of Their Academic Performance." *Community College Review* 29(2): 43–53. https://doi.org/10.1177/009155210102900204.

Fletcher Jason M., and Mansur Tokmouline. 2010. "The Effects of Academic Probation on College Success: Lending Students a Hand or Kicking Them While They Are Down?" *CiteSeerX*: 1–32. http://citeseerx.ist.psu.edu/viewdoc/summary?doi=10.1.1.600.115.

Gabrovsky, Juliana. 2009. "Mock Graduation Shares Goals of DREAM Act." *Daily Bruin*, April 29, 2009. http://dailybruin.com/2009/04/29/mock-graduation-shares-goals-dream-act/.

Goffard, Christopher. 2012. "An Immigrant in Limbo between Two Americas." *Los Angeles Times*, June 8, 2012. http://articles.latimes.com/2012/jun/08/local/la-me-maria-20120608.

James, Cindy L., and Sarah Graham. 2010. "An Empirical Study of Students on Academic Probation." *Journal of the First-Year Experience and Students in Transition* 22(2): 71–92. https://eric.ed.gov/?id=EJ906631.

Jones, Maggie. 2010. "Citizenship for Students | United States: Coming Out Illegal." *New York Times Magazine*, October 21, 2010. https://www.nytimes.com/2010/10/24/magazine/24DreamTeam-t.html.

Kamphoff, Cindra S., Bryant L. Hutson, Scott A. Amundsen, and Julie A. Atwood. 2007. "A Motivational/Empowerment Model Applied to Students on Academic Probation." *Journal of College Student Retention: Research, Theory and Practice* 8(4): 397–412. https://myecc.ecc.edu/excels/Completion/initiative49/Shared%20Documents/Motivationa%20Empowerment%20Model.pdf.

Kelley, Karl N. 1996. "Causes, Reactions, and Consequences of Academic Probation: A Theoretical Model." *NACADA Journal* 16(1): 28–34. https://doi.org/10.12930/0271-9517-16.1.28.

Lindo, Jason M., Nicholas J. Sanders, and Philip Oreopoulos. 2010. "Ability, Gender, and Performance Standards: Evidence from Academic Probation." *American Economic Journal: Applied Economics* 2(2): 95–117. https://doi.org/10.1257/app.2.2.95.

Madera, Gabriela. 2008. *Underground Undergrads: UCLA Undocumented Immigrant Students Speak Out*. Los Angeles: UCLA Center for Labor Research and Education.

McGrath, Shelley M., and Gail D. Burd. 2012. "A Success Course for Freshmen on Academic Probation: Persistence and Graduation Outcomes." *NACADA Journal* 32(1): 43–52. https://doi.org/10.12930/0271-9517-32.1.43.

Menjívar, Cecilia, Leisy J. Abrego, and Leah C. Schmalzbauer. 2016. *Immigrant Families*. Malden, MA: Polity Press.

Mirseyedi, Leila. 2010. "Undocumented Students DREAM of a Better Tomorrow." *Pacific Ties*, December 4, 2010. https://pacificties.org/undocumented-students-dream-of-a-better-tomorrow/.

Nance, Molly. 2007. "The Psychological Impact of Academic Probation." *Diverse: Issues in Higher Education*, November 1, 2007. https://diverseeducation.com/article/10004/.

Perez, Jonathan. 2015. "Challenging the 'DREAMer' Narrative." *The Huffington Post*, November 16, 2015. https://www.huffpost.com/entry/challenging-the-dreamerna_b_6163008.

Pérez, William 2012. *Americans by Heart: Undocumented Latino Students and the Promise of Higher Education*. New York: Teachers College Press.

Pérez, William, and Richard Douglas Cortés. 2011. *Undocumented Latino College Students: Their Socioemotional and Academic Experiences*. El Paso, TX: LFB Scholarly Publishing.

Pérez, William, Roberta Espinoza, Karina Ramos, Heidi M. Coronado, and Richard Cortes. 2009. "Academic Resilience among Undocumented Latino Students." *Hispanic Journal of Behavioral Sciences* 31(2): 149–81. https://doi.org/10.1177/0739986309333020.

Schwiertz, Helge. 2015. "Beyond the Dreamer Narrative—Undocumented Youth Organizing Against Criminalization and Deportations in California." *UCLA Institute for Research on Labor and Employment*. https://escholarship.org/uc/item/0m96d1fm.

Seirup, Holly, and Sage Rose. 2011. "Exploring the Effects of Hope on GPA and Retention among College Undergraduate Students on Academic Probation." *Education Research International* 2011: 1–7. https://doi.org/10.1155/2011/381429.

Tovar, Esau, and Merril A. Simon. 2006. "Academic Probation as a Dangerous Opportunity: Factors Influencing Diverse College Students' Success." *Community College Journal of Research and Practice* 30(7): 547–64. https://doi.org/10.1080/10668920500208237.

Wong, Kent. 2012. *Undocumented and Unafraid: Tam Tran, Cinthya Felix and the Immigrant Youth Movement*. Los Angeles: UCLA Center for Labor Research and Education.

GABRIELLE CABRERA

3

Disrupting Diversity

Undocumented Students in the Neoliberal University

During my time as an undergraduate student, many touted UC Merced (UCM) as having the highest percentage of undocumented students, thereby constructing the university as a welcoming space for this population. The infrastructure on campus, however, proved otherwise. During my time there, the Services for Undocumented Students (SUS) office at UCM was so poorly funded, it consisted of only two cubicles run by a part-time staff of four undergraduate women of color. No matter how many times this statement was repeated in institutionalized UndocuAlly trainings and in SUS and administrative staff presentations, it did not produce sufficient resources. Drawing on UCM as one example of many in the United States, this chapter examines how diversity discourse about undocumented students uses diversity as a commodity. Through my own experiences as an undocumented woman and as an undocumented student conducting research, I interrogate the construction of "undocumentedness" in a space of "diversity." I craft a text that recognizes and follows decolonizing feminist methodologies (Ahmed 2017; Da Silva 2007; Hundle 2019; Mohanty 2003; Smith Tuhiwai 1999) while placing deep significance on the everyday lived experiences and subjective modes of knowledge of undocumented women.

In the contemporary historical context, diversity and multiculturalism are conflated with the success and excellence of universities. In some ways, data on student identities operate to measure the value of a university. Boards of trustees and corporate investors in universities are deeply concerned with

World Report rankings and have engaged in "diversifying" universities to attract more students (see Urciuoli 2003, 2016). During the admissions process, for example, students are voluntarily asked to check their racial identification on an application form. These data are then sent to the office of student life and made available to national ranking systems such as the *World Report America's Best Colleges*. Along with these practices, universities have come to iconize undocumented students as "diverse" subjects who add value to the institution through their experiences of marginalization. What does the university's practice of diversity do to undocumented students and how are undocumented students expected to perform in response?

Through analysis of two case studies, this chapter explores the university as a neoliberal structure (Giroux 2014) that commodifies the experiences and identities of undocumented students. Neoliberal logic is guided by the belief that individual and societal well-being can be achieved through the freedom of global markets and privatization (Harvey 2005; also see Somers 2008). Since UCM is the newest university built in the UC system at a time of increased globalization and economic inequalities, I find it useful to use neoliberalism to call attention to the public–private partnership established by the UC and plenary groups to construct the "Twenty-First-Century American University." UCM, therefore, is a strategic case study that serves as an example for the increasingly corporate practices being adopted by universities throughout the nation. It makes visible the broader problems in higher education, including funding cuts in student programs, slashing of humanities and social sciences courses, lack of security for graduate and undergraduate workers, and the loss of faculty autonomy in university governance—all while administrators are seeking private funding. Following the market demands of the institution, I analyze undocumented students' own practices in marketing their life stories *both* as resistance to and acceptance into the university. Under neoliberal regimes, undocumented students must mobilize their lived experiences (which may include narratives of suffering and trauma) to make political claims.

The first case study examines UCM's use of statistical discourse to index diversity in the university. The second case study provides a history of how undocumented students became a diversity initiative in the UC system under Janet Napolitano's presidency. In particular, I document the university's promotion of a news article about undocumented students after the 2016 presidential election. I problematize the "DREAMer narrative" and stories of resilience to demonstrate the range of exclusions that occur when the discourse on undocumented migrants relies solely on those who embody "good" and "model minority" behaviors. Together, these case studies excavate how and why undocumented students are presented as exhibits—seen as worthy within the control of a curator—the university—as part of a process of commodification of the undocumented condition.

The Twenty-First-Century American University

In a competition to attract students as if they were consumers, colleges and universities develop their own brand. UCM has branded itself as "The first new American research university of the twenty-first century," striving to be seen as a symbol of development, progress, and a hopeful addition to the UC system. By 2020, UCM aims to accommodate 10,000 students and build new classroom and residential buildings, recreational fields, and research labs. UCM aims to uphold the principles of the UC system and its commitment to diversity, multiculturalism, research, and educational access for California residents (see the University of California's Principles of Community). However, as the twenty-first-century university, built at a time of global economic restructuring and public–private partnership between the UC system and private developers, UCM's past and future as an institution is based on neoliberal logic. There was a large push to build UCM in the Central Valley to address social, environmental, and political issues in the Valley. Campus leadership emphasized the economic support that UC would generate for the City of Merced, as well as for California's San Joaquin Valley. The discourse on UCM uplifting the Valley is deployed around the further expansion of UCM as part of the 2020 plan. The university's investments with public–private partnerships are concealed by claims of "tolerable suboptimization" (also see Hundle and Vang 2019), which demand that the university community deal with resource constraints such as lack of staff, faculty, and student spaces and understaffed departments until UCM's 2020 plans are completed. Tolerable suboptimization is a response to questions about the university's productivity; specifically, the means to perform at a level without adequate staff and resources.[1] Neoliberal conditionality is naturalized through the 2020 plan rationale as procedures for expansion and future visions of a cutting-edge UC in the Central Valley mean that faculty and students of color, especially undocumented students, must accept these limitations.

UCM prides itself as a Hispanic-Serving Institution, with over 51 percent of the student body identifying as Hispanic according to 2016–2017 figures (see UCM website). As an institution predominantly comprised of students of color, UCM has mobilized categories of sexuality, gender, class, and race to demonstrate its commitment to inclusion and diversity. I am specifically using data—including percentages, statistics, and graphs—as presented by the university to draw attention to the institution's arbitrary use of figures, but also to highlight ways in which diversity data have depoliticizing effects and conceal a productive role in "minoritizing" students of color and undocumented students. It is through diversity discourse and celebrations of multiculturalism that the neoliberal practices of UCM and the UC system as a whole are legitimized (see Hundle and Vang 2019). Diversity statistics reaffirm the UC's commitment to Regents Policy 4400, the UC system's diversity statement, adopted in 2007. The statement expresses UC's commitment to serve the interests of California, a diverse state, by seeking to "achieve diversity among its student bodies and among its employees."[2] The statistics demonstrate that a large population of first-generation, undocumented, and students of color enroll in the university. Therefore, the logic suggests that campus leadership has promoted these statistics as symbols of diversity and commitment to equity and inclusion. These homogenizing tendencies may serve to conceal inequalities within the university.

ETHNIC AND RACIAL CLASSIFICATIONS AT UCM

The university claims to collect information about citizenship and residence status to better serve students. These data can be used by the university to make claims about multiculturalism and inclusion, but can also be used by students to demand change and make political claims. Statistics are central to the production of modern subjects and serve as a technology of governance. In a practical, policy-based approach, statistics are important for needs assessment and funding. However, statistics construct "regimes of truth": specifically, "truths typically accorded authoritative, scientific validity" in the world (Urla 2012, 112). Diversity is often measured through statistics; social categories are quantified to legitimize specific, authoritarian claims. Statistical classifications are prevalent when documenting diversity in universities, as seen by how UCM classifies their ethnic and racial groups as "diverse." Classifications influence the organization of social life; they reduce the complexity of social phenomena into quantifiable units that aim at making certain political claims. Statistics are not just representational; they are also material. This is evident in how the numbers of racialized and minoritized students in a university are used to represent diversity.

At UCM, like at other universities, undocumented students' citizenship status is "unclassified," while our residence is categorized as "nonresident." The Office of Institutional Research and Decision Support provides campus statistics, survey support, and uses collected data on the campus for decision-making processes. The office defines "nonresident alien" as a noncitizen or nonnational of the United States and someone "who is in this country on a visa or temporary basis and does not have the right to remain indefinitely" (UCM's Office of Institutional Research and Decision Support). Nonresidents are people whose legal permanent residence is outside California. These nonresidents are required to pay out-of-state tuition because they are not residents of California. This categorization of resident and nonresident alien is related to AB 540, which allows California nonresidents to qualify for in-state tuition when they meet specific requirements. These definitions contribute to the discursive production of migrant "illegality" and serve to reinforce the "Other" status of undocumented students. Moreover, the collection of legal status as data functions as surveillance for undocumented people (De Genova 2002, 2004, 2013) and is used to legitimize diversity at UCM.

The Office of Institutional Research and Decision Support follows the standard terminology established by the Integrated Postsecondary Education Data system, a data collection program for the National Center for Education Statistics. It is important to trace the genealogies of these concepts and historicize them under the process of neoliberalizing diversity discourse in broader political processes. The semiotic processes of statistical discourse tell stories about subjects and the institution. These data are deployed to capture and promote diversity and multiculturalism on campus. When published in university brochures and websites, the data communicate a commitment to students from underrepresented communities.

How does the manifestation of diversity in the university reproduce both the neoliberal agendas and racial hierarchies in institutions? Calling UCM "diverse" because of the number of enrolled "minoritized" students has given campus leadership the confidence to use the large number of first-generation, undocumented/DACAmented, and students of color as evidence of a diverse, multicultural, twenty-first-century university. "Minority" functions as a code that allows people to talk about difference in a subdued manner, much like trying to talk underwater. You can talk normally, but the sound that comes out is not transmitted well. Therefore, a crucial discussion of "minority" displaces a conversation about "the more taboo and threatening topic of race and what it entails: racism, white supremacy and racial injustice" (Hundle 2019). The language of "minority" and "diversity" suggests that the university is engaged in initiatives that aim for a multicultural campus community. In the face of such uses of diversity to discuss difference in the university, we must engage and illuminate the processes that conceal the neoliberal productivity of diversity work.

The discussion of statistical discourse and background on UCM, an institution born at the height of increasingly neoliberal policies, dovetails with the two case studies in this chapter. I argue that the university sells undocumented student stories of migration and trauma as a method of cultivating an image of an altruistic, progressive institution. Specifically, my aim is to demonstrate how undocumented students, part of a diversity initiative in the UC, are used as a metric to measure the university's mission of inclusion. I attempt to illustrate how diversity functions as a border for actual transformative work because it conceals inequalities and violence that are imposed on the undocumented student community.

Case #1: Undocumented Students as a Diversity Initiative

During an interview with New American Media,[3] University of California President Janet Napolitano notes that she does not care if students are documented or undocumented, as long as they are good students. In her opinion piece published by SFGate, she asks readers to consider the $5 million given for undocumented student services as a "down payment—one more piece of evidence of [the UC's] commitment to *all* Californians" (Napolitano 2013, emphasis mine). Undocumented students form part of a diversity initiative because we were once *unofficially* excluded from the UC. While undocumented students were able to attend a UC campus with the benefit of in-state tuition in California, it was difficult to complete a degree before the implementation of the California Dream Act (AB 130 and AB 131) in 2012 and 2013, respectively.[4] Before these legislative bills, the UC campuses did not have a protocol for assisting undocumented students financially. Now, the UC plans to move forward with initiatives of inclusion under Napolitano's leadership. Initiatives for inclusion and diversity are seen as a shift toward equity in the university, but only if we understand that the presumed default is the absence of people of color, most especially racialized migrants, within the university. Diversity, therefore, becomes a veil used by the institution to substitute unacceptable things: racism, sexism, heteropatriarchy, homophobia, and transphobia. Diversity is used to obscure; it is "a technique for not addressing inequalities by allowing institutions to appear happy" (Ahmed 2017, 102).

THE NATIONAL SUMMIT ON UNDOCUMENTED STUDENTS

In spring 2015, the University of California Office of the President (UCOP) hosted "The National Summit on Undocumented Students," a conference that sought to "address the needs of undocumented students." Despite its title, the summit was not national, as it only included selected students from each UC campus. Although the purpose of the summit was to assess the needs of undocumented students throughout the UC system, it was planned without the input of undocumented students. The official press release from UCOP notes that Napolitano had identified undocumented students as a key issue since her instatement as UC president (Freeling 2013). There were over one hundred undocumented students in attendance. Undocumented activists, immigration advocates, lawyers, representatives and educators for organizations such as Educators 4 Fair Consideration, and academic researchers were also invited. Undocumented students present expressed that the summit felt like a field site for scholars interested in immigration; the conversation was *on* undocumented students as an academic topic—about us, rather than with us.

Undocumented student attendees critiqued the lack of student input and the number of assumptions regarding our needs by the UC. The rationale set forth by organizers was that moderators would summarize the information from these workshop discussions and present it to UCOP as recommendations. The selected students from each campus were essential to making the decisions for all undocumented students throughout the UC. Feeling uneasy with the planned program, undocumented students met at the hotel pool the night before Napolitano's keynote address. After some deliberation, a protest was planned. The purpose of the protest was to call attention to the lack of student voices in the planning of the program and demand more resources for undocumented students throughout the UC system. During Napolitano's speech, undocumented students stood with our fists up. One student from each campus made a short statement before we walked out to the lobby. We were making claims and calling attention to the precarity undocumented students encounter in the university system. However, the official news, the one historicized by the public media and UCOP, details the disruption by undocumented students of Napolitano's speech during the summit (Richman 2016).

A month later, a draft of the recommendations from the summit was released to the undocumented student summit attendees. The dialogue from the summit was translated into the language of the institution, a language that was deemed legitimate and proper. The draft retained the demands, but the context of the violence undocumented people encounter locally, nationally, and through the university was omitted. For example, during the summit, some undocumented students called for an end to the structural violence and dehumanization imposed on undocumented people who do not fit the "DREAMer" criteria. At the summit, we spoke in groups about how the DREAMer narrative is used to separate and criminalize parents as at fault for bringing undocumented children into the United States. The Student Rec-

TABLE 3.1. UCOP Undocumented Scholar Support from 2014

Financial aid	$100K
Staff	$63K
Career services	$15K
Writing support	$25K
Law clinic	$10K
Emergency funds (for DACA renewals, assistance with other personal fees)	$12K
Total	$230K

ommendations subsection is called "Change the DREAMer Narrative" and is clearly much tamer than our original language:

> Undocumented students are not the models that the media and others paint them to be. For example, statements that refer to undocumented students as being in the U.S. illegally[5] through no fault of their own implies that their parents are criminals.

The university repackaged undocumented students' demands to instead perpetuate another narrative acceptable to the UC.

In addition to the DREAMer narrative, undocumented students were also concerned about the sustainability of undocumented student program services. In October 2013, a few months after Napolitano was appointed president of the University of California system, her diversity initiatives came in the form of $5 million that she allocated for undocumented students in the UC system. The one-time fund was distributed to each campus based on the number of undocumented students enrolled and was set up to recruit undocumented student coordinators, provide academic and career development support, assist in establishing undocumented student centers (as in the case of UCM, these "centers" may consist of a cubicle, makeshift walls, and a white-noise machine), and for financial support. UCM received a total of approximately $230,000 per year over a period of two years. The funds were allocated in the form of emergency funds, financial aid, salary for program coordinators, and career development programs.

UCM received $230,000 per year from UCOP to fund undocumented student services from 2014 to 2016. This information was provided to students who attended the Open Forum for Undocumented Students in the fall of 2016. After providing the breakdown of the 2014 UCOP support for undocumented students and explaining how the original funds were used, students were asked

Disrupting Diversity 73

what we wanted to see for the future of the program. When students recommended that the money be allocated to hire two program coordinators, however, it became clear that there was not enough money for more resources. All of the students' recommendations were met with the response that "it's not in the budget."

The UC Undocumented Student Coalition, which has at least one undocumented student representative from each UC campus, was formed after the summit. The students in the cross-UC campus coalition wrote to UCOP demanding a response for the lack of commitment from Napolitano regarding undocumented students' demands and the renewal of the funds for undocumented student support services. Interested undocumented students were invited to participate in a monthly conference call with UCOP representatives. But there was a lack of transparency from UCOP regarding funding matters. The email letter to UCOP details how Napolitano's $5 million initiative had supported services for undocumented students throughout the UC campuses. The 2013 funds were set to expire in June 2016. Without funding renewal, each UC campus would be required to search for internal and external funding to retain the services for undocumented students, which themselves are already strained by the growing number of undocumented students enrolled in the UC system.

Indeed, structurally, the undocumented student program on each UC campus faces issues of sustainability and lack of funding. The programs must be improved with more staffing and funding, as in the case at UCM. Funding the program provides a better, more cohesive network and support system for undocumented students. Funding is essential for place-claiming and making the university habitable for us.[6] At UCM specifically, this funding provided a coordinator, student coordinator(s), access to legal services, emergency funds, and a support system. The funds have been used to support programs directed at building community and fostering leadership for undocumented students.

In May 2016, a month before the expiration of the 2013 funds and almost a year after the National Summit on Undocumented Students, Napolitano expanded the program by allocating $8.4 million per year over three years to further support undocumented students. While the UCOP website and the official news outlets that historicized this funding suggested that it served as evidence of an inclusive and progressive university system, the funds are split among the nine UC campuses for over three years (UCSF was not included). Therefore, in actuality, some UC campuses receive less money than from the initial funding in 2013. The funding is also divided by the number of undocumented students enrolled on each campus. The UC Undocumented

Legal Service Center, based at UC Davis, will receive $900,000 per year, while the UC Dream Loan Program will receive $5 million per year. The rest of the funds will be allocated for financial support, emergency funds, and staff coordinator salaries. The funding for 2016 and the next three years does not ensure that Napolitano will continue to allocate funds for undocumented students after the three-year period ends. If Napolitano does not renew the funds, the undocumented services on each UC campus will be required to look for alternative means to fund programs.[7] We are at the whim of a "sovereign"—the UC system, a political body founded under the tradition of democratic citizenship but that has shifted to increased privatization of the public university.[8]

Case #2: Undocumented Students as a Public Relations Minefield

Diversity initiatives are not concerned about instituting structural transformation; but rather, they engage in reorganization—the act of "rearranging things so organizations can appear in a better or happier way" (Ahmed 2017, 98). Students of color are used to signify diversity in a series of photographs published by the university, featured on websites and pamphlets. In February 2017, the Education Life Department of the *New York Times* published Patricia Leigh Brown's article, "Creating a Safe Space for California Dreamers." While the primary focus of her article was supposed to be the Fiat Lux Program (FLP), which assists in the transition of first-generation students into college, it shifted to a discussion of undocumented students at UCM. While not all students in FLP were undocumented, students interviewed in the article were all undocumented. Brown states that the FLP was established to reach students "who grew up sleeping on living room floors so the bedrooms could be rented out" (2017). After Brown's description of FLP, she added that "as freshmen, 175 of the scholars, 22 of them undocumented, live together on the upper two floors of Tenaya Hall, sharing sparsely decorated rooms reflective of their modest means—a graduation watch here, a pair of Huaraches there."

While not all undocumented people cross the desert, she appealed to the institutional imagery of an undocumented youth's trek across the United States–Mexico border. Juxtaposing this narrative with undocumented students at UCM, she strung together fragments of life histories, captured a few photographs for the article, and noted the room numbers of her collaborators. Her description of the lived experiences of undocumented students does not deserve discussion in my text because it followed an undistinguished, but prevailing image of lives. She spoke about parents, and how we somehow managed to excel in school, describing one of the students as "like her peers who entered the country illegally," affirming that our presence in the United States, as well as in the university, is abnormal.

Throughout the text, Brown referred to our migration and presence in the United States as "illegal," citing our anxiety and vulnerability with the new presidential regime. She added that one student "saved up money for college by picking plums alongside his mother, who raised three children by rising at 4:30 A.M. six days a week to work in the fields." She ended by stating that, "Collectively, the freshmen in Tenaya Hall are the beacons of a better life." Brown was interested in a particular story: the story of violence, poverty, and resiliency. She implied that the undocumented students interviewed in the article "made it" because these students have been admitted to UCM, despite the violence and trauma they faced while growing up undocumented in the United States.

The snapshots Brown presented appeal to the liberal narrative that undocumented students must improvise but they rise to overcome the trauma of undocumented life. The narratives presented in her text are stories of violence and they parallel the attempts of writers, scholars, and institutions to present undocumented people as able to conform to normative citizenship. Brown's article employed liberal, essentialist lenses in its examination of undocumented students at UCM. Brown noted that we are able to attend university because despite our "illegal" status, we worked hard, and were admitted to the university, just like other Americans who possess values of meritocracy. The article implied that gratefulness should be given to the university for expanding its umbrella of multiculturalism and initiatives of inclusion and diversity to include this population.

The article published students' room numbers and names, releasing the dorm addresses of each student in the article. Publicized in the *New York Times*, this article has been circulated widely by both academics and nonacademics. Some of these scholars, especially those known to conduct research on undocumented communities, celebrate this publication for UCM's efforts to meet the needs of undocumented students. It does not surprise me that these scholars, along with UCM administrators, would commend the article if their names, research interests, and the university's image are uplifted. Following the publication of the article, dialogue with students involved in student government, Associated Students of UCM (ASUCM), noted that the administration was flaunting the article as evidence of the university's diversity efforts. It was not until campus leadership received concerned messages from students, staff, faculty, and community members that they acknowledged the flaws in the article. Brown's decision to publish the full names and room numbers of students in a well-read, global newspaper was unethical.

After I read the article, I called Jane Karr, the editor of the *New York Times*'s Education Life section, as a "concerned reader" and explained that there is private information about the students in the article. Karr claimed that there was nothing wrong with the article because private information was not disclosed. The article contained the featured students' room numbers, an unnecessary piece of information that put our lives in danger, especially when published in a globally read newspaper. Undocumented people already live a precarious life. We are exposed to the possibility of violence every time we speak out, seek justice, and publicly justify our existence in this nation. We are subjected to the violence of explaining why our bodies are within the boundaries of the United States. We are expected to indulge readers with a story about the lack of economic opportunities and violence that we face in our country of origin, while stating that the United States is a land of inclusion, democracy, and opportunity.

The title of the *New York Times* article, "Creating Safe Spaces for California Dreamers," raises the question: What did the university or the *New York Times* do to create a safe space for undocumented students, when the article explicitly provided the room numbers of students? During our conversation, Karr insisted that the *New York Times* does not take stories down. Moreover, she argued that we have "legal papers to be here" and that there is nothing in the article that traces the students' families. In relation to diversity work and the *New York Times*, the article specifically uses "Safe Space" in its title, reminiscent of the way UCM's website claims that the University is a "Safe Space for All." Here, space becomes a metaphorical entity that is created through action and practice. Having a "safe space" means that the space is transformed in a particular way, so students feel supported, secured, and safe in all senses. However, it was this very article that tokenized undocumented students and marked us as success products of the university, as if we are able to thrive because the university allows us to—by providing space for us and allowing us to exist in the university's space.

Figure 3.1 was featured on the official UCM website as part of a slideshow showcasing the campus efforts for diversity, research, and current events. It included a link to the *New York Times* article on undocumented students and the campus's initiatives for "safe space."[9] The summary on the UCM website stated that "The *New York Times* highlights our unyielding efforts to support those from all backgrounds, including first-generation and undocumented students." The article, promoted by the university, remained on the school's

FIGURE 3.1. The twenty-first-century university: the American flag welcomes "minority students" and provides "a safe space for all." Source: https://www.ucmerced.edu/.

website months after its release, even though a segment of undocumented students had condemned it. The chancellor's office released a letter acknowledging that the information released was not appropriate after pressure from students, staff, and faculty allies.[10]

Ironically, a large American flag is featured at the center of the photograph, presumably to attest to ideas of citizenship, democracy, and inclusion of undocumented students at UCM. The American flag, however, is a prime nationalistic symbol which has a history of erasing the violence it has imposed on communities. Here, it is supposed to capture the progressiveness of the twenty-first-century American university that provides a "safe space for all." The discourse of UCM as welcoming undocumented students is reminiscent of the dominant narrative of immigrants arriving in the United States to be greeted by the Statue of Liberty. The use of the American flag in the photograph may be said to parallel the fact that the American flag has been a symbol of assimilation as a survival tactic (see Ahmad 2002) and nationalism when it is waved to represent the exclusion of nonwhites in the United States (Hurd 2008).

The *New York Times* article was emailed to several departments at UCM, as if to celebrate UCOP's initiative: Our good deed is paying off; it was an advantageous decision to expand our multicultural umbrella. This is how the neoliberal university handles diversity. It literally has to use the bodies of undocumented people to prove it is a liberal place that welcomes minority and underrepresented students. Undocumented students are asked to do interviews with these mainstream, traditional platforms to bolster the reputation of the university. Later, an interlocutor commented that good things came out of it because we had concerned readers and allies writing letters and donating to the scholarship fund for undocumented students. These good things included the printing of the university's name in a major newspaper and the validation of the institution's efforts to include undocumented students under the diversity umbrella—the number of undocumented lives in this university's space being an acceptable way to measure diversity, progress, and liberalism. More explicitly, the narratives of poverty and resiliency that surround undocumented students have strong currency in the liberal imaginings of citizenship and provide added value to the university. These "good things," however, came at the expense of not just the violence imposed on the article's interviewees, but also for the undocumented students at UCM who felt uncomfortable and violated with how undocumented people were portrayed.

NAPOLITANO AND THE DREAMER NARRATIVE

After the 2016 elections, Napolitano published an opinion piece in the *New York Times* (Napolitano 2016). News outlets, politicians, and the undocumented community have discussed the possibility of the termination of Deferred Action for Childhood Arrivals (DACA) under Trump's administration. Napolitano attempts to defend DACA, urging readers to consider its benefits by presenting the appealing image of DREAMers. Napolitano discusses her career history as a former U.S. attorney, governor of Arizona (a border state historically known to have punishing laws against immigrants), and president of the UC system. In this op-ed, Napolitano states that she "already knew that many of our immigrant policies made little, if any, sense because they did not prioritize the use of enforcement resources" (2). She plays a neutral position by understanding that the immigration policies "made little, if any, sense" but reaffirms in other parts of the piece the "alien" quality of undocumented people.[11] For example, in terms of immigration, she cites "public safety" for updated enforcement policies that focus on national security (e.g., prioritizing gang members, felons). Napolitano argues that upon realization that Congress would not issue immigration reform, "more needed to be done with respect to one special population—DREAMers" (3). She places significant value on the DREAMers, at the expense of establishing the bad/good immigrant binary. Napolitano states that DREAMers "have become valuable contributors to their community" (3–4). She means to include only those of us who have succeeded in accessing higher education.

Coding the DREAMer as productive and educated, DREAMers are promoted because of our potential economic output—our ability to produce for and be products of the nation-state. DREAMers, or the process of being federally categorized as "DREAMers," perhaps unintentionally but nevertheless implicitly are compared to potential criminals being charged in a case. Napolitano ends with a neutral call for the federal government to be "resourceful." She does not explicitly champion the livelihoods of the undocumented community, or even the DREAMers. Identity becomes disconnected from individual social experience and instead is attached to institutional values by arguing that subjects "marked" (Bucholtz and Hall 2004) as "diverse" contribute to the overall capital of the university. In neoliberal regimes, institutional structures expect individuals with marked identities, such as those communities racialized and marked diverse, to capitalize on and objectify their identities and histories to the university. This history of diversifying universities comes from when boards of trustees recognized the importance of diversity in attracting consumers, such as paying students (Urciuoli 2003). This sets diversity as capital, meaning diversity contributes to the overall attractiveness of the university. Since specific identities (like undocumented) signify capital, the university requires individuals with marked identities to market their identities as something that contributes to the university (Park 2013), effectively concealing broader discussions of language, power, and inequality within and beyond the institution.

People with marked identities are then incorporated into institutions as "value-added" (Urciuoli 2016) through their histories and lived experiences that affirm an institution's diversity criterion. Undocumented students are imagined as quasi-citizens in the national discourse on immigration because of their easily discernible markedness. Despite being marked as "Other" because of their lack of U.S. citizenship status, undocumented youth and students are marked as different from older immigrants—and constructed as productive, highly educated, and almost-American by the mainstream media and some scholarship. Undocumented students and youth are iconized as DREAMers, in a narrative that depends on liberal conceptions of diversity, inclusion, and citizenship. Undocumented youth and students who fit the DREAMer caricature are indexed as worthy and deserving of American citizenship because of potential economic contributions.

While the DREAMer narrative has been reclaimed and appropriated by a faction of the undocumented community, it is also important to highlight that undocumented students and youth also mobilize tropes of deservingness to make political claims. Under neoliberal conditions, "the messiness of marked social identity is reformulated and tidied up as 'diversity'" (Urciuoli 2016, 2). However, the imposed DREAMer identity is made even more complex when it is deployed by undocumented people. Undocumented students and/or youth's educational attainment, use of English, and experience growing up in the United States are perceived as exceptional. These narratives imply that a certain type of undocumented immigrant is more "acceptable"—specifically, more American than another—thus creating a hierarchy and emphasizing a good immigrant narrative. Moreover, the "type" of undocumented immigrant that is coded as more deserving is one that is recognizable to the American public. For example, images of high school and college undocumented graduates are often used to justify proposals for the Development, Relief and Education for Alien Minors (DREAM) Act.[12]

However, in some instances, undocumented people may subscribe to these identities because it provides economic mobility and allows for political claims. The neoliberal regime encourages undocumented students to self-commodify or market histories of trauma and violence and identify with state-ascribed (and self-ascribed) identities like the DREAMer because of its mobility and appeal to the liberal savior trope. Trauma as diversity is scripted to support the institution. Similar to how humanitarian logics depend on individuals to demonstrate their suffering to gain asylum, we are often asked to share our "narrative" and experience living as undocumented students. Sharing our narrative has become a tool for making claims; we are asked to objectify our experience (see Allen 2009; Fassin and Rechtman 2009; Ticktin 2011). As asylum seekers in Lebanon show their scars and wounds, and demonstrate their "victim" status to make asylum claims (Dewachi 2015), a similar expectation of storytelling is anticipated from undocumented students, as seen in the *New York Times* article (Brown 2017).[13] Indeed, storytelling grants us agency and allows us to make political claims, but it has also become commodified by the public discourse that surrounds undocumented youth. Under this neoliberal regime, identity is transformed into a new value system, where individuals are required to negotiate and engage with institutional demands.

Like in Brown's (2017) article, in a liberal society stories of resilience and entrance into the university are positively rewarded. However, the accomplishment is transformed into something the university provided us: undocumented students access higher education because the university and California's AB 540, AB 130, and AB 131 permits us to apply (Abrego 2006, 2008). As an undocumented student active in spaces of support for undocumented communities, I can attest to the fact that undocumented people protested and faced the threat of deportation for speaking against racism in the academy and borders inscribed in our bodies (also see Ono 2012). Primary education may have instilled qualities of Americanness and meritocracy, but the university hammered it into our heads. They cannot bleach the color of skin, but universities can inject ideas of docility, meritocracy, deservingness, capitalism, and heteropatriarchy. Diversity, only in the form of race and citizenship, does not challenge the issue of inequity and lack of security for undocumented students, nor does it take a stance against anti-immigrant sentiment and white supremacy. When undocumented students challenge these structures, we encounter walls, to borrow from Sara Ahmed (2017), and borders that prevent us from accessing these spaces.

Conclusion

Setting the university as a microcosm of state interests (Hundle and Vang 2019), I argue that universities and diversity initiatives may serve as "borders" that function to protect university interests from transformative work. As the "twenty-first-century American university," UCM follows the tradition of its sister campuses by placing deep significance on research, a productive student body, and emphasizing diversity. My discussion of ethnic categories and statistical discourse in the beginning of this essay tries to illuminate the ways in which the physical bodies of students are used to affirm diversity. In regard to undocumented students, labeled as nonresident aliens, I argue that diversity talk and diversity initiatives for our community come in the form of messages that aim to uplift the university as a liberal space.

The undocumented student initiative is a "resource shell" because the funding and resources allocated to undocumented students are granted to appease us, but do not allow us to completely thrive in the university. In conversation with other students as I conducted this project, we demand that the university provide a means of securing jobs for undocumented students (both with DACA and without); have a permanent budget; never have Immigration and Customs Enforcement on campus; train staff, faculty, and students for cultural sensitivity; and seek undocumented student input for all decisions related to our community. In addition, this essay examines how the university uses the bodies of undocumented students (also, more generally, students of color) for public relations purposes to cultivate an image of itself as the twenty-first-century American university—a university that celebrates student success contingent upon academic success and diversity. With the high rate of undocumented students and first-generation students at UCM, the university presents itself as a safe haven for underserved populations. The key point of this essay is to illuminate how the university is willing to sell the stories of violence, pain, and trauma that undocumented students encounter to uplift itself as a liberal, multicultural space that welcomes and provides opportunities for marginalized communities.

The university should not depend on the number of students of color and minorities to demonstrate efforts of inclusion and diversity. In the case of UCM, which is popularly referred to as the "UC for Minorities" because of the student body's demographics (ethnically "minoritized" people, first-generations, a large number of undocumented students), the university needs to provide us the tools to thrive, whether by having more faculty of color, women of color grounded in social justice frameworks in administrative positions, and substantial and sustainable efforts for undocumented students (as well as other marginalized students and communities of color) that do not fall into the trap of resource shells, which are resources provided to students that are minimally funded or unfunded indefinitely and are understaffed, thereby depending on the labor of women (of color), as in the case of SUS.

Universities can be both "homes and non-homes" because the labor to "transform institutions [is] always related to our everyday existence in universities, and our existence in universities is connected to needing to transform the university," and is thus a decolonizing project (Hundle 2019). Universities are home to violent, Eurocentric epistemologies but can also serve as spaces for possibilities and transformation (Moten and Harney 2013; Mohanty 2003). Diversity is not just about producing knowledge about diversity and examining its productivity or how it follows the whim of liberal, normative citizenship; but rather, it is about transforming institutions and making them more habitable for multiple groups of people, most especially migrant women who are often at the margins and working within multiple intersections of identities. In doing diversity work, we must push borders, ceilings, and walls in the university to make them spaces not just to survive, but also to thrive.

NOTES

1. Further information about suboptimal toleration can be found via UC Merced's HR page: https://hr.ucmerced.edu/files/page/documents/webchat_-_wfp_update_qa.pdf.

2. http://regents.universityofcalifornia.edu/governance/policies/4400.html.

3. http://newamericamedia.org/2013/11/qa-napolitanos-vision-for-the-university-of-california.php.

4. AB 130 allows students (both documented and undocumented) from out of state to apply for non-state and non-federally funded scholarships. AB 131 allows students to apply for state-funded scholarships such as Cal-Grants. Together, AB 130 and AB 131 are known as the California Dream Act.

5. The draft recommendation uses the word "illegally."

6. The concept of making the university habitable came from many conversations with Professor Anneeth Kaur Hundle at UCM, in her graduate course, "Feminist Theories: Traditions, Critiques, Praxis."

7. UC Berkeley received a donation from Elise Haas in the fall of 2012 to establish the Robert D. Haas Dreamer Resource Center.

8. Alternatively, UCM can allocate funds for SUS and undocumented students enrolled in the university. UCM, an individual campus, would have to include a budget for undocumented students in its university-wide financial plan. At the time of this writing, UCM has yet to do so.

9. The faces of undocumented students are not present at the website. The photograph used as the backdrop for the article shows the incoming class of students who participated in the mandatory ASCEND conference hosted by UCM.

10. See the released letter here: https://chancellor.ucmerced.edu/content/our-commitment-uc-merced-dreamers.

11. Alien could arguably be read as "illegal" and "criminal" (see Rosas 2010, 2016; De Genova 2002).

12. The DREAM Act is a federal legislative proposal first introduced in 2001 that aimed to provide a pathway for legal residency and later, citizenship, to "qualified" undocumented applicants.

13. Next time someone wants to hear my narrative, life story, oral history, or see my scabs or evidence of my self-imposed inflictions, I will show them my expired work authorization cards, passport, and letters from USCIS.

REFERENCES

Abrego, Leisy J. 2006. "'I Can't Go to College Because I Don't Have Papers': Incorporation Patterns of Latino Undocumented Youth." *Latino Studies* 4(3): 212–31. https://doi.org/10.1057/palgrave.lst.8600200.

Abrego, Leisy J. 2008. "Legitimacy, Social Identity, and the Mobilization of Law: The Effects of Assembly Bill 540 on Undocumented Students in California." *Law and Social Inquiry* 33(3): 709–34. https://doi.org/10.1111/j.1747-4469.2008.00119.x.

Ahmad, Muneer. 2002. "Homeland Insecurities: Racial Violence the Day after September 11." *Social Text* 20(3): 101–15. https://muse.jhu.edu/article/31937.

Ahmed, Sara. 2017. *Living a Feminist Life*. Durham, NC: Duke University Press.

Allen, Lori A. 2009. "Martyr Bodies in the Media: Human Rights, Aesthetics, and the Politics of Immediation in the Palestinian Intifada." *American Ethnologist* 36(1): 161–80. https://doi.org/10.1111/j.1548-1425.2008.01100.x.

Brown, Patricia Leigh. 2017. "Creating a Safe Space for California Dreamers." *New York Times*, February 3, 2017. https://www.nytimes.com/2017/02/03/education/edlife/daca-undocumented-university-of-california-merced-fiat-lux-scholars.html.

Bucholtz, Mary, and Kira Hall. 2004. "Language and Identity." In *A Companion to Linguistic Anthropology*, edited by Alessandro Duranti, 369–94. Malden, MA: Blackwell Publishing.

Da Silva, Denise Ferreira. 2007. *Toward a Global Idea of Race*. Minneapolis: University of Minnesota Press.

De Genova, Nicholas P. 2002. "Migrant 'Illegality' and Deportability in Everyday Life." *Annual Review of Anthropology* 31(1): 419–47. https://doi.org/10.1146/annurev.anthro.31.040402.085432.

De Genova, Nicholas. 2004. "The Legal Production of Mexican/Migrant 'Illegality.'" *Latino Studies* 2(2): 160–85. https://doi.org/10.1057/palgrave.lst.8600085.

De Genova, Nicholas. 2013. "Spectacles of Migrant 'Illegality': The Scene of Exclusion, the Obscene of Inclusion." *Ethnic and Racial Studies* 36(7): 1180–98. https://doi.org/10.1080/01419870.2013.783710.

Dewachi, Omar. 2015. "When Wounds Travel." *Medicine Anthropology Theory* 2(3): 1–82. doi.org/10.17157/mat.2.3.182.

Fassin, Didier, and Richard Rechtman. 2009. *The Empire of Trauma : An Inquiry into the Condition of Victimhood*. Princeton, NJ: Princeton University Press.

Freeling, Nicole. 2015. "UC Hosts National Summit on Undocumented Students." *UC Newsroom*, May 22, 2015. https://www.universityofcalifornia.edu/news/uc-hosts-national-summit-undocumented-students.

Giroux, Henry A. 2014. *Neoliberalism's War on Higher Education*. Chicago: Haymarket Books.

Harvey, David. 2005. *A Brief History of Neoliberalism*. New York: Oxford University Press.

Hundle, Anneeth. 2019. "Decolonizing Diversity: The Transnational Politics of Minority Racial Difference." *Public Culture* 31(2): 289–322. http://search.proquest.com/docview/2220757675/.

Hundle, Anneeth Kaur, and Ma Vang. 2019. "Thinking the Twenty-First Century Neoliberal Research University: Preliminary Reflections on Opportunity, Risk and Solidarity at the New University of California." *Critical Ethnic Studies* 5(1–2): 174–204.

Hurd, Clayton A. 2008. "Cinco de Mayo, Normative Whiteness, and the Marginalization of Mexican-Descent Students." *Anthropology and Education Quarterly* 39(3): 293–313. https://doi.org/10.1111/j.1548-1492.2008.00023.x.

Mohanty, Chandra Talpade. 2003. *Feminism without Borders: Decolonizing Theory, Practicing Solidarity*. Durham, NC: Duke University Press.

Moten, Fred, and Stefano Harney. 2013. *The Undercommons: Fugitive Planning and Black Study*. Wivenhoe, UK: Minor Compositions.

Napolitano, Janet. 2013. "Napolitano Lays Out Ambitious Agenda for UC." *SFGate*, November 2, 2013. http://www.sfgate.com/opinion/article/Napolitano-lays-out-ambitious-agenda-for-UC-4947752.php.

Napolitano, Janet. 2016. "The Truth about Young Immigrants and DACA." *New York Times*, November 30, 2016. https://www.nytimes.com/2016/11/30/opinion/the-truth-about-young-immigrants-and-daca.html.

Ono, Kent A. 2012. "Borders That Travel: Matters of the Figural Border." In *Border Rhetorics: Citizenship and Identity on the US–Mexico Frontier*, edited by D. Robert DeChaine, 19–32. Tuscaloosa: University of Alabama Press.

Park, Joseph Sung-Yul. 2013. "Metadiscursive Regimes of Diversity in a Multinational Corporation." *Language in Society* 42(5): 557–77. https://doi.org/10.1017/S0047404513000663.

Richman, Josh. 2016. "Undocumented Students Disrupt Janet Napolitano's Speech at UC Summit." *Mercury News*, August 12, 2016. https://www.mercurynews.com/2015/05/07/undocumented-students-disrupt-janet-napolitanos-speech-at-uc-summit/.

Rosas, Gilberto. 2010. "Cholos, Chúntaros, and the 'Criminal' Abandonments of the New Frontier." *Identities* 17(6): 695–713.

Rosas, Gilberto. 2016. "The Border Thickens: In-Securing Communities after IRCA." *International Migration* 54(2): 119–30.

Smith Tuhiwai, Linda. 1999. *Decolonizing Methodologies: Research and Indigenous Peoples.* New York: Zed Books Ltd.

Somers, Margaret R. 2008. *Genealogies of Citizenship: Markets, Statelessness, and the Rights to Have Rights.* Cambridge: Cambridge University Press.

Ticktin, Miriam Iris. 2011. *Casualties of Care Immigration and the Politics of Humanitarianism in France.* Berkeley: University of California Press.

UCM Office of Institutional Research and Decision Support. 2017. "Institutional Research and Decision Support." *University of California, Merced.* https://irds.ucmerced.edu/.

Urciuoli, Bonnie. 2003. "Excellence, Leadership, Skills, Diversity: Marketing Liberal Arts Education." *Language and Communication* 23(3): 385–408. https://doi.org/10.1016/S0271-5309(03)00014-4.

Urciuoli, Bonnie. 2016. "The Compromised Pragmatics of Diversity." *Language and Communication* 51: 30–39. https://doi.org/10.1016/j.langcom.2016.07.005.

Urla, Jacqueline. 2012. *Reclaiming Basque: Language, Nation, and Cultural Activism.* Reno: University of Nevada Press.

GABRIELA MONICO

4

American't

Redefining Citizenship in the U.S. Undocumented Immigrant Youth Movement

The 2016 U.S. presidential election, and the subsequent Trump administration, unleashed a nativist wave of anti-immigrant rhetoric and draconian immigration policy and enforcement (Beinart 2016; Ford 2017). While the intensity of these attacks on migrants and other oppressed peoples signaled something specific about this new presidential administration, state-based nativist ideas, rhetoric, and policies are not new. At different points in time, this sort of state-based nativism has been codified, systematized, and instrumentalized, coming to define in implicit and explicit ways who is American and exclude those who fall short (Ngai 2003).[1] In the process, various historically marginalized groups of people have been excluded (Patel 2015; Ruswick 2013). Similar to moments in the collective national past, defining who is deemed worthy of being American today has real effects on people's lives, including the eleven million undocumented people in the United States (Krogstad et al. 2017).

Exclusionary definitions of belonging lead to a binary distinction between those who are deserving of being American on the one hand, and those who are undeserving on the other (Keyes 2014; Nicholls 2014). This phenomenon is not unique to nativist rhetoric, however; it is also present in discourse in support of immigrants employed by some activists, legislators, and the media. An important example is the campaign to support the Development, Relief and Education for Alien Minors (DREAM) Act.

Undocumented immigration has been a visible issue of contention and public discourse for decades. Since 2001, however, much of the policy conversation has focused on the DREAM Act. This proposed legislation would provide a pathway to citizenship for undocumented young people (Batalova and McHugh 2010).[2] In spite of Congress's inability to enact legislation to regularize the status of the broader undocumented population, the fight to pass the DREAM Act has provided a space for undocumented student movements to grow and attain significant legislative victories at the federal, state, and local levels (Gonzales 2008). Some of these victories include the California Dream Act, which provides wider access to financial aid for undocumented students, and most notably the Deferred Action for Childhood Arrivals (DACA) program implemented in 2012, which provides a two-year deportation reprieve to those who meet its requirements.[3] While these policy victories have made a meaningful difference on the ground, it is important to question how the DREAM Act came to almost singularly be the policy prescription for undocumented immigration, when it would benefit so few of the undocumented residents of this nation.

The mobilization to pass the federal DREAM Act has popularized a narrative that excludes those who would not qualify (Nicholls 2014). Due to the DREAM Act's stringent criteria, a significant number of undocumented young people would not be able to obtain legal immigration status if the bill were passed into law (Batalova and McHugh 2010). In fact, a report from the Migration Policy Institute revealed that about 67 percent of undocumented youth are ineligible. The DREAM Act's parameters not only leave out large sectors of the undocumented population but have also shaped the discourse of immigration reform.

Legislators, the media, and some DREAM Act supporters have articulated an "aspiring American" narrative, which rests on the portrayal of the potential beneficiaries as law-abiding, high-achieving students (Keyes 2014). Importantly, embedded in the discourse are arguments steeped in a meritocratic ideal, positing these young people as deserving of citizenship because they have worked hard in ways that are valued in society. This captures the influence of "market citizenship," which rewards human potential and economic contributions with belonging and citizenship (Nawyn 2011; Nicholls 2014). On December 6, 2017, California Senator Kamala Harris made the following remarks in favor of the DREAM Act:

> Let's be clear that these DREAMers who received DACA status, they study in our colleges, they serve in our military, they work in Fortune 100 companies. And they are contributing to our economy in a way that we all are benefiting. If DACA recipients were deported, it is estimated that Califor-

nia would lose $11 billion a year. The United States economy as a whole would lose an estimated $460 billion over a decade. (Harris 2017)

Harris's remarks convey the idea that DACA recipients' deservingness stems from their hard work and economic contributions to the United States.

Although the ideas above powerfully shape the discourse, there has been recognition within the DREAM Act movement, as well as the larger immigrant rights movements, that these mainstream views that have defined the "ideal" undocumented immigrant are exclusionary (Negrón-Gonzales 2015; Nicholls 2014). In response, some activists are employing different rhetoric that challenges these views by calling for a vision of immigration reform that includes all 11 million undocumented residents.

My experience as an undocumented young person placed me in the middle of these different, and at times competing, perspectives and discourses within immigrant rights groups. I was intrigued by these conversations, which motivated me to explore different articulations of belonging and rhetoric used by immigrant rights groups. This led me to take up this project in which I examine the work of The Collective, a Northern California undocumented group that challenges the DREAM Act discourse. Through participant observation and interviews, I seek to answer the following questions: (1) How do young activists left out of the DREAM Act discourse navigate the concept of market citizenship? (2) How do they frame their claims of citizenship and belonging in the United States?[4] I find that undocumented young people who participated in this study recognize, question, and challenge the meritocratic claims embedded in mainstream immigration discourse. They also actively explore how these claims exclude and even commodify those who are supposed to benefit from this framing.

Through their organizing, art, and political education work,[5] study participants recognize themselves as human beings and seek to humanize all undocumented immigrants. As part of this process, The Collective articulates claims of belonging around a human rights frame. They believe that everyone should have the opportunity to see their dreams realized, regardless of their immigration status and meritocratic "deservingness." Study participants do not view themselves as "American" (at least not in the traditional sense) because of their experience of marginalization, exploitation, and exclusion in the United States. They believe that even if undocumented immigrants were given the opportunity to regularize their status, they would still be economically and socially marginalized in the United States. They recognize the need to advocate for legislation that addresses these broader issues.

The Collective also asserts citizenship and belonging by claiming a special connection to the land through Indigeneity, a schema superseding the nation-state that serves as an explicit critique of nativism. I find that as participants explore their Indigenous roots and the concept of Indigeneity, they articulate a vision of transnational citizenship and some identify as Indigenous. Cultivation of this identity is done in The Collective's practices such as healing circles and artwork employing Mesoamerican symbols and motifs. There are many ways in which Indigeneity claims could be problematized; however, I do not feel qualified to do so.

It is important to critically examine the implications of mainstream views on citizenship and belonging because they affect the rights and well-being of millions of people in fundamental ways. My work provides insight into a broader vision of immigrant rights, belonging, and citizenship as conceived through the work of a group of individuals at the margins of society. These individuals deal with a body of intersecting identities but share a common liberatory vision, and articulate claims of belonging to American society in a uniquely broad way.

Evolution of the Immigration Debate and Its Implications

Historically, immigration policies have been shaped by social beliefs about who deserves to be officially included in society (Ngai 2003). Upon the signing of the U.S. Declaration of Independence of 1776, citizenship was restricted to property owners, which in those times was a right only bestowed on white males. Decades later, the 1790 Naturalization Law limited naturalization to "free white" immigrants (Fox and Bloemraad 2015, 181). Voting and citizenship laws that followed excluded populations that have been present in the United States throughout its history, including Native Americans, African Americans, and women (Marston 1990; Lipsitz 1995). Later, policies excluded immigration from Asia and placed quotas on other countries, all the while welcoming migration from Northern and Western Europe (Ngai 2003; Massey 1995).

In 1882, the Chinese Exclusion Act made it illegal for Chinese workers to immigrate to the United States and for Chinese nationals to become U.S. citizens (Ngai 2003, 44). This was the first of a series of Chinese exclusion laws that remained in place for more than 60 years (Lee 2003). The 1924 National Origins Act set quotas on the number of immigrants from outside of the Western Hemisphere in order to "preserve the ideal of U.S. homogeneity" (U.S. Department of State, Office of the Historian). Decades later, during World

War II, Executive Order 9066 stripped Japanese and Japanese Americans' fundamental civil rights by forcing them into internment camps (Ngai 2003, 196). Even though the passage of the Immigration and Nationality Act of 1965 reformed immigration laws, it still excludes legal migration of certain groups of people, as it created a "preference system" of family and occupational categories (Massey 1995). The high number of undocumented people currently present in the United States has resulted in a vigorous immigration debate (Vaughns 2005) and the community organizing of undocumented youth has played a fundamental role in shaping this debate.

Over many decades, undocumented youth have played active roles in immigration law and policy—from *Plyler v. Doe* (1982), where the Supreme Court ruled that K–12 public schools were prohibited from refusing undocumented students, to Senate Bill 699 (2018), a New Jersey law that allows undocumented students to receive financial aid at New Jersey universities (Hing 2018; Rincon 2008; Seif 2004; Abrego 2008). Since 2001, however, the DREAM Act has had a dominant presence in this debate. Since only one in three undocumented youth finishes high school, the bill would provide relief to only 33 percent of the total number of undocumented youth (far more restrictive than the DACA program implemented in 2012, which may benefit individuals who did not attend college) (Batalova and McHugh 2010).

The stories of DREAM Act–ineligible youth have largely been left out of the immigrant rights debate. Many encounter personal and institutional obstacles that prevent them from completing their K–12 education; in fact, out of the 65,000 undocumented immigrant students that graduate from U.S. high schools every year, just 5 to 10 percent attend college (Passel 2003). These statistics are supported by academic literature that explores the legal and economic barriers that undocumented youth encounter, which prevent them from achieving socioeconomic mobility and negatively affect their life chances (Abrego 2006; Gonzales 2011). This paper highlights this population by focusing on a community group that advocates for DREAM Act–ineligible youth.

Often, as a response to the ways in which undocumented immigrants are portrayed as criminals by nativist, right-wing groups and politicians (Lal 2010; Nicholls 2014), some immigrant rights groups and supporters counter that narrative by highlighting the stories of academically exceptional undocumented students (Nicholls 2014). This advocacy, which focuses on the more "deserving," captures the influence of market citizenship in defining who has the right to be fully incorporated into U.S. society. Market citizenship is the idea that citizenship should be conferred on people because of their economic output, which leads to the formulation of exclusionary definitions of membership (Nawyn 2011, 680). This idea is embedded in the rhetoric employed in support of the DREAM Act, which depicts undocumented students as individuals who have the potential to contribute to the U.S. economy. Of course, immigrant labor has long held a central place in the American imaginary of citizenship, and it is found in the ways many undocumented people make claims of belonging. This is illustrated by rhetoric employed during the 2006 immigrant protests, in which citizenship claims were framed around the idea of undocumented people being hardworking and possessing other deserving qualities, like family and American values (Gleeson 2010; Bloemraad and Voss 2011).[6]

Methods

This study employs ethnographic data and interviews collected during one year of continuous research at The Collective,[7] an immigrant rights group led by undocumented youth and sponsored by a local nonprofit organization. The Collective began around 2010 with a handful of undocumented Latino (Latinx) high-school-aged students from an urban area in Northern California. After recognizing that most immigrant youth were being excluded in the immigration debate, the youth committed themselves to advocate for the 67 percent of undocumented young people who would not be eligible for the DREAM Act were it to pass. During the study, the organization was made up of fifteen active Latino (Latinx) youth between the ages of fourteen and nineteen who attended the same high school in Northern California. Most of the youth were undocumented, and the few who were not belonged to mixed-status families (where some family members are undocumented).[8] When data for this study were collected, all of the active members of The Collective resided in the same medium-sized, economically and racially diverse city in Northern California. Black residents are the city's single largest ethnic group, followed by non-Hispanic whites, and Latinos (U.S. Census Bureau 2011). Most of The Collective members reside in the predominantly Latino (Latinx) majority areas of the city in low-income neighborhoods that have been historically affected by (and stereotyped with having) high crime rates and low-resource public schools.

This study took place from February 2012 to January 2013 and it unfolded in three phases. (1) First, I reviewed literature, media, and art produced by the group. (2) After obtaining permission from the leaders, members, and their parents, I conducted participant observation at meetings and activities until the study's conclusion. (3) I conducted one-on-one interviews beginning in July 2012. This allowed me to establish trust and rapport before asking group members to discuss their experiences. I carried out much of the ethnographic fieldwork for this study as part of an assignment for an undergraduate course in the American Cultures Engaged Scholarship Program at the University of California, Berkeley.

A Personal Note on Positionality and My Experience as an Undocumented Student Researcher

My decision to work on this project is rooted in my lived experiences as an undocumented scholar-activist. I migrated from El Salvador at age sixteen and I was undocumented from 2005 through 2015. Shortly after my arrival in the United States, I became involved in the immigrant rights movement. My involvement in activism increased after enrolling at UC Berkeley, where, along with others, I advocated (often motivated as a matter of basic survival) for increased access to educational resources, financial aid, and institutional changes for undocumented students. When the sustained collective efforts of undocumented youth at the federal, state, and local levels yielded, respectively, DACA, the California Dream Act, and the Undocumented Student Program at UC Berkeley, I had the breathing room and opportunities to explore my research interests (as did many other of my undocumented peers on campus and nationwide). I became interested in studying issues surrounding youth who fall outside of the DREAM Act discourse. I took special interest in exploring the claims of belonging made by this population because through my own experiences I gradually learned to question claims of meritocracy embedded in the DREAM Act discourse. When I arrived in the United States, I believed in the American Dream and had middle-class aspirations influenced by my upbringing. However, as the years went on I began to question these ideas as I witnessed and experienced forms of exclusion that affect many immigrant communities.

While my experiences as an undocumented person allowed me to understand some of the intricacies of the undocumented experience, I quickly realized that my own experience was different from those of my study participants. Though I was undocumented, I had been able to pursue higher education and become one of those students whose stories have become part of the dominant discourse of immigration. Conducting this project led me to further reflect on my experience and see the link between power and hierarchy (positionality) to the creation of knowledge (epistemology) (Pillow 2003).[9] Understanding positionality and where I stand with respect to power in relation to others has been particularly helpful in preparing me to learn, accept, respect, and deeply appreciate new perspectives. In this process, I learned to acknowledge that while my past experiences of being undocumented are helpful, I also needed to recognize the privileges I have. This helped me realize that although, to a certain extent, I considered myself an insider, being part of the larger community of unauthorized immigrants does not solve relations of power that I would encounter as a student researcher.

The opportunity to directly work with The Collective allowed me to build relationships with my participants in an authentic way. Past studies on ethnographic fieldwork indicate that "highly participatory roles in which the researcher performs the activities that are central to the lives of those studied . . . provides special opportunities to get close to, participate in, and experience life in unknown settings" (Emerson et al. 1995, 4). By working alongside the participants in this study, I was able to establish meaningful relationships and share experiences with them, deepening my understanding.

The DREAM Act Rests on False and Harmful Notions of Merit

There's always an obstacle that's stopping you from reaching your goals, no matter how hard you work, you are never going to get ahead.—Rosa

Meritocratic arguments portray DREAM Act–eligible undocumented youth as hardworking and deserving. When U.S. Senator Dick Durbin (D-IL) delivered a speech on the Senate floor in support of the DREAM Act in 2010, he described young undocumented people in the following manner:

> They are student council presidents, they are valedictorians, they are junior ROTC leaders, star athletes . . . Why shouldn't our economy benefit from the skills these young people have obtained here? It is senseless for us to chase out the home-grown talent that has the potential to contribute so significantly to our society. They're the ones who are going to start companies, invest in new technologies, pioneer medical advances. (Durbin 2010)

Senator Durbin's words exemplify how legislators and the media often rely on the myth of meritocracy. These depictions are problematic because they position some people as deserving of citizenship at the expense of others; if one is not successful, the presumption is that the reason is that she or he did not try "hard enough." The consequences of this market-citizenship based rationale serve to create and perpetuate exclusionary definitions of membership (Nawyn 2011). Based on my observations, members of The Collective reject the market citizenship arguments as false and harmful.

Participants consistently demonstrated support for the idea that the impact of merit on life outcomes is vastly overestimated (McNamee and Miller 2004). Through their lived experience, they have come to accept that working hard does not necessarily lead them to the American Dream. Paula and Rosa,[10] two Collective members, reflected on the futures they saw for themselves as people and as undocumented youth. Rosa said she would like to become a nurse in the future saying, "I have been treated differently just because I wasn't born here . . . there's always an obstacle that's stopping you from reaching your goals, no matter how hard you work, you are never going to get ahead." Paula then said that she knows of undocumented friends who have to drop out of school and work out of necessity, "friends who have to worry about providing food on the table, so their brothers and sisters have something to eat." Rosa and Paula speak to the structural obstacles that prevent undocumented young people from reaching their dreams and goals, or as authors put it, their "social incorporation" and "transition to adulthood" (Abrego 2006; Gonzales 2011). For Rosa, given the dire economic circumstances of the community in which she lives, her perspective of not being able to "get ahead" is understandable. For many undocumented people, as Paula pointed out, school cannot always be the priority in the face of economic necessity.

Members of the collective believe the obstacles they face are common in the undocumented community because of the hardships faced by their own family members and their own perception that workers such as day laborers are exploited. This point is illustrated by Mariana, who stated the following:

> I don't think there's an American dream. I had to learn that when I was really young. There is no American Dream. I don't know if I had high expectations when I was smaller, but I would just see my parents go to work every day and then they came back really tired. I always saw my family working. My friends' friends were always working, and I would see people on TV and I would see *las novelas* [the soap operas] and people who didn't have to go to work and I was like, "oh, they're living hella fancy" and I started realizing stuff like that really young. Since I was young, I knew that everybody worked so much, and I was like, "where's the American Dream?" and you just walk into the streets and see *jornaleros* [day laborers]. They're just there waiting for a job.

Mariana also recounts this from her work with The Collective:

> [W]e had a project where we interviewed *jornaleros* and I remember I was talking to this *jornalero* . . . He was saying that a lot of people would play with them and they would open the door for them to get into their cars but then they would just leave just to see them fighting each other for a job. They talked about how people would sometimes talk shit about them. They were like, "a lot of us don't know English but you don't have to know English to know that they are being disrespectful to you. He was just telling me how it was him and two other guys living in an apartment and he didn't make a lot of money. I was like, "do you think it's different [in the U.S.]?" He said, "it's very different here." And he remembered that he didn't expect it to be like that. And he was telling me about *la pasada* [the border crossing/journey]. He was from Guatemala and you know it's worse for them. He said that he had a friend who lost his legs, and I remember he got emotional, he didn't want to cry because I guess we were all girls and he was like, "Yeah I had a friend who jumped, and he slipped and then his legs got cut off." And he got really emotional and he kinda stopped talking about it. That convinced me that there is no American Dream.

Unlike previous studies in which undocumented youth appear to "internalize expectations of merit" (Abrego 2006, 227), the participants in this study appear to question meritocracy, and in turn, market citizenship. This is further illustrated by Paula's contribution at a group discussion centered on a video clip about human rights violations that take place at the Mexico-U.S. border:

> Paula raised her hand and said that while it is important for the group to know about the issues in the clip, we also needed to keep in mind the problems that happen in the U.S. In a tone that evoked frustration she said, "You all realize that we could get killed just because of the color of the shoes we wear . . . what is the *sur* (south)? or the *norte* (north)? what matters is that we are brown and that we go through these problems now because we have struggled for too long. Yes, we live in the U.S., but we have always lived under the poverty line. I think many of us would still be poor *even if we had papers*" (italics added for emphasis). Everyone nodded to Paula's words and the room got quiet. (Fieldnotes)

As Paula mentioned, members of The Collective find themselves struggling against structural obstacles in their daily lives. Their self-perceived marginalization serves as proof that hard work does not lead to economic mobility. In her comment, she makes reference to gang violence and to two prevalent gangs in her neighborhood, *Sureños* and *Norteños*, and highlights a number of problems faced by immigrant communities in her neighborhood, such as gang violence and poverty. Both Rosa's and Paula's remarks in this section show their rejection of meritocracy and indirectly market citizenship because these concepts do not align with the socioeconomic realities in which they live. This informs their skepticism of rhetoric that indirectly blames them for "not working hard enough" to deserve citizenship.

Market Citizenship Reduces Immigrants to Economic Actors

The government doesn't really care about us, they care about the labor
—Patricia

The members of The Collective reject market citizenship as the basis for claiming citizenship or belonging because it dehumanizes through its unattainable parameters. I observed members discuss what they consider to be a historically exploitative and unequal relationship between the United States and immigrant labor, which forms the basis for their rejection of market citizenship.

At a meeting, The Collective screened the film *Sleep Dealer* (Rivera 2008), a work of speculative fiction[11] that depicts a dystopian Tijuana, Mexico, in the near future. In the film, the Mexico–U.S. border has been permanently closed and walled off, and immigration has been banned. The border is now completely militarized, with drones regularly using lethal force to deter immigration and drug smuggling. Instead of having laborers physically present in the United States, laborers in Mexico employ cybernetic nodes to control robotic bodies located in the United States to perform manual labor very similar to work that they do presently.

The youth engaged in a long and heated discussion about *Sleep Dealer*. While the subject of the conversation started with members drawing parallels between the militarization of the Mexico–U.S. border today and in the "not-so distant" future depicted, it shifted to a discussion about labor exploitation and dehumanization:

> Patricia said, "Did you all pay attention to what the woman said to her co-worker towards the end of the movie? Something like, "we give the United States what they've always wanted, all the work-without the workers" . . . I was like 'She's so right!' when I saw that." From then on, they kept on discussing how, throughout their lives, they have witnessed people in their communities being abused and exploited by employers

for many years. Mario added, "Just like in the movie, they treat us as robots. The government doesn't really care about us, they care about the labor. That's just wrong" [. . .] Towards the middle of the discussion, the discussion leader interjected and said "So what do you all think about this movie and legislation like the DREAM Act or even immigration reform? Any connections?" People in the group mentioned that they believed this legislation was created, in part, because the U.S. is interested in the labor of the potential beneficiaries but does not actually care for their personhood. (Fieldnotes)

The Collective members challenge market citizenship with the critique that historically the arguments used in support of proposed legislation to regularize undocumented immigrants' legal status has commodified immigrants. Such arguments see immigrants primarily as potential beneficial assets to the United States economy. In the DREAM Act this is focused on providing labor to the white-collar and military sectors, but such arguments are also employed by those seeking to pass comprehensive immigration reform in conjunction with guest worker and agricultural worker programs, which legalize the exploitation of workers who are not provided the same protections of pay as they are entitled to (Southern Poverty Law Center 2013). The Collective recognizes that these proposals do not address the economic and labor exploitation of immigrants but seek to regularize it.

Moving Away from a Definition of "American" That Excludes

I can't call myself American. If anything it's American't . . . the American dream is only a Dream and nothing else.—Adela

Study participants do not view themselves as "American" because of their experiences of exclusion in the United States. These experiences include inequality, poverty, lack of educational resources, and racial prejudice. Participants believe that even if undocumented immigrants were given the opportunity to regularize their status, they would still face dehumanization and exclusion in the United States. Juan Jose, who moved to the United States with his family when he was a one-year-old, recounts growing up in a city of Northern California:

> I live in the flats of . . . [name of city]. You know, the everyday struggle, with liquor stores, gangs, drugs, you know . . . But it's kind of nor-

mal for brown folks to live in low-income communities since we have been excluded from so many things. There's a lot of diversity in [name of city], but you can see the gap . . . you can notice the types of places where there's more brown and black folks and where there's not.

When asked if he sees himself as American, he says that although "he was practically born here," he does not see himself as American. Juan Jose claims that the history and cultural values that he has been taught by his parents are different from "what America has done and created . . . capitalism."

Mariana, who grew up in the same neighborhood as Juan Jose, said: "A lot of people that I grew up with . . . a lot of my friends and my brother's friends . . . they're either dead, locked up, or got deported." She adds that shootings near her home happen every week, but the experience has become normal to her. When asked if she sees herself as American she says, "I'm not American. America hates 'illegals' so much so why would I consider myself American?"

Members of the collective recognized that they would not see themselves as American even if they were granted citizenship status. Adela, a member of the group who is a U.S. citizen from a mixed-status family says:

> I am a citizen, but I don't consider myself American. Somebody who feels like they're American is somebody who has power. Like if you look at someone who is in power, that's what it means to be American. I don't see my people being represented so I can't call myself American. If anything it's American't . . . The American dream is only a dream nothing else. It only happens to people with privilege and money because that's how society's run, with money.

It is clear from the statements above that experiences of exclusion have led the members of The Collective to associate the term "America" with privilege, power, and capitalism, which contribute to maintaining the marginal social space in which they find themselves.

Articulations of Belonging That Humanize Immigrants

Through their words and actions, study participants recognize themselves and undocumented immigrants as human beings. As part of this process, The Collective articulates claims of belonging around a human rights frame. They believe that undocumented immigrants should be entitled to human rights and the opportunity to see their dreams realized, regardless of their immigration status and deservingness.

FIGURE 4.1. No human being is illegal, and each one has a dream (2011).

This human rights frame employed by The Collective can be witnessed through the language, symbols, and images on their murals. The aesthetics of the group's works is closely tied to an understanding of what they perceive to be the underlying causes of immigration to the United States. During the fall of 2011, every time I stepped in and out of the building where meetings took place, I ran into a mural titled "No Human Being is Illegal, y Cada Uno Tiene Un Sueño (and each one has a dream)" (Figure 4.1) that The Collective painted in the summer of 2011. The language of the mural suggests a rejection of the label "illegal" and an attempt at humanizing immigrants by saying that everyone has a dream. This also serves to reject the rhetoric of the DREAM Act by interpreting the term "dreamer" broadly, in contrast to the restrictive definition that has been used as part of the DREAM Act.

The images in the mural depict the journey of crossing the border; after embarking on such a dangerous trip not all immigrants arrive in the United States. People of all ages, including children, cross the border. This mural is highly valued by The Collective not only because of its artistic merit, but also because of the powerful message it conveys. The images depict the realities and hardships many immigrants experience while trying to get to the United States. This mural calls for the humanization and recognition of all immigrants.

Belonging through Connection to the Land Based on Indigeneity

We all come from Indigenous cultures, we are all from somewhere.—Mariana

Along with making claims based on human rights, The Collective articulates a claim of citizenship and belonging through connection to the land based on Indigeneity. An example of this is also present in the mural shown in Figure 4.1, which contains Mesoamerican symbols like the Olmec head, jaguar, and the plumed serpent. This Indigeneity supersedes the nation-state, even borders. I witnessed members conduct a healing ceremony circle where they burned copal like Indigenous people that they refer to as "ancestors," from Mesoamerica did.[12] During the ceremony as each person passed the copal incense, everyone was given time to reflect about the good and bad moments of the year while the others listened. Mariana, one of the oldest members in the group, said during the ceremony, "[w]e all come from Indigenous cultures, we are all from somewhere." This would support the argument that there are ways that locate citizenship beyond the boundaries of the nation-state, which articulate visions of transnational citizenship that blur the line (Bosniak 2000, 449). For members of The Collective, their perceived Indigeneity forms a basis for claiming belonging in this land, even if they are marginalized by the state.

Participants take an interest in exploring their Indigenous roots and the concept of pan-Indigeneity not only to articulate a vision of transnational citizenship, but also to protest the stigma that Indigeneity carries in their countries of origin and in the United States. During their interviews, some participants identified as Indigenous while others identified as *mestizo*. Many of them claimed that they grew up "not knowing" about their Indigenous roots and of the colonial and historical relationship between Spain and Latin America. In most cases, the respondents' parents would refuse to engage in conversations with them about Indigeneity given the stigma it carries in both their motherlands and in the United States. This is clearly illustrated by Mariana, who claims to be Mixtec:

> I remember I would hear one of my relatives speaking a different language over the phone and I would ask my mom "what is he speaking?" She would just ignore me. One time she finally told me that it was Mixtec but she would've never told me if I had not asked her. Later on, I learned that when she was my age she used to be ashamed. She never spoke Mixtec, she taught herself to forget the language, and she did. She recently told me that when she was young in Mexico she saw an Indigenous lady who was selling potatoes. She said that people would

just steal them away from her but my mom just stood there watching and I was like, "why just watch?" and she said, "it's hard because if you help them they start thinking that you are one of them." So yeah, I have learned that we all come from Indigenous cultures but a lot of us forget about them. A lot of us are taught to hate ourselves.

Mariana's mother's decision demonstrates the costs of racism, prejudice, and dehumanization of Indigenous people in her society. Arguably, what led her to hide and reject Indigenous modes of conduct, language, and cultural practices was the portrayal of Indigenous culture as inferior, undeserving, and not belonging. When these ideas become embedded within Indigenous populations, marginalized people feel pressure to assimilate. I find that study participants seek to reconnect with what they believe to be their Indigenous roots because by claiming a connection to their Indigeneity, they cope with marginalization and rejection in the United States and their country of origin by reclaiming their Indigeneity.

In the United States, an increasing number of Latinos (Latinx) self-identify as Indigenous (Decker 2011). In some of these cases, individuals descend from Indigenous people, but are not members of an Indigenous Tribal Nation (Bautista 2019). Indigeneity claims of this nature can be problematized as they can lead to the erasure of Indigenous people in the United States and Latin America (Bautista 2019). At the same time, as more Latinos (Latinx) identify as Indigenous, there has been a growth in the presence of Indigenous diaspora from Latin America, which has led communities and scholars to engage in conversations that encourage a critical exploration of the issues above and the ways in which this diaspora is "shifting and raising questions about transnational meanings of race, place, and indigeneity." (Blackwell, Boj-Lopez, and Urrieta 2017, 126).

Without opining on the claims to Indigeneity made by members of The Collective, I do believe that it is important to note that the immigrant rights movement is diverse, and there are activists of many backgrounds who may not recognize an Indigenous space as a familiar one. On the other hand, there might be a chance for understanding and collaboration if we consider the words of Mariana, that "we are all from somewhere."

Critical Pedagogy in Schools and Organizing Spaces

I think I am politically conscious because of the things that I've been through and the things that I've seen my family go through. But the education I received in high school . . . I think everything started to make sense there. It was like a puzzle, and then all the pieces came together.—Luz

It is important to note that a recurrent theme in interviews and observations, which influenced the formulations of belonging and thinking of the study participants, is the exposure to critical pedagogy[13] that allowed them to further understand and reflect on their social and political realities. Most of my study participants were first exposed to critical pedagogy in high school and some in middle school. The mission of the high school that most Collective members attend reads, "[o]ur work is grounded in a theoretical framework that enables our students to analyze history, literature and the world around them in terms of oppression and liberatory action." Luz says,

> In middle school, I used to have a lot of trouble in my history class. I would try to pay attention, but the subject was not relevant to me. I always flunked it. Once I got to my high school, I started learning about different types of histories, not this western white history that we are always taught. I was learning about the black community and my community . . . about all these things that were interesting to me, and all of a sudden, my history grades went up. I think I am politically conscious because of the things that I've been through and the things that I've seen my family go through. But the education I received in high school . . . I think everything started to make sense there. It was like a puzzle, and then all the pieces came together.

Luz is suggesting that there seems to be an awakening once the youth make a connection between their lived experience and what they are being taught at their school; in this case, an independent high school.

In her interview, Luz added that before attending high school she would see and live in oppression, but she could not give a name to it. One of her most memorable moments in school was learning about South African apartheid and having a conversation after school with one of her teachers about "how things like the South African apartheid happened in Mexico . . ." The connections that Luz makes between Mexican and South African apartheid show how students apply the critical pedagogy lens to their lived experience.

In addition to their high school's framework, respondents have claimed that a Raza Studies afterschool class, of which about two-thirds of The Collective members attend, has been a space where they have been further exposed to critical pedagogy. This program began in the city where they live in 2008 and it is fully funded by their school district in response to community advocacy efforts. The two main components of the program consist of (1) providing an overview of the history of Latinos (Latinxs) in the United States and the impact of racism on the community, (2) and learning about civic participation and activist organizing. Mariana, who has been in the Raza Studies class since ninth grade says,

> We started learning about the Indigenous people who got colonized and I remember I was like, "what?! I never knew this," then I talked to my mom about it and she was like, "well I didn't know this either." And then I started learning about Emiliano Zapata and Cuahutemoc . . . learning all these things made me feel so empowered.[14]

This Raza Studies class has allowed the youth to learn more about their roots in a transnational sense, by learning about Indigenous history in the United States and Latin America, as well as different national histories, and about Latino (Latinx) leaders from the community who have organized communities to win rights, resources, and recognition. To some, this class has provided a space in which to learn that they have the power and potential to organize effectively and contribute to social justice in their communities.

Not everybody in The Collective had the opportunity to attend the Raza Studies class. Yet, the youth who could not be in the class were able to learn and engage in some of its content and in critical pedagogy through their peers. An example of this is Juan, who says, "I couldn't make it because I had soccer practice but my friend, Mariana, would use the knowledge that she had learned to teach it to me." The high school curriculum and the Raza Studies class are not the only spaces where there is growing critical pedagogy. The process is continuous and is replicated in organizing spaces like The Collective.

Conclusion

Throughout this study based on The Collective I sought to answer (1) how young activists left out of the DREAM Act navigate the concept of market citizenship and (2) how they frame their claims of citizenship and belonging. The Collective rejects market citizenship based on their lived experiences of marginalization. I have observed collective members recount that facing structural and economic oppression has led them to believe that meritocracy does not necessarily "get you ahead." The Collective puts forth its own claims of belonging. They claim belonging from Indigeneity and human rights. Through these claims, they demand that immigrants be treated like human beings and free from harm and exploitation.

I hope that this project will serve as a guide to others who are interested in studying undocumented youth, especially those that are left out of the DREAM Act discourse. The generalizability of these findings may be limited by an important factor. My study participants are concentrated in an area of Northern California that is considered to be a "liberal" space and has a widely recognized history of activist movements, which might influence the way my participants organize and frame their belonging. However, I believe that it would be a worthwhile guidepost to contrast different geographical areas, populations, and methods.

The Collective not only offers us important lessons about activism and the struggles faced by youth ineligible for the DREAM Act but also challenges us. It challenges the mainstream assumptions, that even other undocumented youth may hold without critical reflection. It also challenges individuals to reexamine meritocratic claims and assess how these claims of "deservingness" exclude the people that are supposed to benefit from such a movement. This challenge is not only to the DREAM Act, though that is the piece of legislation du jour, but all immigration reform that excludes, dehumanizes, and divides immigrants into any categories. It challenges the historic economic inequality and exploitation suffered by immigrants—past, present and future. Most fundamentally, it asks us what it means to belong.

NOTES

1. The United States has had a long history of nativist policy and rhetoric. Past nativist waves led to shifts in immigration law and policy that deliberately excluded certain groups of people. Examples include the internment of individuals of Japanese ancestry during World War II, and the Chinese Exclusion Act of 1882, which prohibited all immigration of Chinese laborers.

2. At the time of this writing there are five different DREAM Act–like proposals that were recently introduced in the U.S. Congress: 2019 DREAM and Promise Act, BRIDGE Act, Hope Act, and SUCCEED Act. The SUCCEED Act, the most conservative proposal, has some provisions that are similar to the DREAM Act but lays out a much more restrictive path to citizenship. It would require applicants to wait fifteen years to apply for U.S. citizenship; it would also exclude individuals with minor offenses and prevent lawful permanent resident beneficiaries from sponsoring family members, including immediate relatives (National Immigration Law Center 2017).

3. On September 5, 2017, President Trump announced an end to the DACA program. However, a preliminary injunction issued in January 2018 by a judge in San Francisco, California, has temporarily stopped Trump's order to end the program. The program continues to be in effect while the Supreme Court considers a decision on the matter.

4. In order to protect study participants, pseudonyms have been employed in this paper.

5. At the time of this study, members of The Collective engaged in various kinds of work to advance the rights of immigrants. Their organizing included participation in protests demanding that Wells Fargo Bank divest its holdings in the Corrections Corporation of America (CCA) and the GEO Group, private prison companies that

run immigration detention centers. Their artivism consisted in the creation of murals depicting a series of narratives that speak to the stories of particular segments of the undocumented population that are not often highlighted by mainstream media. The group also engaged in political education, a collective process of studying and discussing issues relevant to their mission.

6. In 2006, millions of people participated in protests that began in response to proposed legislation known as HR 4437, which would have raised penalties for undocumented immigration and classified undocumented immigrants and anyone who helped them enter or remain in the United States as felons. It is important to note that not all undocumented people make claims solely on their economic productivity; some also emphasize notions of social citizenship (Brown 2011). Social citizenship is based on a sense of belonging to a state; exemplified by literature that suggests that undocumented students belong to the United States because they have grown up "American" (Perez 2009). Social and market citizenship are not mutually exclusive.

7. To protect the identities of study participants, "The Collective" is used in lieu of the real name of the group.

8. Families in which one or more members are unlawfully present in the United States.

9. I decided to practice *reflexivity* and examine critically the nature of my research process. I focused on the strategy of *reflexivity* by being aware of my position and observing myself through the use of reflexive notes to myself. At the end of every meeting I observed and interviews, I wrote notes for myself about my own behavior and any pressing thoughts and questions about what I had just observed.

10. Pseudonyms have been used in order to protect participants.

11. The speculative fiction genre encompasses narrative fiction with supernatural or futuristic elements.

12. Copal is a name given to the resin of a tree that is particularly identified with the aromatic resins used by the cultures of pre-Columbian Mesoamerica as ceremonially burned incense and for other purposes.

13. Critical pedagogy is a philosophy of education heavily influenced by the work of Paulo Freire. In the foreword to *Pedagogy of the Oppressed* (1968), Shaull (2006) posits that education can either function as a tool to facilitate the incorporation of the attitudes of the present system into younger generations and maintain the status quo, or become a "practice of freedom" by which people see reality through a critical lens and learn how to participate and engage in a transformation of their world.

14. Emiliano Zapata was a leading political figure in the Mexican Revolution of the early twentieth century. Cuauhtémoc was the last Aztec ruler of Mexico.

REFERENCES

Abrego, Leisy. 2006. "'I Can't Go to College Because I Don't Have Papers': Incorporation Patterns of Latino Undocumented Youth." *Latino Studies* 4(3): 212–31.

Abrego, Leisy. 2008. "Legitimacy, Social Identity, and the Mobilization of Law: The Effects of Assembly Bill 540 on Undocumented Students in California." *Law and Social Inquiry* 33: 709–34. https://www.jstor.org/stable/20108779.

Batalova, Jeanne, and Margie McHugh. 2010."DREAM vs. Reality: An Analysis of Potential DREAM Act Beneficiaries." *Migration Policy Institute*. http://www.migrationpolicy.org/research/dream-vs-reality-analysis-potential-dream-act-beneficiaries.

Bautista, Romario. 2019. "My Thoughts on Indigeneity, as an Indigenous Person." *Dichos de Un Bicho Blog*, February 24, 2019. https://dichosdeunbicho.com/my-thoughts-on-indigeneity-as-an-indigenous-person/.

Beinart, Peter. 2016. "The Republican Party's White Strategy." *The Atlantic*, July/August, 2016. https://www.theatlantic.com/magazine/archive/2016/07/the-white-strategy/485612/.

Blackwell, Maylei, Floridalma Boj Lopez, and Luis Urrieta Jr. 2017. Introduction of "Special Issue: Critical Latinx Indigeneities." *Latino Studies*. 15: 126–37.

Bloemraad, Irene, and Kim Voss. 2011. "The Immigration Rallies of 2006: What Were They, How Do We Understand Them, Where Do We Go?" In *Rallying for Immigrant Rights*, edited by Kim Voss and Irene Bloemraad. Berkeley: University of California Press.

Bosniak, Linda. 2000. "Citizenship Denationalized." *Indiana Journal of Global Law Studies* 7: 447–509. https://www.repository.law.indiana.edu/ijgls/vol7/iss2/2.

Brown, Hana. 2011."Refugees, Rights, and Race: How Legal Status Shapes Liberian Immigrants' Relationship with the State." *Social Problems* 58: 144–63.

Decker, Geoffrey. 2011. "Hispanics Identifying Themselves as Indians." *New York Times*, July 4, 2011. https://www.nytimes.com/2011/07/04/nyregion/more-hispanics-in-us-calling-themselves-indian.html.

Durbin, Dick. 2010. DREAM Act Floor Speech. *Citizen Orange*, August 6, 2010. http://www.citizenorange.com/orange/2010/08/dick-durbins-recent-senate-flo.html.

Emerson, Robert, Rachel Fretz, and Linda Shaw. 1995. *Writing Ethnographic Fieldnotes*. Chicago: University of Chicago Press.

Ford, Matt. 2017. "President Trump's Immigration Policy Takes Shape." *The Atlantic*, February 21, 2017. https://www.theatlantic.com/politics/archive/2017/02/trump-immigration-deportation-memo/517395/.

Fox, Cybelle, and Irene Bloemraad. 2015. "Beyond 'White by Law': Explaining the Gulf in Citizenship Acquisition between Mexican and European Immigrants, 1930." *Social Forces* 94: 181–207. https://doi.org/10.1093/sf/sov009.

Gleeson, Shannon. 2010. "Labor Rights for All? The Role of Undocumented Immigrant Status for Worker Claims." *Law and Social Inquiry* 3: 561–602. https://www.jstor.org/stable/40783684.

Gonzales, Roberto. 2008. "Left out but Not Shut Down: Political Activism and the Undocumented Student Movement." *Northwestern Journal of Law and Social Policy* 3: 1–22.

Gonzales, Roberto. 2011. "Learning to be Illegal: Undocumented Youth and Shifting Legal Contexts in the Transition to Adulthood." *American Sociological Review* 76: 602–19.

Harris, Kamala. 2017. Senate Floor Remarks on Protecting Dreamers. December 6, 2017. https://www.harris.senate.gov/news/press-releases/senator-harris-floor-remarks-on-protecting-dreamers.

Hing, Julianne. 2018. "A Win and a Loss for Dreamers' Fight for In-State Tuition." *The Nation*, April 18, 2018. https://www.thenation.com/article/a-win-and-a-loss-in-dreamers-fight-for-in-state-tuition/.

Keyes, Elizabeth. 2014. "The DREAM Act, Immigration Reform, and Citizenship." *Nevada Law Journal* 17: 101–55. https://scholars.law.unlv.edu/nlj/vol14/iss1/5.

Krogstad, Jens Manuel, Jeffrey Passel, and D'Vera Cohn. 2017. "5 Facts about Illegal Immigration in the U.S." *Pew Research Center*, April 27, 2017. http://www.pewresearch.org/fact-tank/2017/04/27/5-facts-about-illegal-immigration-in-the-u-s/.

Lal, Prerna. 2010. "Most Racist Political Campaign Ads 2010." *Prerna Lal Blog*, October 10, 2010. http://prernalal.com/2010/10/most-racist-political-campaign-ads-2010/.

Lee, Erika. 2003. *At America's Gates: Chinese Migration During the Exclusion Era, 1882–1943*. Chapel Hill: University of North Carolina Press.

Lipsitz, George. 1995. "Possessive Investment in Whiteness: Racialized Social Democracy and the 'White' Problem in American Studies." *American Quarterly* 3: 369–87.

Marston, S. A. 1990. "Who Are the People?: Gender, Citizenship, and the Making of the American Nation." *Environment and Planning* 8: 449–58.

Massey, Douglas. 1995. "The New Immigration and Ethnicity in the United States." *Population and Development Review* 3: 631–52.

McNamee, Stephen, and Robert Miller. 2004. "The Meritocracy Myth." *Sociation Today* 2: 1.

National Immigration Law Center. 2017. "2017 Legislation to Protect DREAM Recipients/Immigrant Youth." *National Immigration Law Center*, October 2017. https://www.nilc.org/wp-content/uploads/2017/10/Dream-2017-legislation-compared.pdf.

Nawyn, Stephanie. 2011. "I Have so Many Successful Stories: Framing Social Citizenship for Refugees." *Citizenship Studies* 15: 679–93.

Negrón-Gonzales, Genevieve. 2015. "Undocumented Youth Activism as Counter-Spectacle: Civil Disobedience and Testimonio in the Battle around Immigration Reform." *Aztlan: A Journal of Chicano Studies* 40: 87–112.

Ngai, Mae. 2003. *Impossible Subjects*. Princeton, NJ: Princeton University Press.

Nicholls, Walter. 2014. "From Political Opportunities to Niche-Openings: The Dilemmas of Mobilizing for Immigrant Rights in Inhospitable Environments." *Theory and Society* 43: 23–49.

Passel, Jeffrey. 2003. "Further Demographic Information Related to the DREAM Act." *The Urban Institute*, October 21, 2003. https://www.nilc.org/wp-content/uploads/2015/11/dream_demographics.pdf.

Patel, Leigh. 2015. "Deservingness: Challenging Coloniality in Education and Migration Scholarship." *Association of Mexican American Educators Journal* 9: 11–21. http://amaejournal.utsa.edu/index.php/amae/article/view/268.

Perez, William. 2009. *We Are American: Undocumented Students Pursuing the American Dream*. Sterling, VA: Stylus Publishing.

Pillow, Wanda. 2003. "Confession, Catharsis or Cure? Rethinking the Uses of Reflexivity as Methodological Power in Qualitative Research." *International Journal of Qualitative Studies in Education* 16: 175–96.

Rincon, Alejandra. 2008. *Si Se Puede! Undocumented Immigrants and Higher Education*. New York: LFB Scholarly Publishing.

Rivera, Alex. 2008. *Sleep Dealer*. Directed by Alex Rivera. Maya Entertainment, DVD.

Ruswick, Brent. 2013. *Almost Worthy: The Poor, Paupers, and the Science of Charity in America*. Bloomington: Indiana University Press.

Seif, Hinda. 2004. "Wise Up! Undocumented Latino Youth, Mexican American Legislators, and the Struggle for Higher Education Access." *Latino Studies* 2: 210–30.

Shaull, Richard. 2006. Foreword to *Pedagogy of the Oppressed*, by Paulo Freire. New York: Continuum.

Southern Poverty Law Center. 2013. "Close to Slavery: Guest Worker Programs in the United States." *Southern Poverty Law Center*. https://www.splcenter.org/sites/default/files/d6_legacy_files/downloads/publication/SPLC-Close-to-Slavery-2013.pdf.

U.S. Census Bureau. 2011. "U.S. Census Bureau Projections Show a Slower Growing, Older, More Diverse Nation Half a Century from Now." https://www.census.gov/newsroom/releases/archives/population/cb12-243.html.

U.S. Department of State, Office of the Historian. "The Immigration Act of 1924 (The Johnson-Reed Act)." https://history.state.gov/milestones/1921-1936/immigration-act.

Vaughns, Katherine. 2005."Restoring the Rule of Law: Reflections on Fixing the Immigration System and Failed Policy Choices." *University of Maryland Law Journal of Race, Religion, Gender and Class* 5: 151–86. https://digitalcommons.law.umaryland.edu/rrgc/vol5/iss2/2.

GABRIELA GARCIA CRUZ

5

Contesting "Citizenship"

The Testimonies of Undocumented Immigrant Activist Women

Growing up, I was told that my life was defined by the "illegality" of my body in a place I could not call home. I, like many others, migrated with great hope. However, the reality that became my life in the United States was different than what I had hoped for; *el sueño* transformed into a life in the shadows—unseen and unheard. I have used my lens as an undocumented person to analyze citizenship, governance, illegality, and civic engagement through a gendered framework. I, like the women I interviewed, have faced the nation-state's tactic of fear to keep us silent and under control—tactics which have sought to keep us from owning our presence in this country and seeing ourselves as political agents capable of making change. My aim in this chapter is to highlight the ways in which, despite this anti-immigrant context, undocumented women have deconstructed their identity as "illegals" and developed as powerful, active members of their communities. More importantly, through their activism undocumented women have learned to advocate for themselves regardless of their status. As active members of their community they have been able to establish a feeling of belonging. In this context, belonging pushes the limitations of "citizenship," where undocumented women have reclaimed their space, and a sense of community.

My involvement in the undocumented immigrant rights movement from 2006 to 2018 gave rise to an alarming observation: the undocumented community was being fractured. During my early involvement, I recall mothers marching demanding safer lives for their children. This coincided with the rise of the Development, Relief and Education for Alien Minors (DREAM) Act Movement, which focused on the struggles of undocumented youth who arrived at a young age and were pursuing higher education. These young people were seen as exceptional, both because they were raised in the United States and because they were in college. This exceptionalism allowed undocumented youth visibility within the debate around immigrant rights, in a way that was very different from their non-DREAMer counterparts, who struggled to be seen. Witnessing this division was foundational for me because, despite my educational privilege, I did not identify as a DREAMer. My upbringing gave me an understanding of the nuance caused by the division. I was intimately connected with the awareness of all the things that were sacrificed so that I could have more resources. I took notice that it was always stories like mine that made it onto national television networks and social media, but never stories like that of my mother's. I believe these voices, which have been excluded and sidelined, have the potential to change and unify the movement. That is why my focus in this chapter is on undocumented women who are not DREAMers but who through their activism are changing the political landscape around illegality, citizenship, and belonging.

Globally, since 2010 there are an estimated 210 million people living outside their country of origin.[1] Issues surrounding citizenship and migration are incredibly complex due to the myriad forms of legality that are granted by nation-states. Millions of border crossings happen every day around the world; an occurrence which in the United States is persistently framed as an issue of national security. However, the movement of bodies across international borders must be seen within the broader context of the production of hostile environments for those deemed as the "other." The United States serves as an example of anti-immigration enforcement reactions caused by the movement of bodies into its territory. Because migration is a phenomenon that is experienced differently by social groups, there is a need for more academic attention to and analysis of this subject from the perspective of those on the ground.

Federal inaction in ending the legal violence of the immigration system has forced many undocumented immigrant women to become political activists and agents of change. The goal of my research is to further add to the academic work that exists on the meaning of "citizenship" for undocumented immigrant activist women. I ask how does transnational migration shape notions of belonging for undocumented immigrant activist women? How does engagement in political activism against state-based immigration enforcement lead undocumented women to challenge notions of citizenship and "illegality"? I argue that undocumented women continually navigate fear in spaces that they inhabit, but that speaking out, becoming engaged, and sharing their testimonies results in personal transformation and a feeling of belonging, resulting in the creation of communities of political power. My research aims to contribute to existing scholarly work on undocumented women by specifically highlighting how they embody resilience and resistance.

Gendered Migration and Citizenship/Illegality

My contributions are focused on the political agency of undocumented women and the impact they make in a nation that limits their rights. Through a gendered framework I examine the concepts of "state of emergency," "illegality," and "civic engagement" to analyze how undocumented immigrant activist women challenge the notion of "citizenship" through civic engagement. This research considers "governmentality and governance" in relation to surveillance of undocumented people, which perpetuates the placement of immigrant women in the position of the "other." However, my findings demonstrate that undocumented women refuse to abide by the nation-state's use of fear and instead create communities of belonging.

The nation-state's power over its subjects is challenged by the movement of bodies through its borders, yet the moment a person crosses the border they become subject to the nation-state's power (De Genova 2009, 450). The power of the state for this purpose is defined as a structure that allows the subject to access resources, safety, and representation (Oliviero 2013, 4–5). However, access is granted to a select group of people based on their immigration status. As a result, the movement of bodies through transnational borders creates a "state of emergency" (De Genova 2012, 130). Using a neo-Marxist approach, Nicholas De Genova discusses the state of emergency as "a method used by the nation-state to continue its sovereign power over its subjects" (De Genova 2009; 450). This declaration gives the nation-state complete discretion over governance of these subjects by any means; legal or undocumented. Citizenship is a tool to bestow rights on certain members deemed worthy, a distinction that is made sharply through the exclusion of others (Oliviero 2013). "Bare life" is a product of sovereign power; it "expresses our subject on to political power"[2] (De Genova 2012, 133). On the other hand, "labor–power" is the way migrants are only seen as a means to produce labor. This labor is then commodified for sale on the market. In the international division of labor, De Genova argues that immigrant labor mobility becomes flexible and subject to demand at any time (global space) (De Genova 2012). Further expanding on De Genova's argument, I highlight the process of resistance against the nation-state's subjugation.

With efforts at addressing the state of emergency in the context of migration, Oliviero analyzes the link to gender and race as the discourses that drive national precariousness and belonging (Oliviero 2013). Oliviero discusses how the rhetoric of protecting the security of vulnerable national citizenry is used to justify the legal treatment of undocumented migrants and their U.S. citizen children (Oliviero 2013, 4, 15). As a result, she argues that gender and ethnic discourses enable extremely troubling reorganizations of "formal citizenship" and anti-discrimination frameworks (Oliviero 2013, 10–13). This state of emergency, as I will demonstrate, is used as a means to justify fear and control through policies and practices such as racial profiling and discriminatory laws.

Sarikakis argues that the status of the migrant subjects is characterized by a loss of communication rights (Sarikakis 2012, 801–4). She notes those times as "policies of exemption and personhood," stating that precisely under these conditions the rights to communicate are the most crucial (Sarikakis 2012, 811). Lack of communication, freedom, and silent majorities of migrants connect to the broader context of the immobilization of women migrants by the process of silencing. The discussion begins by contextualizing communicative aims in personhood, citizenship, and legitimacy (Sarikakis 2012). The activism of undocumented migrant women, then, can be seen as a reclamation of voice within a context of silencing. The neglected sites of growing political activism among immigrant communities and their push to bring attention to their presence is a crucial aspect in understanding forms of resistance. On the other hand, Weil (2011) argues for the need to develop agents of social change within the context of economic globalization; political actors who are willing to transform society. Weil suggests that the development of social agents requires not only an alternative theory of development but also a collective action and horizontal collaboration (Weil 2011, 628). This includes the sharing of experiences, the conciliation of interests, and visions of new constructed alliances.

In this work, I highlight how undocumented women use their voices to demand their right to exist. Beyond the right to citizenship, these women are advancing a platform and creating communities of political power and community engagement. I argue that in the case of undocumented women, the limitation in their relationship with the nation-state leaves them to create and challenge the power over their presence. I share testimonies of undocumented women to illustrate how the nation-state attempts to enforce its power through tactics of fear and how their reframing of belonging challenges these practices.

Methods and Positionality

The seeds of this research were planted during my time with the San Francisco Organizing Project (SFOP), a not-for-profit, nonpartisan organization, working on a nationwide Campaign for Citizenship. The Campaign for Citizenship is a project of PICO (People Improving Communities through Organizing) National Network, representing immigrant families and people of faith, working to win citizenship for 11 million aspiring Americans. Through this organization, I was introduced to community activist networks around the country, which allowed me to connect with the work other undocumented people were doing and witness the transformation of undocumented women involved in grassroots community empowerment. By the time I began working with SFOP, I had been involved in the undocumented movement for over a decade and had participated in diverse organizations with different activism approaches, yet this was the first time I encountered a group that positioned self-worth as a central part of activism. I conducted five interviews with undocumented women living across California—in Bakersfield, Los Angeles, San Francisco, and Fortuna. I traveled throughout California interviewing undocumented women, who through their efforts had transformed the notion of citizenship through civic engagement.

My first interview was in Bakersfield, with Sofia, a woman in her mid-20's, an immigrant from Mexico who identified herself as a community organizer for Faith in Action Kern County. I was referred to Sofia through community leaders in San Francisco. Sofia carried herself with confidence and certainty. She had begun her political and community engagement in her late teens, when she was recruited by community leaders working for PICO National Network. She spoke about the difficulties of living in a conservative area and how it shaped her activism and engagement. I then continued my journey further south, where I had scheduled interviews with community leaders from Orange County Congregation Community Organization (OCCCO) and San Diego Organizing Project (SDOP). I first met with Andrea, a nineteen-year-old woman whose mother was also an active OCCCO member. As a result of their shared political work, Andrea's interview covered not only her own experience but also her mother's story. My two-week journey continued to San Diego. However, with the rise in hostility against immigrants during that time, my interviews in San Diego were canceled. Thus, I used the time to gather participatory observations that would contextualize the interviewees' environment. I returned to San Francisco, where I interviewed four women whom I had befriended during the year I resided in the area. They are Camila, Silvia, Lizbeth, and Esperanza. Their ages varied from early twenties to mid-fifties and they had migrated from various places in Latin America including Guatemala, Mexico, Paraguay, Peru, and Venezuela. In San Diego, San Francisco, and Fortuna, I conducted participant observations by attending meetings, building relationships with community members, and in civic engagement actions led by their leaders.

All participants are women over the age of eighteen who had been engaged in the Campaign for Citizenship for at least one year; I use pseudonyms to protect their identities. I only spoke Spanish while conducting this research, which allowed me to connect with participants in their native language and on their own terms. As a researcher, it was emotionally difficult to process the journeys of these women, because this also necessarily involved reflecting on my own situation. It was a humbling experience to learn about the work of women who are engaged in their communities and willing to empower others, despite their own positions of vulnerability.

Experiencing Fear as a Mechanism of Control

Nativist groups that target immigrants ignore the complicated history of U.S. law and immigration, and how often migration is the result of U.S. intervention in other countries. Nativist groups promote the idea of the contemporary "illegal criminals" who broke the law while they simultaneously romanticize the migration of their European ancestors by claiming that their families migrated legally (Schrag 2010). Since its inception, the United States has created a "state of emergency" against immigrants, which has entailed limited legal protection while giving the nation-state complete power to enact discriminatory policies in the name of national security. The state of emergency targets undocumented communities, subjecting them to legal punishment such as detention and deportation, and therefore creating a climate of increased fear within the undocumented community. Immigrants have to be cautious about who they engage with and how they go about their daily lives.

Having undocumented status shapes the lives of immigrants by separating them from the legal protection of the nation-state, thus making them vulnerable targets from a number of directions. Socially and politically, the dominant narrative has cast undocumented immigrants as criminals who are taking over the country. During my interview with Camila, she described how this narrative has impacted her identity, saying "The dominant narrative tells you that you are not part of American society. They tell you that you have to be a certain way" (Interview, August 5, 2014). She explains that even people of the same race who are documented will face discrimination from the system. The use of the "other" is a way to exclude people from belonging. For people like Camila, this meant that she was unable to see herself as part of her community because she was continually considered as an outsider due to her immigration status. Camila went on to explain how difficult it is to ignore her "illegal"[3] status. She stated, "It's something so difficult to leave behind, especially when you are creating a new beginning . . . the type of abuse, the embarrassment [you go through] reminds you of what you live, until you enter a deep depression." Camila left Mexico in search of safety from physical and sexual abuse. She had a desire to start a new life and forget the pain she had endured. However, Camila describes the difficulty in overcoming the trauma, given that fleeing also meant that she became undocumented.

> Afterwards everything started becoming more complicated because unfortunately racism is much stronger. Solely by looking like you're from somewhere else changes your life completely, because you are worth nothing to people. At jobs they pay you what they want because you don't belong to this world, to this city, to this country. They abuse you in jobs, of your innocence, it's the reality of this country. Because it's really supposed to be a place of opportunity built by immigrants, but the reality is different. We suffer discrimination at work because of our origin, because of the accent and because I can't speak English. (Interview, August 18, 2014)

Rather, she continued to face the trauma caused by her past and the pain was amplified by the discrimination she faced. The constant fear is a reminder to undocumented people that due to their undocumented status they are not protected.

In this political context, fear works as a tool to limit the participation of undocumented women in American society, by controlling various aspects of their daily life. The women in my study had to navigate fear to access safety, resources, and to develop political agency. Women felt particularly vulnerable in work spaces. Widespread anti-immigrant hostility creates an environment in which employers who know their status subject these immigrants to abuse under the threat of being reported. One of the main driving forces for migration across borders is caused by lack of economic opportunities. These women occupy lower-paying jobs, which often opens them up to job discrimination and harassment. The lack of government-issued identifications such as a social security number amongst undocumented communities limits access to resources including in the areas of education, jobs, and housing. Camila stated, "At work they pay you whatever they want because we don't belong in this world, city or country" (Interview, August 18, 2014).

Employers, however, are not the only ones who abuse and attack undocumented immigrant women. Indeed, their legal status makes them vulnerable to various forms of abuse. For example, a woman who had embarked on a pilgrimage from San Francisco to Bakersfield as part of her activist work told me of a specific encounter that revealed the difficulties that undocumented women face. In speaking with immigrant women who worked in the agricultural sector, a prominent theme that arose was their experience of sexual assaults perpetuated by undocumented men. Lizbeth describes how "[she] walked through those fields, and saw those women, who were undocumented and afraid, by [their] own people, who [were] facing the same oppression. Having them say something, for me, was empowerment, where you get to that point, [that I didn't] want to be quiet anymore" (Interview August 20, 2014). In most cases, undocumented women avoid reporting any type of abuse due to fear of deportation.

Women in my study often talked about their fear of coming into contact with authorities. They knew that immigration enforcement practices have the potential to turn their lives upside down. The fear of deportation and getting separated from their families, for example, means facing the possibility of losing everything they risked their life for. The women I interviewed cited the economic difficulty and violence in their country of origin as reasons for migration. Camila concluded, "there is a great fear that I will not find any opportunities and have to return with nothing." Two of these women, moreover, were raped by a family member and they feared for their lives prior to migration. Under the threat of being deported back to a place where they experienced such violence, many women prefer to avoid police, even if it means having to let crimes against themselves go unpunished. This vulnerability as women marks their migration stories in the multiple ways that their gender makes them targets for violence.

It is understandable, then, that undocumented people do a lot to remain in the shadows, including silencing their pain and not reporting when they are victims of abuse by others, leaving them vulnerable to legal scams, wage theft, racial discrimination, and domestic violence. For many, reporting an abuse requires them to interface with the system they are hiding from. This also leads to abuse and violence at the hands of police through a lack of due process, verbal abuse due to language barriers, and racial discrimination and racial profiling. Silvia described how her landlord raised her deposit by $500 because she did not have a social security number. "He told me that I wouldn't get my deposit back. That was $1,500 I would never see again" (Interview, August 20, 2014). She had no other option but to accept these conditions, for fear of retaliation. According to Camila, the fear of being detained and deported paralyzes her. She states that "undocumented people fear being detected and deported to a country with situations that you don't want to relive."

Undocumented women experience fear in many of the spaces that they navigate. Even when they become activists, they face risks in speaking out. One woman, for example, relayed an experience she had while participating in a lobbying visit in which she was threatened by a member of the House of Representatives, who told her that now that he had her information she would be in danger and "you illegals watch out." The constant fear is a foundational part of daily life experienced by undocumented women, limiting their full inclusion in society and brokered through a lack of access to resources and equal opportunity. The possibility of being detected and deported is a threat they must confront on a daily basis, particularly because being sent home for many of these women means being sent to a place where they were subjected to violence.

One of the repercussions of this ever-present fear is that the secrecy that is seen as a protective measure isolates undocumented people from each other. The fear of being arrested causes undocumented immigrants to make their presence invisible even to those who may be of support (Oliviero 2013; Weil 2011). Isolation is caused by the legal restrictions that undocumented immigrants face, limiting their acceptance in the communities in which they reside. People who may be experiencing the same thing will be unaware that others are experiencing it. Camila describes her culture as one that does not speak and remains silent. The women in this study described multiple forms of isolation in their community. One interviewee commented that appearing like an outsider signals to others that you do not belong (Interview, August 20, 2014). This can include things like not speaking the language and moving into a new community where others don't know you.

The United States–Mexico Border in 2014
As the news focused on the record numbers of unaccompanied children arriving at the border, anti-immigrant hostility grew against the newcomers and those who were already settled in the United States. Having trav-

eled from northern to southern California, I witnessed the intensity of fear along the border. The increase in hostility created more fear and uncertainty, which limited my ability to interact with people living in the border areas. Though these hostilities may have flared up during this period, as I understood from study participants, they were already present in these communities before 2014. The border areas between the United States and Mexico are known for harboring anti-immigrant groups, such as the "Minutemen Project," referred to by the undocumented communities as "caza inmigrantes" (immigrant hunters). In 2005, San Diego established a group of their own called, San Diego Minutemen (SDMM). This group is known to patrol the border, often armed, and act aggressively toward undocumented migrants. Because status is not immediately visible, this group and others like it rely on racial profiling, threatening people they perceive as "illegal." The Southern Poverty Law Center (SPLC) reported that SDMM has been the focus of several police investigations for its harassment of immigrant communities. According to their own materials, SDMM seeks:

> To demand maximum border security, oppose illegal immigration in all parts of San Diego County, and to assist the U.S. Border Patrol in securing the U.S.–Mexican Border from terrorists, criminals, drugs, and illegal aliens. We act on behalf of and in accordance with the United States Constitution and Bill of Rights. We oppose the racist Aztlanders, Reconquistas, and all other anti-American groups and vow to expose their true agendas. (N.R.G. 2004)

The participant observation data I collected captured this hostile environment that was a part of daily life for undocumented women residing near the border; several interviews I had already set up were understandably canceled once I got to San Diego. One participant told me, "perdóname compañera, pero no puedo ir a nuestra cita hoy" (sorry comrade, but I will be unable to attend our appointment today). I told her not to worry and asked if she would talk to me over the phone instead. Our conversation was short, as I could sense she was lost in thought. She explained that her children were scared to leave her sight and she promised them she would stay with them. Groups like SDMM reinforce the physical claim to divisions between the "native" and the "illegal," regardless of age. The hostility aimed in that moment at refugee children provided a clear message of animosity to all other migrants, thereby increasing the fear among undocumented mothers that they may be separated from their families.

My investigation took place between National City and San Ysidro, right near the international border crossing. Communicating in Spanish with locals encouraged them to feel comfortable talking to me. Out of curiosity, I asked one of the locals where the nearest sightseeing point for the border wall was. People were cautious, telling me to be careful because according to them, "Si tomas la calle equivocada, vas a tener problemas" (If you take the wrong street, you will run into problems). The fear among the Spanish-speaking population residing along the U.S.–Mexico border was palpable during this period.

As I approached San Ysidro, the town bordering the U.S.–Mexico border, I began to notice more police presence throughout the city. As I walked around the city of San Ysidro, I could see the visible exertion of state power, possibly also due to the military bases located in surrounding areas. After finally reaching the fence that separated both countries, I began to notice how those around me were racially profiling me. I was constantly watched over. The walking passage to the wired fence was patrolled by various forms of military-styled enforcement. As my heart raced, I stood to examine the voyage of bodies in transition, monitored by people with a government-issued identification, both domestic and international.

From where I stood, I could clearly see the Mexican flag and the densely populated city of Tijuana on the other side. The United States and Mexico have a history of fluid migration; the United States for years has been dependent on cheap Mexican labor, but the crossing is militarized and conveys the message of danger for those coming from Mexico.

On my journey out of San Diego, the U.S. Department of Homeland Security conducted a checkpoint. Every person passing that checkpoint had to provide a U.S. identification to prove his or her legal status. Preparing to pass through this checkpoint and fearing for my own safety, I was reminded of the power fear holds. Undocumented people living in the United States face constant reminders of their "illegal" status. These constant threats, therefore, create a psychological impact on their personhood (Hayden 2010). It is the feeling that is focused on survival. This experience causes an internalization of the Other. According to Hayden, in the eyes of those in power and in communities unfamiliar with immigrants, "'Illegal' immigration status becomes a sign of other forms of illegality and illicit activity, even to the point of excluding the undocumented from the category of 'human beings'" (Hayden 2010, 160). Being in that situation, and despite my knowledge of the structural forces that shape my life, I felt the intense fear of the state that the undocumented women in my study shared with me.

"Obama escucha, estamos en la lucha":
Sharing Our Testimonies

Given such a violent political, legal, social, and economic context, it is incredibly inspiring to then witness the political agency of undocumented women. Social transformation through speaking out, community engagement, and testimonies serve as the most crucial components of how undocumented activist women are contesting citizenship. What does it mean to be a noncitizen of a country while trying to fight for rights? Why is it important? Borrowing from Nicholas De Genova's (2012) concept of social becoming and transformation, my research illuminates the ways in which undocumented women are transformed through the process of becoming activists. This transformation enables undocumented women to develop a sense of belonging through the spaces created through their political and community engagement processes. This process involves sharing, claiming, and acknowledging their stories.

During my interviews, I asked the women to reflect on themselves before and after their involvement in the movement. Lizbeth described herself as a different person:

> I wasn't aware that I could create social change; I didn't know that undocumented people could fight for their rights, so it was really eye opening. SFOP has been life changing, it has changed my mind, what I want my past to be, and it helped me find myself. I was shy, and reserved, someone who was always afraid to be loud and be who I was. But it [SFOP] helped me find my voice and help others. It was so cool to see and acknowledge that power is beautiful, and we could do something as people. (Interview, August 5, 2014)

Lizbeth's feelings were common among the women I interviewed; the fear that had been such a central part of their lives also served as a catalyst to define themselves as people capable of making change. Undocumented activist women became aware of their political agency through active participation in organizations like SFOP.

Strict immigration policies and the fear of deportation often cause undocumented immigrant women to hide their status and therefore contribute to social isolation, leaving them to deal with the difficulties of being undocumented and alone. Through participant observation, I was able to witness the social transformations of undocumented activist women who chose self-agency and rejected the nation-state's narrative that they do not belong. My initial participatory observation with SFOP began with attendance at weekly meetings and methods of grassroots organizing. The meetings represented a space that encouraged women to speak about their stories as a form of truth and encouraged their political participation. Camila, an SFOP undocumented activist stated, "I've learned that if we share, we are able to let go of the fear and unite." Speaking out marked the first step to social transformation, often initiating the process of healing. Similarly, Andrea, an OCCC undocumented activist, added that she had to choose what she wanted and decided that living in fear was no longer an option. This motivated her to make her story public with a promise to herself and to her community that she would no longer live with this unbearable fear.

These women spent a lot of time engaged in this work and though it could be considered yet another drain on their limited time, the frame of engagement was shifted from something that felt "time-consuming" to something that felt worthwhile because it was a community-building effort. Camila had been involved in an organization prior to her involvement with SFOP, where time had always been an issue. She said that forms of political participation like protests and marches had become a privilege for activists who could afford to attend. She perceived her engagement as solidarity with others, as she felt that they all make a difference in their own form. Yet she still felt marginalized if she did not have the time to fully engage.

Sofia, an undocumented organizer and activist residing in Bakersfield, described how in Campaign for Citizenship, she felt that participation at all levels was accepted, whether you had only a little bit of time or a lot of time to devote to the work. She knew that engaging marginalized communities who had spent long hours working was a difficult process. Therefore, the fact that engagement at whatever level of time commitment that was possible was welcomed gave these undocumented women a sense of power. Another member of SFOP, when asked about engagement, responded by saying, "In SFOP you give where you can and help how you can. That way we all feel like we are all doing something." Transforming how women thought about their engagement opened the door for others to contribute without feeling judgement that they were not doing enough. They built their community by understanding and valuing each individual.

Leadership and growth were promoted through participation in weekly meetings and committees. The meetings were structured to include introductions, check-ins, reflection, next steps and improvements, and were led by volunteers. The meetings focused on how to dismantle power dynamics by empowering people to act. Each meeting, regardless of whether new members were present, started with people introducing themselves, sharing their credentials as community leaders representing SFOP, and what brought them there. They were also invited to share how they were doing through a check-in question. These components encouraged participants to acknowledge themselves as leaders. The first few times, I clearly noticed the participants' hesitation to claim their leadership. Undocumented communities who live their lives "in the shadows" are accustomed to remaining quiet, fearing that their status will be discovered. Through ongoing empowerment and engagement with their community, these participants were pushed to claim their leadership and identify themselves as leaders, allowing for a collective understanding of how the fight for citizenship is a part of a bigger fight for human dignity and the right to belong.

The frame of belonging through human dignity encourages a shared meaning of citizenship among undocumented people. During my participant observation in Fortuna, I was able to witness the meaning of this testimony. Fortuna is in the process of becoming part of the PICO National Network, and the meetings that I attended were for people beginning to claim their story as power and resistance. Experienced community leaders testified about the power they had received once they claimed their human dignity. Camila stated:

> When I began to attend the meetings, that's when I began to realize what the organization [PICO] does, how they work and support us. I became part of that movement. At the same time, I felt that I was becoming part of a place. I had value, and like everyone we have helped; they all have a value that is unbreakable, a value that God has given us. That's where I connected with myself. I feel like I have the value and the voice needed to express what I want, not only for me but also for everyone because we are all the same. (Interview, August 18, 2014)

Another interviewee stated that it was more than a battle for citizenship but rather to demonstrate their worth as a people (Interview, August 18, 2014).

The Campaign for Citizenship was used as a platform to engage in issues that affected 11 million undocumented people, not just DREAMers. The undocumented activists who were engaged in this work were able to develop identities rooted in their experiences as undocumented people, while also acknowledging that they were more than just their undocumented status. During a demonstration outside of the San Francisco Immigration Customs and Enforcement office, the activists chanted "¡Obama escucha, estamos en la lucha!" ("Obama listen, we are in the fight"). I heard them while still several blocks away: the voices of these women were loud, clear and concise. De Genova suggests that women who are activists are able to engage in civil society, resulting in their ability to define and construct their social community (De Genova 2009). While participating in a national leadership training, I witnessed these women develop their political capacities and skills. The intensive week-long training focused on tools to "find their prophetic voice," an in-depth review of theory, and the practice of grassroots organizing. The training opened spaces of dialogue around issues of state-based repression occurring in their communities including black imprisonment, police brutality, Native American water/environmental rights, and family separation through deportation.

The importance of sharing testimony was both a spiritual practice as well as an essential part of the organizing work for the women I interviewed. When asked whether they defined themselves as citizens they often responded with a "yes," because they defined citizenship as one's proclaimed active participation and desire to contribute to the place they reside in. The testimonies that they shared asserted the women's feeling of "presence" and "belonging," and therefore "citizens." The testimonies of undocumented women activists demonstrate the resistance against the legal political power that they are denied by the state; by publicly telling their stories, they claimed their presence and political power.

Creating and Empowering Nuestras Comunidades
The social transformation these undocumented women underwent was rooted in the creation and empowerment of their communities. The desire to become active members of their communities represented the empowerment of the people in their surroundings, with hope to "break free of the chains." One of the women who shared her testimony explained that her migration left her with the traumatic experience of growing up without knowing her father for six years of her childhood. Family separation was a common feature in their stories and led undocumented activist women to form bonds with one another based on their testimonies. Undocumented people often have difficulty claiming their presence due to years of remaining silent. These patterns of silence, rooted in fear, prevent stories from connecting people who are facing similar circumstances. Several of the women I interviewed stated that engaging others and finding these commonalities was a method to build community with one another in order to continue the fight.

During the initial process of social transformation, women responded that they felt alone, with a lack of connection to a community. The separation of their families meant that the traditions they held dear were often left behind, leaving them to figure out how to create new ones within the context of a hostile environment. For example, some women like Lizbeth are separated from family due to economic circumstances. Lizbeth describes her migration from Mexico to Los Angeles and then to San Francisco as forced, because she was forced to migrate out of economic necessity. For her, engagement in activism was eye-opening because it made her realize that she wasn't alone and that she was a survivor of anti-immigrant laws. She continued to develop herself and her identity through the work of acting as an agent of political change for her community. The vision that undocumented leaders had was to engage other community members in the work that they did and liberate and empower those like them. The unity they had built for their community gave them a space that acknowledged their presence. Camila stated that in order to change the system they had to modify how they were defining community-building. Community- and relationship-building were crucial in avoiding state-based enforcement, such as "retenes" (ICE checkpoints and raids). Women spoke about the importance of letting their compañeros (comrades) know that they were in trouble, because though at times they felt isolated with nowhere to go, the work they did together meant that they were a community, that they had come together as family. The lack of resources they navigated on a daily basis meant that that feeling of being alone was often overpowering, so developing a trustworthy network and community was very meaningful to them. This created community signified a space to feel like they belonged, regardless of their legal status.

The ability to create new communities and being empowered through this creation allowed undocumented activist women to share the ways in which they resist the dominant narrative of their "illegality." Many of them spoke about their motivation derived from personal experiences of feeling alone. An interviewee said "I just felt like I was invisible, I thought that I was powerless" (Interview, August 3, 2014). SFOP encouraged her to continue her participation while developing and exposing her to self-empowerment.

Concluding Reflections

The time I spent with undocumented activist women shaped my core understanding of community engagement and belonging and provided me with the lens to reimagine and envision a place where citizenship does not dictate self-value. The stories of these women demonstrated a social transformation from a place of fear to empowerment. The way they organize is rooted in the belief that relationship-building can create solidarity and political change and their actions demonstrate frameworks of belonging. Through them, I learned about resistance through storytelling and the importance of learning about these stories because their voices are illuminating the resistance embedded within the undocumented community.

Through the lens of the undocumented women we are able to imagine community-building that is rooted in love, self-acceptance, and resiliency; their work has paved the way to an inclusive vision of political agency and the tools needed for social transformation. In the current political climate, it is crucial that immigrant movements learn to provide space so that undocumented women can also lead. Unless this is done, the debate over undocumented people's rights will continue to leave out those who are most impacted.

NOTES

1. http://www.unfpa.org/pds/migration.html.

2. De Genova uses Agamben's (1998) notion of "bare life" to position the framework.

3. I use the term "illegal" to refer to the societal structure that has attempted to push undocumented people out of legal protection.

REFERENCES

Agamben, Giorgio. 1998. *Homo Sacer: Sovereign Power and Bare Life*. Stanford, CA: Stanford University Press.

De Genova, Nicholas. 2009. "Conflicts of Mobility, and the Mobility of Conflict: Rightlessness, Presence, Subjectivity, Freedom." *Subjectivity: International Journal of Critical Psychology* 29(1): 445–66. https://doi.org/10.1057/sub.2009.22.

De Genova, Nicholas. 2012. "Bare Life, Labor-Power, Mobility, and Global Space: Toward a Marxian Anthropology?" *CR: The New Centennial Review* 12(3): 129–52. https://www.jstor.org/stable/41949805.

Hayden, Bridget. 2010. "Impeach the Traitor: Citizenship, Sovereignty and Nation in Immigration Control Activism in the United States." *Social Semiotics* 20(2): 155–74. https://doi.org/10.1080/10350330903565865.

N.R.G. Concepts Inc. 2004. "San Diego Minutemen." http://unitedstates.fm/sdmm.htm.

Oliviero, Katie E. 2013. "The Immigration State of Emergency: Racializing and Gendering National Vulnerability in Twenty-First-Century Citizenship and Deportation Regimes." *Feminist Formations* 25(2): 1–29. https://www.jstor.org/stable/43860684.

Sarikakis, Katharine. 2012. "Access Denied: The Anatomy of Silence, Immobilization and the Gendered Migrant." *Ethnic and Racial Studies* 35(5): 800–16. https://doi.org/10.1080/01419870.2011.628036.

Schrag, Peter. 2010. "The Unwanted Immigration and Nativism in America." *Immigration Policy Center*: 1–11. https://www.americanimmigrationcouncil.org/research/unwanted-immigration-and-nativism-america.

Weil, Patrick. 2011. "From Conditional to Secured and Sovereign: The New Strategic Link between the Citizen and the Nation-State in a Globalized World." *International Journal of Constitutional Law* 9(3–4): 615–63. https://doi.org/10.1093/icon/mor053.

CAROLINA VALDIVIA

6

Undocumented Young Adults' Heightened Vulnerability in the Trump Era

I was thinking maybe I need to go back to therapy and I have never been on medicine before, but maybe it's time because it's a lot to take in emotionally . . . This is definitely very stress-inducing. I mean, this country is going to kill me of a heart attack or something because it's constantly being on alert . . . constantly being in fight-or-flight mode.

—Veronica, 32-year-old DACA beneficiary

Veronica grew up in the United States and has lived here for over twenty-five years. As she expressed, at this particular moment in her life she finds herself for the first time considering taking medicine to help her cope with stress. When we spoke, Veronica mentioned the great stress she is undergoing as she navigates everyday life as an undocumented immigrant under the Trump administration. As a result of changes in immigration policy and enforcement efforts under the current administration, Veronica is now struggling with the uncertainty surrounding the Deferred Action for Childhood Arrivals (DACA) federal program.[1] She is also experiencing heightened feelings of anxiety and fear. In this chapter, I explore what it means to navigate everyday life while undocumented under the Trump administration for immigrant young adults like Veronica who have lived in the United States for years and must navigate an increasingly hostile political climate.

Although anti-immigration policies and enforcement efforts have been on the rise for several decades, we are entering yet a new phase under the current administration. On January 25, 2017, for example, just a few weeks after the inauguration, the Trump administration issued an executive order aimed at increasing the number of detentions and deportations. The following month, on February 21, the Department of Homeland Security (DHS) stated on their website that they would not "exempt classes or categories of removal aliens from potential enforcement." DHS further noted that, "all of those in violation of the immigration laws may be subject to enforcement proceedings, up to and including removal from the United States." The administration also enabled the expansion of the 287(g) program, which allows law enforcement officers in certain localities and states to act as immigration officers.

This memo stands in sharp contrast to one that was issued on June 17, 2011, under the Obama administration. In the 2011 memo, immigration officers were advised to consider several factors to decide if and to what extent they should enforce the law against any particular individual. To decide whether prosecutorial discretion was warranted, immigration officers were asked to consider factors such as the following: "the person's ties and contributions to the community, including family relationships; whether the person has a U.S. citizen or permanent resident spouse, child, or parent; the person's pursuit of education in the United States, with particular consideration given to those who have graduated from a U.S. high school or have successfully pursued or are pursuing a college or advanced degrees at a legitimate institution of higher education in the United States."

Although it is important to keep in mind that the contemporary wave of mass deportations began to unfold during the Obama administration (Golash-Boza 2015, 6), under the Trump administration we are seeing changes in immigration policy and enforcement that yield a qualitatively different experience of what it means to be undocumented in the United States. Unlike the 2011 memo, which provided a temporary layer of protection for undocumented immigrants who met several of these conditions (and had the evidence and resources to fight their case), the 2017 memo essentially placed any and all undocumented immigrants who come into contact with immigration officers at equal risk for deportation and thus effectively heightened their vulnerability.

This new historic reality facing undocumented immigrants brings to bear a level of vulnerability to detention and deportation not seen since the previous wave of mass deportation which occurred over a half-century ago.[2] The number of immigration-related arrests across the country has increased by nearly 40 percent from January to June 2017 (Pickoff-White and Small 2017); a record number of noncitizens are waiting for an immigration court hearing (more than half a million) (Cohen 2017); and even DACA beneficiaries are being detained (Lynch 2017).[3] In this chapter, I argue that these changes to immigration policy and enforcement in the Trump era are exacerbating the effects of illegality—resulting in heightened feelings of uncertainty, vulnerability, stress, and anxiety that immigrant young adults and their families experience on a daily basis.

In the sections that follow, I first provide a review of the literature, paying close attention to how the lack of legal immigration status affects the lives of undocumented immigrants and their families. I then discuss the data from which I draw for this chapter, including a note about my positionality as both an "outsider" in my role as a researcher and an "insider" as someone who grew up undocumented in San Diego County for over a decade. Following the section on methods, I discuss in greater depth what it means to be undocumented under the Trump administration for the immigrant young adults I interviewed, with a particular focus on how it affects important aspects of their daily routines and mental health.

Literature Review

To be able to understand what it means to be undocumented under the current presidential administration, it is important to first examine the literature on illegality. As a theoretical concept, illegality moves beyond a purely juridical understanding of an individual's lack of legal immigration status to one that encapsulates both (1) the *production* of illegality (i.e., the mechanisms and policies that make individuals undocumented and that regulate their movement) and (2) its *condition* (i.e., migrants' lived experiences) (Abrego 2014, 71; Chavez 2007, 192–95; De Genova 2002, 423; Menjívar and Kanstroom 2013, 5–13).

Existing scholarship on the condition of illegality illuminates the detrimental effects that the lack of legal immigration status has on undocumented immigrants' daily routines. In an effort to avoid possible encounters with police or immigration officers, undocumented immigrants may limit their time spent outside of the home, withdraw from community events or avoid driving (Dreby 2015, 26; Negrón-Gonzales 2013, 1287; Schmalzbauer 2014, 59; Valdivia 2019, 112). They may also incorporate strategies to try to "pass" as documented (Garcia 2014, 1905–8; Gonzales 2015, 105). For example, undocumented immigrants may attempt to "act normal" around police, drive newer cars, adjust their appearance, and only speak English in public settings. The fear of deportation has also prevented parents from enrolling their U.S. citizen children in public programs (even though they are eligible) because they fear that they (i.e., the parents) could be identified as undocumented and potentially turned over to immigration officers (Yoshikawa and Kholoptseva 2013, 1; Zatz and Rodriguez 2015, 55). The fear of deportation profoundly shapes decisions about where families can live and travel (Asad and Rosen 2018; Valdivia 2019).

The lack of legal immigration status also takes a toll on the mental health of undocumented immigrants and their immediate family members. More specifically, the fear of deportation and limited opportunities for undocumented immigrants can manifest itself in anxiety, depression, and stress (Dreby 2015, 48; Gonzales 2015, 115). Among undocumented young adults, the fear of deportation may be felt most profoundly when they make the critical transition into adulthood and "learn to be illegal" (Gonzales 2011). Notably, U.S. citizen children with undocumented parents also share in the risks and limitations associated with the lack of legal immigration status. For example, given that encounters with the police may place undocumented immigrants in deportation proceedings (Golash-Boza 2015, 6), and their children, regardless of their own immigration status, often learn to also fear the police (Abrego 2019, 15; Dreby 2015, 47; Enriquez 2015, 9; Valdivia 2019, 109), scholars find that U.S. citizen children experience high levels of anxiety and depressive symptoms; they also often report trouble sleeping and concentrating at school due to the fear that their parent(s) may be deported (Brabeck, Lykes, and Hershberg 2011, 283). Similarly, even undocumented young adults who have benefited from the DACA program remain fearful that their loved ones may be subjected to deportation (Martinez and Salazar 2018; Patler et al. 2015; Roth 2018).

These fears are exacerbated during times of heightened enforcement (Dreby 2015, 26). Drawing from four years of ethnographic research with Mexican families in Ohio and New Jersey, Dreby (2015) found that the intensification of immigration enforcement has fostered a culture of fear within undocumented communities. Many of the women interviewed referenced the economic hardships that their female friends underwent after the deportation of their husbands. Although many of the interviewees had not been directly affected by a deportation, knowing about the hardships experienced by their female friends was enough to heighten fear over the possibility of deportation.

Methods

Following the inauguration of the Trump administration, I embarked on an ethnography to understand how undocumented immigrants and their loved ones perceive, experience, and respond to the threat of deportation; and in some cases, how they cope with the aftermath of an actual deportation. I began by interviewing immigrant young adults (between the ages of 18 and 36) who fall into one of two groups: (1) A group of respondents who have not had a family member deported, but have a family member who is undocumented, and as a consequence, live with the perpetual fear that their family member *could* be deported; and (2) respondents who have had an immediate family member deported from the United States.

To date, I have conducted fifty-two interviews. Interviews ranged from one to four hours in length and took place in settings where participants felt most safe and comfortable (e.g., their homes, school classrooms, local parks). At the time of the interviews, thirty study participants had benefitted from DACA, fourteen were U.S. citizens, six were ineligible for DACA due to the program's strict age requirements, and two were former DACA beneficiaries who had recently transitioned into legal permanent residency. Among noncitizen respondents, age at arrival in the United States ranged from only four months to sixteen years. While most participants are of Mexican descent, interviewees also hail from Costa Rica and South Korea. To protect participants' identities, I have replaced their names with pseudonyms.

A Note on Positionality

Having grown up undocumented in San Diego County for over a decade, I am deeply committed to conducting research with and for undocumented communities. I was introduced into the world of research as an undergraduate. At the time, there was a project on campus that aimed to explore the educational experiences of undocumented college students. I remember that I reached out to the professor leading the initiative even though I was initially concerned because this would be my first time disclosing my immigration status to someone outside of my inner circle of friends and family. Looking back, I am glad I took the risk. The opportunity to participate as an interviewee (and a few months later as an interviewer when the project expanded) was both meaningful and empowering, precisely because a fellow undocumented student interviewed me and connected me to a wealth of resources available to me despite my undocumented status. My participation in the project transformed my educational trajectory by providing me with invaluable research, organizing, and mentoring experience.

To this day, I continue to participate in a number of research projects, either as an interviewer or interviewee. More specifically, I have had the opportunity to lead or co-lead projects that examine the online and offline organizing efforts of immigrant young adults, the political participation of undocumented young adults across the country, the effects of DACA, and more recently, the experiences of educators and counselors who work with undocumented high school students.

For this book chapter, I am drawing on interviews from my dissertation project to explore the consequences of immigration enforcement on the lives of immigrant young adults and their families in San Diego County, California. To be sure, my personal experiences growing up undocumented have shaped many of the stages of this project. For example, my personal background facilitated my access to potential participants. It also encouraged me to engage in a reflexive model of research where there is constant dialogue between the social scientist and the people under study. This approach "embraces not detachment but engagement as the road to knowledge" (Burawoy 1998, 5). It entails paying attention to one's multiplicity of identities and its implications for research. Throughout the research process, I wrote memos about my own personal experience in the field, including emerging ideas, questions, and challenges. In the findings section and conclusion of this chapter, I included some of these insights where appropriate.

Constantly on Alert: How the Trump Administration Affects Immigrant Young Adults' Daily Routines

Under the current administration, immigrant young adults find themselves constantly on alert. They are frequently hearing concerning news about immigration, especially about raids and deportations targeting undocumented immigrants across the country. The following are examples of recent news headlines: "Trump's policies at work: ICE deports an immigrant mother in the middle of the night" (Lopez 2017); "A Young Immigrant Spoke Out About Her Deportation Fears: Then She Was Detained" (Hauser 2017); and, "ICE Detains Salvadoran Immigrant during Annual Check-in in Houston" (Flynn 2017). Notably, these news articles often feature the stories of immigrants who were temporarily protected (whether informally or formally) from the threat of deportation during previous administrations: undocumented mothers, DACA beneficiaries, and immigrants with pending cases who had to regularly check in with immigration officers.

Isabel, a 23-year-old DACA beneficiary, described the constant exposure to news about deportations under the Trump administration as heartbreaking:

> Every day I am on Facebook I see something about someone being in detention or about to be deported. Or in the news, now that I have cable, it's constantly someone . . . I was watching the news about a family saying good-bye at the airport because the dad was about to be deported . . . It is heartbreaking because you think about, "what if that was my family? What if that was my mom? Or what if that was my brother?" And it's hard because you don't want to see that happen.

Although Isabel and her two siblings are DACA beneficiaries, when she hears that an undocumented community member is being deported, she is forced to immediately think about her own family being separated. These articles therefore should not be taken as merely journalists' accounts of deportations. Through the eyes of those directly affected by immigration enforcement efforts, these concerning news items remind undocumented immigrants about their own and their loved ones' precarious status.

Under the Trump administration, young adults have also heard frequent rumors about immigration raids happening in their community. For example, on Wednesday, August 30, 2017, the following message circulated via social media, e-mail, and text message about a possible raid that was scheduled for the coming days in San Diego County:

> We have received this from a very reliable source: ICE plans to make a massive raid in North County [San Diego] this Friday, September 1st in the morning. It may last all day. They know where undocumented [immigrants] live and work. DACA [beneficiaries] please beware given 45's recent statements.

By the end of the day, there were more details:

> You will recall that I posted an alarm about a possible ICE raid this Friday in north county San Diego. This is now confirmed. I assume the raids will include the cities of Escondido, San Marcos, Vista, Valley Center, and Oceanside. I cannot confirm that DACA students will remain safe.

Although there was no information about the original source, the message had reached undocumented immigrants and allies. Community members then forwarded it to their families and friends as a safety precaution. I personally remember first seeing the message on my social media accounts. Many of the young adults I spoke with had also received the message via their e-mail, social media accounts, and/or phones from trusted community members. Despite a handful of clues that seemed to indicate that the information was indeed only a rumor, the disturbing message created a lot of fear, anxiety, and confusion among undocumented and mixed-status families because no one would really know for certain if this was a rumor or not until the day the raids were supposedly to have occurred. I remember having trouble sleeping the night the message was circulating. When I was not busy trying to trace the source of the message to confirm its validity, I was concerned about the people close to me (both in and outside of my research project) who are undocumented and live with the omnipresent threat of deportation. Flor, a 25-year-old DACA beneficiary in a mixed-status family, recalled receiving the message late at night on the 31st:

> I was texting other people and they're like, "yea it's just a rumor, but they're just asking people to be careful." So I was actually already like asleep, but then I just texted my sister . . . I told her, "hey can you tell the parents just to be careful." And then I sent them a picture [of the message]. "I don't know if this is true or not but just tell them to be careful tomorrow."

On September 1st, the family took additional preventive measures. For example, Flor's younger sister, Karla (who is a U.S. citizen) accompanied her mother, Raquel, to work. Because Raquel is undocumented and works cleaning homes in north county San Diego, her daughters were especially worried that she might be a target for immigration officers. In case the messages were true, Karla decided to join her mother as they drove around the city on September 1st. By the end of the day, Flor and her family were safe. They did not hear or see any more information about the raids. It was confirmed that the previous messages were only rumors. The family could breathe again.

Just a week later, however, a similar message gained traction. Only this time, the message was about raids scheduled across the country. Speculative messages about possible raids have surfaced quite frequently under the Trump administration. As evidenced by the experiences of young adults like Flor, these messages exist in the public realm and yet they have powerful ramifications in the private lives of undocumented immigrants and their families. It is precisely the waiting period—from the day the rumor reaches the undocumented community to the day the raids are rumored to occur—that heightens levels of risk and uncertainty that inevitably lead undocumented and mixed-status families to experience increased feelings of fear, stress, and anxiety.

Regardless of whether the messages are true or false, families have to confront the possibility of being forcefully separated and prepare accordingly.

Immigrant young adults in San Diego County have also noticed a dramatic increase in immigration enforcement after the Trump administration was inaugurated. Not only have they heard more stories about community members being apprehended, but they have also seen border patrol cars more frequently, either driving through the streets or parked near freeway entrances and exits. I interviewed Valeria, for example, who spoke vividly about the times she has seen immigration officers near her home. She is a thirty-one-year-old young woman who immigrated to the United States with her mother and brothers to reunite with their father. Valeria was just four years old at the time; she has lived in the United States ever since and was able to apply for DACA. Valeria recalled her experiences about growing up undocumented in San Diego County, including more recent changes in immigration enforcement she has seen in her neighborhood:

> I have seen . . . like I told you that I work in the evenings and so sometimes I get out at midnight. And at midnight I have seen that *la migra*, border patrol is nearby . . . by Panda [Express]. They are just right there . . . I have seen them more than a couple of times there because it's close to the freeway . . . because of that I feel scared for my mom and my dad because they [immigration officers] might apprehend them one day if they want to stop them.

Interviews with young adults who have grown up in San Diego County, along with participant observations, confirmed the presence of immigration officers in predominantly Latino neighborhoods and during dawn or dusk when people are traveling to/from work. Indeed, when I was driving to and from interviews, I often saw immigration officers. Participants recalled feeling tense, attempting to act "normal" when in public, and checking in with their family members immediately after seeing immigration officers or learning about a possible raid.

When I spoke with Flor, she referenced recent news articles about two undocumented parents of four U.S. citizen children who were apprehended and detained by immigration officers in National City, which is located less than forty miles away from north county San Diego where Flor and her family have lived for over a decade. When Flor's family heard about the news, they began to discuss the possibility of deportation and took preventive measures. Flor's mother, Raquel, mentioned that "if that happens we need to have the house under Gabriel's name [Flor's younger U.S. citizen brother]." Flor elaborated and told me that the family had actually done this and more already:

> They actually sent the paperwork out because my brother is not really here so when he was here he signed that paper . . . we [also] have savings that they tell us about . . . I tell them too if they do get apprehended I will be in charge of my siblings.

In addition to undocumented parents turning over home ownership to a U.S. citizen child and allocating emergency funds, family members also memorized each other's phone numbers, made sure their identification cards (e.g., passports, state IDs) were up to date, and updated emergency contact information in school records. Following the 2016 presidential elections, an immigrant rights organizer and I convened an immigration forum open to the undocumented community in San Diego County. At the event, we presented on the most recent and projected immigration policy changes and facilitated a discussion around possible emergency plans. I vividly remember that at the event an undocumented mother asked if she should apply for her children's U.S. passports. On the one hand, she wanted her young children to have their passports ready, especially after her fear of deportation heightened following the election results; on the other hand, she worried that by submitting her children's applications, she may come to the attention of immigration officers. As undocumented immigrants' fears of deportation enter the conscious level very frequently under the current political climate, they find themselves weighing the benefits and potential negative consequences before employing preventative measures, even when these should be straightforward bureaucratic processes.

Not all preventive measures are as straightforward. Importantly, undocumented parents express growing concerns and fears about what would happen to their young children if they were apprehended. To prepare, some families started looking into the adoption process for the U.S. citizen children to remain in the United States with citizen caregivers in the case of family separation. In other instances, the oldest sibling would volunteer and mentally prepare for taking responsibility for her/his younger siblings, as was the case with Flor. This often involved difficult conversations. For example, Denise, a twenty-nine-year-old DACA beneficiary, shared with me that after the elections, the increasing news about deportations prompted her mother to make plans for the young children in the family:

> When Trump got elected, you'd see a lot of [news about] deportations on the media . . . so then our communities got scared and my parents

got scared so then my mom, she decided . . . she was making this plan in her head, "Ok, so we have to go to an attorney and get Elizabeth [Denise's younger nineteen-year-old sister, who is a U.S. citizen] to be responsible of all of your siblings." And I remember telling her, "why Elizabeth? I am the oldest. I am the one responsible of my brothers . . . of my siblings. Why are you having her be the responsible one?" She said, "because you don't have secure status either."

This conversation greatly impacted Denise. As the oldest sibling living at home with her parents, Denise has taken on various responsibilities to help her siblings throughout the years. She often drives them to/from school or soccer practice. She also assists them with their homework and is always encouraging them to pursue a college education. To Denise then, it made the most sense that she would be the one responsible for her five younger siblings if the family's nightmare came true one day and both parents were deported. However, Denise's mother was also concerned about her temporary status, noting that even with DACA, her future in this country is not guaranteed. This experience reveals the ways in which immigration policies and enforcement powerfully shape family dynamics. In the case of Denise, this experience highlighted her limitations when it comes to taking care of her siblings. In Denise's words, "that was the first time where my status made an impact when it comes to my siblings because my sister that has status here was taking my position of me being the oldest and of me being the second mom of my siblings."

Some participants also turned to organizing or providing legal assistance in their local community as an attempt to address the detrimental effects the current administration is having on undocumented communities. These young adults expressed that they wanted to turn their fear into action by helping families in similar situations. Some of the young adults planned community meetings to inform their neighbors about the latest changes in immigration policy, others organized antideportation campaigns or attended rallies, and a handful of others were part of civil disobediences aimed at fighting for a path to citizenship for all undocumented immigrants.

As the experiences of Flor, Valeria, Isabel, and Denise demonstrate, undocumented and mixed-status families have been prompted to constantly think about and discuss the potential ramifications of a family member's deportation. These thoughts, conversations, and plans are further influenced by members' immigration status, age, gender, and birth order. They can also create tensions between siblings. It is not surprising then that the constant stress has repercussions on the well-being of all members in undocumented and mixed-status families. In the section that follows, I explore in greater depth how the heightening of immigration enforcement under the current administration affects young adults' mental health.

Consequences for Young Adults' Mental Health
Emilia's experience vividly illustrates the amount of stress and uncertainty that undocumented young adults are exposed to under the current administration. Having grown up in San Diego County since she was six years old, Emilia shared with me that she never felt the full weight of what it meant to be undocumented until more recently, following the 2016 presidential election results. It was then that she had to relive painful memories; namely, the day she realized she was undocumented. She explained:

> I didn't really like to think of my situation and I was really good at it . . . I didn't really have to deal with it until . . . when Trump got elected. Then that scaredness [sic] that I felt when I was little came back [crying] . . . And it's like an ongoing feeling like yeah I'll have fun, you'll see me smile, you'll see me laugh, I'll go out with my friends, but at the end of the day that's how I feel. At the end of the day when I'm alone you realize who you are and everything, and as much as I try to push that feeling away it's still there, it won't go away. That's why with the whole political talk that I hear every day, and with DACA going on, it just got to the point where I'm just like, "I'm done, I'm over it" [crying]. And it sucks because I want to have that mentality where I'm just like, "I'm done. I want everything to be done. If they're going to send me back, send me back," but I just can't be living like this.

As Emilia shared, young adults have to constantly confront feelings of uncertainty under the current administration. In some instances, the force of these emotions has led young adults to suddenly break down in tears both during and outside of the interview setting. While Emilia felt protected from deportation as a DACA beneficiary under the Obama administration, many beneficiaries like her no longer feel protected under the current administration. Even before Trump was inaugurated, several news reports surfaced about the precarious state of DACA and its beneficiaries. And on September 5, 2017, the Trump administration officially terminated the program, leaving thousands of young adults in limbo. At the time of this writing (May 2018), the decision is still in limbo in the courts, adding to young adults' need to stay informed and therefore exposed to persistent stress.

Following the 2016 presidential elections, undocumented young adults who are not eligible for DACA have also struggled mentally preparing for another four years without any form of immigration relief. Karina, a thirty-three-year-old undocumented woman, expressed how difficult it has been for her to be working in low-paying jobs that are not related to her career goals, despite having earned a bachelor's degree, due to her immigration status. Although Karina has lived in the United States for over fifteen years and is passionate about pursuing a career in the medical field to help underserved communities, she is unable to qualify for DACA because of its exclusionary age requirements. Subsequently, she is unable to legally work in the country.[4] She shared with me how this reality has affected her emotionally:

> I am not living a normal life. It is affecting my stress. My emotional, physical, everything... There are days that I am very energetic and very positive, but there are days that I feel very down. There have been times where I am at work and I can't control my emotions and I start crying at work [*crying*] and then I have to hide because I don't want anyone to see me. It's hard.... There are times when I don't want to, but all of the sudden I just cry. When I get home after a long day, I feel super tired. I have my to-do list, but for the most part I never follow my to-do list because I am so tired.

With the current administration, not only does Karina have to experience heightened levels of stress and anxiety related to the increasing immigration enforcement efforts she is seeing in her community, but she also has to contend with the reality that she will not have access to any form of immigration relief for at least another four years. Under all these pressures, Karina shared with me that she has not been eating well; she was recently diagnosed with anemia because her iron levels reached an all-time low. She is also unable to get enough rest or have enough time and energy for herself. During the interview, I could see that this has all taken a toll on Karina's health. She broke down on multiple occasions, especially when we spoke about the current political climate, her jobs as a housecleaner and server, and her plans for the future.

Interviews with multiple members of the same family unit also revealed that entire families are deeply affected by the current political climate. I had the opportunity to speak with Gabriella, for example, a twenty-eight-year old DACA recipient whose two younger siblings also have DACA and whose mother is undocumented. She shared with me how the concerning news on immigration has affected her and her family members:

> I'm currently going through depression, anxiety . . . Out of nowhere I just cry. I just get anxious and I am married now and my husband . . . he just sometimes doesn't know what to do because sometimes you're watching the TV and you're seeing the news that something is happening and you just start crying . . . My family is going through that as well because my mom went through that, I am going through that, and right now my brother is going through that as well.

During the interview, Gabriella also shared that she has been experiencing stomach pains and her brother has been struggling to eat as a result of the stress they are undergoing during these turbulent political times. She elaborated on her brother's condition:

> My brother told my mom the other day, he even said these words, "I don't even think I can continue walking" . . . After everything happened with Trump, for him it was . . . I would say that was the time I saw him really really worried.

On a separate occasion, I had the opportunity to speak with Gabriella's younger sister, Isabel. When I asked Isabel how the news about immigration policies and enforcement efforts affect her emotionally, she expressed the following:

> It makes me sad because like I said I think about me being in that situation and it stresses you out more because you know you and your family don't have papers. You worry about that and even though you have DACA or . . . even if you are a resident and you have family [members] that don't have papers, you're still stressing out, you're still worried because you don't want to see your family go through that.

Following the 2016 presidential elections, Isabel's condition worsened. She had to seek medical attention:

> My doctors actually gave me medication for depression because I stress out and I cry, but sometimes I don't cry and I let it build up. I was actually seeing a psychologist because I couldn't take it anymore. I was not eating. I was not sleeping because it's really stressful.

Notably, I only came across two cases where young adults were able to receive medical attention to cope with feelings of depression and anxiety. Isabel and another young woman, Cristina, were currently seeing a psychologist and taking antidepressants. More often than not, young adults struggled on their own as they tried to cope with the heightened awareness of their family's vulnerability to deportation. Many young adults were hesitant to seek medical care, either because they did not have access to health insurance or because they did not want their parents to find out so as not to add another source of worry for them.

Immigrant young adults who have experienced the trauma of seeing a loved one apprehended were also undergoing increased levels of stress and depression. During the summer of 2017, I met Sofia, a twenty-three-year-old DACA beneficiary whose father was deported in 2010. The entire family was devastated at the time; Sofia's mother had recently given birth to a boy. They could not imagine a future where they would have to live divided by the United States–Mexico border. After a few attempts, Sofia's father was able to return to the United States. However, because his only option was to return unauthorized (as is the case with most deportees), the family fears that one day he could be deported again. These experiences motivated Sofia to pursue a career as a lawyer. She is currently a full-time college student and a legal assistant at an immigration law office. Sofia is passionate about working with families who have been directly affected by the detention or deportation of a loved one. As one of the few legal assistants in the office, Sofia is often the first to receive the news that a community member has been detained and/or deported. She shared with me just how often this occurs, especially under the Trump administration:

> After the elections I felt like it was just every week that we were getting at least one phone call that somebody was getting detained, and "oh my god, what is going on?" And obviously that causes a lot of anxiety . . . it was a very emotional time those very first few weeks and even now it [still] feels like it's an emotional rollercoaster, like we're okay for a little bit and then the next horrible thing happens.

Sofia elaborated to share how this affects her mental health:

> It takes a toll even though it's not my family members. I don't know these people. And it's just . . . since I've been in that position I feel like it hits me the most at work. And obviously I can't cry at work so you know sometimes I go home and I'm just sad for the day.

On the one hand, Sofia is actively preparing for a career as an immigration lawyer. As a legal assistant, she has access to invaluable experience in the field of immigration law. On the other hand, the fact that Sofia is directly working with families affected by deportation frequently brings to the surface traumatic memories associated with her father's deportation; these are memories that the family is afraid of having to relive and subsequently cause feelings of fear, stress, and depression.

Conclusion

Under the Trump administration, immigrant young adults find themselves having to constantly think about one of their greatest fears—having one or more family members deported. This heightened awareness of the family's vulnerability to deportation disrupts young adults' sense of reality. One day their family is safe and united, and the very next day it could be torn apart and forced to live divided by the United States–Mexico border. Perpetually imagining the worst-case scenario leads young adults to experience sustained periods of depression, anxiety, stress, and/or psychosomatic symptoms, such as stomach pains and headaches. These feelings inevitably affect important aspects of their lives, such as their ability to participate at school and work, and in the household and community.

As both an insider and outsider, I am witness to the uncertainty, vulnerability, and barriers that undocumented immigrants confront. These become most evident particularly during turbulent times. For example, multiple sources were reporting that the Trump administration would soon terminate the DACA program during late August and early September 2017. Headlines such as the following increasingly surfaced in people's social media and e-mail accounts: "Trump is Considering Ending DACA, but Hasn't Decided, Aides Say" (Bennett 2017); "Trump Seriously Considering Ending DACA, with 6-Month Delay" (Haberman and Thrush 2017); and, "700,000 People Could Lose Their Jobs if Trump Ends DACA" (Marcus 2017). In the midst of all this uncertainty, immigrant young adults would suddenly break down when discussing their plans for the future during the interview. Questions about the future inevitably required young adults to think about multiple scenarios, such as the possibility of DACA ending and/or being separated from a loved one due to a deportation. Personally, I could not help but constantly think about those closest to me (both within and outside of the research project) whose lives would be deeply affected by the decision to terminate DACA. Many of them would have to find new jobs, likely ones that were not related to their career goals and that paid much lower wages. A few of them would have to postpone their plans of applying to graduate school. I knew that many of their future plans would have to drastically change if they suddenly lost their DACA status.[5]

As policymakers continue to consider anti-immigrant policies and enforcement efforts, it is imperative to shed light on the various ways in which the lack of legal immigration status profoundly affects the everyday lives of undocumented immigrants and their loved ones. This chapter revealed the stressors, pains, and uncertainties that immigrant young adults in San Diego County in particular are experiencing as a consequence of the current political climate. Their stories remind us of the importance of serving both as witnesses and actors in the struggle for immigrants' rights; until the day that undocumented immigrants' dignity, humanity, and rights are recognized, regardless of their immigration status.

NOTES

1. On June 15, 2012, the Obama administration announced the DACA federal program, which provides temporary relief from deportation and work authorization for eligible undocumented young adults. Every two years, beneficiaries have to apply to renew their DACA. Five years later, in September 2017, the Trump administration rescinded the program, preventing young adults from submitting initial DACA applications and leaving current DACA beneficiaries in greater uncertainty.

2. In 1954, over one million Mexican nationals were deported under "Operation Wetback" (Garcia 1980).

3. The DACA program provides eligible undocumented youth with temporary work permits and relief from deportation. The Obama administration first announced DACA on June 15, 2012. Five years later, on September 5, 2017, the Trump administration terminated the program. At the time of this writing, the Supreme Court is considering a determination on the program's future.

4. To be eligible for DACA, applicants must have arrived in the United States. before reaching their sixteenth birthday. Having arrived in the United States just a few months after turning sixteen, Karina has been left out of the program.

5. At the time, it was still unclear how the DACA program would come to an end. That is, it was unclear if current DACA beneficiaries would have to immediately return their permits (and subsequently lose the temporary protection from deportation and work authorization overnight) or if they would be able to keep their permits at least until the initial date of expiration they were given.

REFERENCES

Abrego, Leisy J. 2014. *Sacrificing Families: Navigating Laws, Labor, and Love across Borders*. Stanford, CA: Stanford University Press.

Abrego, Leisy J. 2019. "Relational Legal Consciousness of U.S. Citizenship: Privilege, Responsibility, Guilt, and Love in Latino Mixed-Status Families," *Law and Society Review* 53(3): 641–70. https://doi.org/10.1111/lasr.12414.

Asad, Asad L., and Eva Rosen. 2018. "Hiding within Racial Hierarchies: How Undocumented Immigrants Make Residential Decisions in an American City," *Journal of Ethnic and Migration Studies* 45(11): 1857–82. https://doi.org/10.1080/1369183X.2018.1532787.

Bennett, Brian. 2017. "Trump is Considering Ending DACA, but Hasn't Decided, Aides Say." *Los Angeles Times*, August 31, 2017. http://www.latimes.com/politics/washington/la-na-essential-washington-updates-trump-is-considering-ending-daca-but-1504212086-htmlstory.html.

Brabeck, Kalina M., M. Brinton Lykes, and Rachel Hershberg. 2011. "Framing Immigration to and Deportation from the United States: Guatemalan and Salvadoran Families Make Meaning of Their Experiences." *Community, Work, and Family* 14(3): 275–96.

Burawoy, Michael. 1998. "The Extended Case Method." *Sociological Theory* 16(1): 4–33.

Chavez, Leo R. 2007. "The Condition of Illegality." *International Migration* 45(3): 192–96.

Cohen, Kelly. 2017. "Immigration Court Backlog Hits Record High in April." *Washington Examiner*, May 15, 2017. http://www.washingtonexaminer.com/immigration-court-backlog-hits-record-high-in-april/article/2623150.

De Genova, Nicholas. 2002. "Migrant 'Illegality' and Deportability in Everyday Life." *Annual Review of Anthropology* 31: 419–47.

Dreby, Joanna. 2015. *Everyday Illegal: When Policies Undermine Immigrant Families.* Oakland: University of California Press.

Enriquez, Laura E. 2015. "Multigenerational Punishment: Shared Experiences of Undocumented Immigration Status within Mixed-Status Families," *Journal of Marriage and Family* 77(4): 939–53.

Flynn, Meagan. 2017. "ICE Detains Salvadoran Immigrant during Annual Check-in in Houston." *Houston Press*, February 24, 2017. http://www.houstonpress.com/news/ice-detains-el-salvadorian-immigrant-during-annual-check-in-in-houston-9225511.

Garcia, Angela. 2014. "Hidden in Plain Sight: How Unauthorised Migrants Strategically Assimilate in Restrictive Localities in California." *Journal of Ethnic and Migration Studies* 40(12): 1895–1914.

Garcia, Juan R. 1980. *Operation Wetback: The Mass Deportation of Mexican Undocumented Workers in 1954.* Westport, CT: Praeger.

Golash-Boza, Tanya. 2015. *Deported: Immigrant Policing, Disposable Labor and Global Capitalism.* New York: New York University Press.

Gonzales, Roberto G. 2011. "Learning to be Illegal: Undocumented Youth and Shifting Legal Contexts in the Transition to Adulthood." *American Sociological Review* 76(4): 602–19.

Gonzales, Roberto G. 2015. *Lives in Limbo: Undocumented and Coming of Age in America.* Oakland: University of California Press.

Haberman, Maggie, and Glenn Thrush. 2017. "Trump Seriously Considering Ending DACA, with 6-Month Delay." *New York Times*, September 3, 2017. https://www.nytimes.com/2017/09/03/us/politics/trump-daca.html.

Hauser, Christine. 2017. "A Young Immigrant Spoke Out about Her Deportation Fears. Then She Was Detained." *New York Times*, March 2, 2017. https://www.nytimes.com/2017/03/02/us/immigrant-daca-detained.html.

Lopez, German. 2017. "Trump's Policies at Work: ICE Deports an Immigrant Mother in the Middle of the Night." *Vox*, February 9, 2017. https://www.vox.com/policy-and-politics/2017/2/9/14560258/guadalupe-garcia-de-rayos-deportation-trump.

Lynch, Jamiel. 2017. "DREAMer Speaks Out on Immigration, Gets Arrested by ICE." *CNN*, March 2, 2017. http://www.cnn.com/2017/03/01/us/dreamer-arrested-jackson-mississippi/index.html.

Marcus, Josh. 2017. "700,000 People Could Lose Their Jobs if Trump Ends DACA." *Vice*, August 29, 2017. https://news.vice.com/en_us/article/qvzx9d/700000-people-could-lose-their-jobs-if-trump-ends-daca.

Martinez, Lisa M., and Maria del Carmen Salazar. 2018. "The Bright Lights: The Development of Oppositional Consciousness among DACAmented Latino Youth." *Ethnicities* 18(2): 242–59.

Menjívar, Cecilia, and Daniel Kanstroom, eds. 2013. *Constructing Illegality in America: Immigrant Experiences, Critiques, and Resistance*. New York: Cambridge University Press.

Negrón-Gonzales, Genevieve. 2013. "Navigating 'Illegality': Undocumented Youth and Oppositional Consciousness." *Children and Youth Services Review* 1284–90.

Patler, Caitlin, Jorge A. Cabrera, and the DREAM Team Los Angeles. 2015. "From Undocumented to DACAmented: Impacts of the Deferred Action for Childhood Arrivals (DACA) Program." *UCLA IRLE Reports*. https://escholarship.org/uc/item/3060d4z3.

Pickoff-White, Lisa, and Julie Small. 2017. "Immigration Arrests Increase in Northern California." *KQED*, August 16, 2017. https://ww2.kqed.org/news/2017/08/16/immigration-arrests-increase-in-northern-california/.

Schmalzbauer, Leah. 2014. *The Last Best Place? Gender, Family, and Migration in the New West*. Stanford, CA: Stanford University Press.

Valdivia, Carolina. 2019. "Expanding Geographies of Deportability: How Immigration Enforcement at the Local Level Affects Undocumented and Mixed-Status Families." *Law and Policy* 41(1): 103–19.

Yoshikawa, Hirokazu, and Jenya Kholoptseva. 2013. "Unauthorized Immigrant Parents and Their Children's Development." *Migration Policy Center*.

Zatz, Marjorie S., and Nancy Rodriguez. 2015. *Dreams and Nightmares: Immigration Policy, Youth, and Families*. Berkeley: University of California Press.

MARIA LILIANA RAMIREZ

7

Beyond Identity

Coming Out as UndocuQueer

I don't know what was harder: to say that I was gay or to say I was undocumented... I have a hard time knowing where people stand. Even I've met other gay friends that are actually out, men and women, and then all of a sudden I come to find out that they are extremely anti-immigrant. I have to be very careful. Just because a person is gay doesn't mean that they're going to accept the other. —Kassandra, age thirty-six

Amid the heated debate around undocumented migration in the United States, undocumented individuals are increasingly dehumanized and criminalized.[1] This gives way to the notion of a "bad" or "undeserving" immigrant as ingrained in both immigration law and political rhetoric. Policy makers have normalized the idea that undocumented immigrants are "illegal" and in this way, undocumented immigrants are criminalized, deemed undesirable and even dangerous to the nation.

Historically, immigration laws have differentiated "good" immigrants from "bad" immigrants through distinctions including race, gender, and sexuality. While gays and lesbians were addressed in 1917 when U.S. immigration law was modified to ban "persons with abnormal sexual instincts" from entering the United States, this exclusion was further entrenched under the Nationality Act of 1952. The Immigration and Nationality Act of 1952 specifically excluded "[a]liens afflicted with a psychopathic personality, epilepsy, or a mental defect." Thirteen years later, in 1965, Congress eliminated epilepsy from that clause and replaced it with the phrase "sexual deviation."

While the Immigration and Naturalization Act of 1965 discarded the use of a quota system to focus on family reunification, it maintained a specific racial, patriarchal, and heteronormative order in which the heterosexual family unit becomes an institutionalized access point for legal migration. Moreover, the level of access was dependent on a racial hierarchy embedded in the U.S. immigration system, in which Canadian or European heterosexual family claims were more valued than Latin American or Caribbean heterosexual family claims (Luibhéid 2008). In the 1965 Act's banning of gay and lesbian immigrants under the category of sexual deviants, it emphasized a preference for heteronormative families for economic purposes, which expected fathers to work and mothers to be consumers (Luibhéid 2008). Although the ban on gay and lesbian immigrants was lifted in 1990, the distinction between "deserving" and "undeserving" continues to persist throughout the nation's immigration discourse and rhetoric. Moreover, it is within and through this distinction that heterosexuality continues to be embedded in the nation's vision of "deservingness" for immigrant families. One example of how this rhetoric is present even within pro-immigrant discourses is when heterosexual undocumented immigrants are highlighted as the good immigrants.

"Deserving" immigrant narratives emphasize a belonging to the nation-state by upholding key ideals of nationalism such as economic contributions to the state, instead of defying the role of the nation-state (White 2014). Thus, immigrant narratives based on deservingness are part of an assimilationist strategy where the goal is to be accepted into the nationalist fabric by proving one's ability to integrate into capitalism. Such a course further perpetuates the exclusion of "undesirable" immigrants who are less economically productive, and therefore less desirable.

Narratives in support of the Development, Relief, and Education for Alien Minors (DREAM) Act and the Deferred Action for Childhood Arrivals (DACA) program fall in line with assimilationist strategies based on deservingness. Therefore, scholarship that has attempted to provide a more humanizing narrative of being undocumented based on deservingness risks perpetuating similarly exclusionary and assimilationist narratives. Given that the scholarship on undocumented migration is largely dominated by a heterosexual focus, it further positions queer migrants in the category of bad immigrants. Being rendered invisible in academic scholarship perpetuates a heteronormative portrayal of who undocumented immigrants are. Thus, it is important to explicitly focus on excluded subgroups within the undocumented community when we discuss the resistance of those within this community, including an examination of the experiences of queer undocumented individuals.

While an individual's undocumented immigration status generates obstacles in accessing education and employment, it also involves a complicated and multifaceted experience of "coming out" in romantic relationships and friendships. In order to illuminate the complexities of the experience of being undocumented and queer, I make use of Deleuze and Guattari's (1987) rhizome. In their introduction to *A Thousand Plateaus: Capitalism and Schizophrenia*, Deleuze and Guattari define the rhizome as a subterranean assemblage varying in form, where any of its parts can connect to another. An assemblage being a network of connections that constantly deterritorialize and reterritorialize, the rhizome does not rely on any one part of the assemblage for its existence or for self-definition. Instead, the rhizome is composed of multiplicities that do not dominate each other. All multiplicities are connected and coexist along with each other. The rhizome opens an abstract space to further think about the possible intimacies of queerness along with an undocumented status.

Through the Deleuzian framing of a rhizome, coming-out experiences of undocumented queer individuals are rearticulated in a series of meaningful events that allow for the self-recognition of an undocumented and queer existence. As Jasbir Puar (2013) explains, theorizing assemblages has implications for the future of feminist knowledge production. Deviating from reductionist identity politics, assemblages (1) "de-privilege the human body as a discrete organic thing"; (2) "do not privilege bodies as human, nor as residing within a human/animal binary"; (3) consider signification as "only one element of many that give a substance both meaning and capacity"; and (4) considers categories such as race, gender, and sexuality as "events, actions, and encounters, between bodies, rather than simply entities and attributes of subjects" (Puar 2013). A queer praxis of assemblage insists that reclaiming the nation's most perverse beings considers queerness as fundamentally antinationalist and unintelligible to state practices of surveillance and control (Puar 2005). Following Puar's use of assemblages as a form of feminist knowledge production resistant to identity politics, I argue that the Deleuzian framing of rhizomatic assemblages or connections is productive in reframing the experience and existence of being undocumented and queer beyond the limitations of identity.

In this study, I attempt to provide a theoretical contribution that challenges voyeuristic narratives such as those of a "master status" (Gonzales 2016), which totalizes and reduces the experiences of undocumented immigrants to legal status. As Gabrielle Cabrera thoroughly explains in an earlier chapter of this book, academics and non-academics alike are interested in making undocumented immigrants intelligible through narratives of violence, trauma, and resiliency. Through my exploration of coming out as undocumented and queer, I argue that an individual's existence is not overdetermined by an immigration status. Rather, I highlight the ways in which undocumented queer people make sense of themselves without exclusively relying on their undocumented immigration status. To avoid perpetuating a voyeuristic narrative of consistent suffering, I center agency and resistance enacted by undocumented queer individuals through the Deleuzian concept of the rhizome. Unlike the typical liberal narratives of resistance that center notions of meritocracy, I explore how undocumented queer immigrants claim agency and resistance through their own understandings of being.

Following a brief review of the literature, I have divided this analysis into two main sections. The first section, "Coming Outs" examines the various modes of "coming out." I explore how the various planes of consistencies inhabiting the rhizome map the possibilities of coming out as undocumented and queer. I argue that the multiplicities embedded in planes of consistencies open up a space in which multiple ways of being coexist with one another. Unlike the notion of a master status, no single form of identification or immigration status is embodied over the other. On the contrary, they exist simultaneously and do not rely on each other for existence. This signals a fluidity in understanding the self that is not totalizing. Additionally, the planes of consistency also map intimacies of romance and trauma apparent in negotiating an undocumented status and sexual orientation. I then move to the second section, "'UndocuQueer' as an Assemblage." Here, I outline the limitations and possibilities of the UndocuQueer movement. I argue that although the UndocuQueer movement serves for political visibility, it reifies bounded notions of identity possibilities based on fixed categorization of undocumented and queer. I ground that argument by emphasizing my interlocutors' rejection of the term UndocuQueer as a form of identity.

Literature Review

Early scholarship on undocumented students heavily focused on the obstacles related to obtaining a higher education (García Peña 2012; Lopez 2010; Patel 2013; Perez 2009; Soltis 2015). The earliest research took place prior to "undocumented-friendly" (Suárez Orozco et al. 2015) policies and examined experiences before the passage of AB 540 or the California Dream Act, and before the signing of the executive order authorizing DACA. Since then, scholars have been following the development of such policies to discover their effects on the lives and self-understandings of undocumented youth. The earliest undocumented-friendly policy in the state of California was AB 540, which not only opened educational opportunities, but also destigmatized the identities of undocumented students (Abrego 2008; Negron-Gonzales 2014). With this early piece of policy, undocumented students began to use shorthand terms such as AB 540 instead of bluntly stating their undocumented status. This strategy of using a shorthand term to express an undocumented identity has continued to evolve, along with policy changes and the development of the undocumented youth social movement. This trend can be seen with the early use of the term "DREAMers" after the push for a federal DREAM Act, and currently with some undocumented youth calling themselves "DACAmented" after the executive order authorizing the DACA program. Although research on "DREAMers" or "DACAmented" individuals has served to highlight the connection between policy and identity formation among undocumented youth, it also creates a dangerous idea of a homogenous identity and recreates supposed divisions between so-called deserving and undeserving immigrants. Further, it actively erases the existence of other identities experienced by undocumented youth, such as being queer.

With the recent emergence of activism strategies such as "undocumented and unafraid" and "coming out of the shadows," researchers began to look at the coming-out aspect of the undocumented experience (Negron-Gonzales 2014). This body of literature connects the strategies used in the LGBT movement with strategies adapted by the undocumented youth movement, including the UndocuQueer movement (Nicholls 2013; Terriquez 2015; White 2014). It is here where undocumented queer individuals are finally acknowledged by discussing the concept of a "double coming out." A double coming out is unique to the undocumented-queer experience because individuals must navigate coming out not only as queer but also as undocumented. This attempt to break the heterosexual narrative of undocumented youth or their activism continues to be one-dimensional. It demonstrates the structural intersectionality of the UndocuQueer movement but does not go further than that to show its contribution or cost to the overall undocumented youth movement. It does not fully discuss the experience of being undocumented and queer.

Anthropological work on migration and queer studies holds potential in further exploring the experience of being both undocumented and queer. Queer anthropologists have had a long-standing conversation about not only the function but also the meaning of categories used as sexual identities

(Lewin and Leap 2002; Boellstorff 2007; Weston 1996). Further, queer studies in anthropology has begun to concern itself with questions of intersectionality and the relationship between sexuality and globalization (Boellstorff 2003, 2007). In his essay "A Queer Itinerary: Deviant Excursions into Modernities," Martin Manalansan IV (2003) uses notions of home to anchor the experience of queer migrants from the Philippines in the United States (including those who were undocumented). Manalansan (2003) disrupts the concept of home from being attributed with nostalgia and safety by also including violence and betrayal. In an almost oxymoron, he describes home for the queer migrant of color to mean being placed and displaced. This evokes Anzaldua's (1987) borderland studies, where homophobia is described as the fear of going home. Homophobia is not necessarily always most present in the public sphere, but rather in the most intimate and familial spaces. That is where the fear of homophobia lies for queer migrants of color.

Methodology

With IRB approval, I conducted ten in-depth interviews with undocumented students in Southern California who identified as queer between June 20 and September 28, 2016. The interviews focused on the individuals' undocumented status, queerness, and their coming-out stories with family, friends, and coworkers. All interviews were audio recorded and transcribed verbatim. The recruiting process was based on a snowball sample method to expand the diversity in educational background of my participant pool. I reached out to old high school classmates, current college peers, and then to individual people of color and LGBTQ+ organizers at the school and community levels. Individuals agreed to participate with the acknowledgement that the study was not paid and were given the option to be represented by a pseudonym or their real name.

The criteria for participant selection required that students: (1) were undocumented—DACA or non-DACA; (2) self-identified as non-heterosexual; (3) were current students, on a break, or had graduated from an institution of higher education. Individuals were at different levels of their education: one had just finished a master's degree, another was taking a break before transferring to a four-year institution, and the rest were between their third and fourth year of their bachelor's degree. The individuals I interviewed were between the ages of twenty and thirty-six and identified as gay, lesbian, bisexual, pansexual, queer, or did not identify with any label that would signal a sexual orientation. Seven women and three men were interviewed, and all had emigrated from

Mexico. Not all participants benefited from DACA, AB 540, or the California Dream Act. I include the experiences of those who do not qualify for any undocumented-friendly policies because this exclusion in itself is an important element of the navigation of their identities. In particular, with the implementation of DACA, the narratives from non-DACA-eligible undocumented individuals have been marginalized within immigration scholarship. Given that this project aimed to obtain in-depth interviews with people who are made vulnerable for multiple reasons, this study does draw on a small sample size. Though I do not claim that the findings are statistically significant, the interviews provide deep insights into these particular experiences.

My position as an undocumented queer student gave interlocutors a comfort level to express concerns that they may not freely have expressed to a non-undocumented, or non-queer, researcher. Indeed, one participant, named Carlos,[2] before and after the recording continuously expressed his concern and discomfort with what he called the "fetishizing" of non-undocumented people doing research on undocumented individuals. Having participated in various research projects, he felt as if his story had been exhausted by past researchers. Although a few had knowledge of my undocumented status before the interview, most did not know either my undocumented status or that I identify as queer. Even those who knew I am undocumented did not know I am queer. However, without exception, all participants asked me with curiosity about my status or sexual orientation at some point during the interview. Given that for most participants, our interview session was our first meeting, we built rapport during the minutes prior to and throughout the interview. Coming out to them as queer and/or undocumented became a crucial opportunity to build trust, since at that moment interlocutors spoke in a more relaxed tone.

Although interlocutors and I shared many similarities in our trajectories of being undocumented queer students, there were also several significant points of distinction. Like and unlike some of my interlocutors, I had access to all of California's undocumented-friendly policies (AB 540 and California Dream Act) and I held DACA. This is important not only because some of the interlocutors did not qualify for these benefits, but also because many undocumented students continue to struggle for access to U.S. universities. Institutional barriers continue to be in place that prevent undocumented students from accessing a higher education, and therefore very few of us have had access to graduate programs or the possibility of becoming professors. These structural barriers at the university and state level have excluded undocumented people from being knowledge producers of their own experiences.

Even when given access to academia, undocumented students continue to be relegated to research objects and expected to perform their status in a way that falls into the trope of the never-ending suffering undocumented immigrant who needs to be saved.

I share this to point out that even as graduate students or as researchers, undocumented academics continue to have unequal access to resources that are accessible to U.S. citizen scholars researching undocumented communities. There continues to exist unequal power dynamics between undocumented people and U.S. citizen scholars even when undocumented individuals make it into academic spaces. While scholars of color engaging in research on undocumented communities face institutional challenges in making a place for themselves in academia, their U.S. citizenship enables them to have easier access to higher education and funding. On the other hand, undocumented scholars have limited access to higher education, internal university funding, and external funding opportunities. At no fault of immigration scholars who are U.S. citizens, citizenship status continues to produce structural inequalities and hierarchies that exclude undocumented immigrants in and outside of academia. Regardless of what political decisions are made regarding undocumented immigration, immigration scholars that are U.S. citizens will be immune from deportation and will continue to be employed and lauded for producing research on undocumented communities.

Coming Outs

The experience of coming out as undocumented lies in various planes of consistencies linked to each other but manifested in distinct and nonlinear ways. In these planes, undocumented individuals negotiate the acceptance of an undocumented status and sexuality. Coming out for undocumented queer individuals does not take place as a linear process or narrative, but instead manifests as multiplicities. Coming out happens more than once, to multiple people, and in multiple spaces. The multifaceted aspect of coming out as undocumented and queer links to intimacies of desire that are in tension with daily interactions with racism, xenophobia, and homophobia in the United States.

My conversation with Christian,[3] age twenty, revealed that an influential factor in navigating coming out as undocumented was his comfort level with both his immigration status and sexual orientation. While Christian was more comfortable with his queerness, he struggled to disclose his undocumented status in intimate relationships outside of family. In Christian's first romantic relationship, he did not disclose his undocumented status due to his partner's conservative political views on immigration, but now—two years later—he tries to disclose his status early in relationships. Christian explained,

> I just let them know in casual conversations rather than sit them down and be like I'm undocumented. I think I've gotten more comfortable with my undocumentedness in the last two years. It's not a big deal; it doesn't make me less than anything . . . it literally means nothing. Like it does in certain contexts in ways. But like does it define, is it my full identity? Not really. Like yes and no. So if somebody doesn't want to date me because I'm undocumented or whatever it's dumb yeah . . . So I feel more comfortable letting people know, whoever I'm talking to, like yeah I'm undocumented. It's just a part of my identity. I'm in this type of situation.

The experiences of trauma and love are merged by the fear of rejection when imagining coming out as undocumented in a romantic context. Experiencing pain along with romance in the same plane of consistency rearticulates an intimate relationship between an undocumented status and sexual orientation. Christian's articulation of coming out to those he dates demonstrates a tension in how he had to constantly rearticulate how he presented himself to others. Even when disclosing his undocumented status, he did not shape his entire sense of being around his immigration status. These feelings of uncertainty, despair, and transgression are inevitably connected to the daily interactions with racism, xenophobia and homophobia. An undocumented status, like sexual orientation, is thus experienced in the form of a fragment in which it is credited as being only part of a way of being.

Similarly, Kassandra expressed having a harder time disclosing her undocumented status than her sexual orientation. Kassandra explains the following as her process of coming out as undocumented to her friends:

> I'm very out as a lesbian to my closest friends. Not all of them know [I am undocumented], still up to now, even after knowing me for years a lot of them don't know . . . I think sometimes I keep that out on purpose because sometimes I just want to talk about normal things and not feel so . . . vulnerable. Because then there's the chance they might pity me and that's something I hate, that I absolutely hate. I have different things that I say, for example when they would say why don't you know how to drive? I would say, I bike instead. I love biking because I don't want to be an extra car on the streets. Things like that . . . I find ways to

delude that conversation. And they end up thinking I'm an interesting person, very eccentric. So I just keep it out because I don't want to feel different from them.

Sometimes not coming out as undocumented is not only about safety concerns, but also about creating distance from the emotional baggage an undocumented status carries. Kassandra does not come out as undocumented to some of her friends, not because she feels shame about her legal status or feels unsafe, but because it gives her a space where she does not feel the traumatic weight of being undocumented. For that moment, she does not have to explain the legal implications of her status and thus does not relive some of the traumatic aspects of being undocumented. Both Kassandra and Christian regain their agency in balancing how much power and control they consciously give their undocumented status.

Undocumented individuals are in constant negotiation with their undocumented status and with retaining agency against the current and historical xenophobic political climate that relentlessly tries to strip them away from that possibility. They are able to maintain agency—by not disclosing their undocumented status, they manifest it in their experiences as a fragment of how they understand themselves and not. Coming out as undocumented is rhizomatic in its nature since it cannot help but evoke experiences related to the individual's sexual orientation. In that way, the experience of being undocumented is intimately connected to the experience of being queer.

Navigating the rhizome is abstract in its nature but it is lived in concrete experiences. Such an experience is the process of coming out as queer because one must navigate coming out in multiple planes. These multiple dimensions of coming out link together to form a heavier emotional experience that includes variations of happiness, sadness, and other emotions that cannot be reduced to words. Like the rhizome, there is no linear process in coming out as queer. Below I explore how both Kassandra and Italia[4] demonstrate in their coming-out stories that, although they both experienced a lack of support from their families when coming out, the impact of their coming-out experiences did not follow a linear path. Kassandra was heartbroken after she experienced her first same-sex relationship break up, and her mother became suspicious of her behavior. Since Kassandra kept her relationship a secret from her mother, her mom did not automatically suspect a breakup. Instead she thought Kassandra was doing drugs. Kassandra explains,

> [A]t some point I was just so devastated that I had to tell her after she had left that well it turns out she and I were dating and you know I'm

gay. Her first reaction was: I won't kick you out of the house as long as you don't tell your dad. You can't tell anyone. You tell your dad [and] I will kick you out of the house. So, I kept quiet for a while because there was nowhere I could go and I was about 20–21 years old at the time. So, at some point I got a job and rented a room with a friend and I moved out.

Although Kassandra had come out, her mother's reaction pushed her back into being closeted. Because Kassandra was denied a chance to be completely out with her family, she felt pressured to move out. A parent's reaction of not talking about homosexuality or pretending as if the coming-out conversation had never happened attempts to erase the individual's queer identity as part of the family's dynamic. In the face of family rejection, coming out can be experienced as a constraining, traumatic, and vulnerable moment. While the words said at the moment of coming out can be painful, silence and erasure of that moment also create moments of violence. Keeping quiet after coming out becomes a survival tool to avoid any further pain. This is reminiscent of Anzaldúa's shadow beast that lives inside an individual in the attempt to suppress unacceptable parts for fear of family rejection. Anzaldúa (1987) argues that to live in fear of rejection is to live in a constant confrontation with the shadow beast. This shadow beast teaches not only to fear a possible rejection, but also to fear one's nonconforming sexual orientation. In a sense, to fear rejection is to fear one's self. The trauma and vulnerability Kassandra experienced when dealing with coming out as undocumented is linked yet separated by the intimate wound caused by coming out as lesbian to her family. In a very rhizomatic manner, through the intimate wound, the space of the planes in which coming out as queer takes place is expanded. She experiences intimate wounds in different planes of consistencies: one occurs in the intimacy of her family unit, and the other occurs in public spaces where she must navigate the state.

On the other hand, Italia's coming-out story came about from a forced circumstance. Her partner was kicked out of her home after her parents discovered their relationship, which led to Italia having to come out to her family as well. Their families finally accepted their relationship almost five years after their coming out, but as Italia explains, it was a slow process:

Well it's going to be five years next year. So, it's been four and a half years since then. My partner's family took a while to come around. They didn't want to see me, not even in pictures. Nothing. Like in Spanish you say, "no quiero verte ni en pintura" ["I don't want to see you even in pictures"]. Literally that. They would even ask my partner to take off my picture from Facebook. It took them up until recently a few months ago for her mom to see me . . . But when she moved back after she graduated, she was like, I have to move out so we started living together. So, I think that's when her parents started seeing that it's an actual thing, it's serious, they are living together. A few months ago, they went over to our apartment, her mom did. Then I have gone over now like her mom talks to me and her dad talks to me. There's still a lot of things we don't really touch on or we avoid the conversation but you know, baby steps kind of thing.

While the pain Italia experienced related to coming out began with the moment of coming out to her family and with the coming out of her partner, it was not limited to only that moment. Instead that pain continued throughout the years post–coming out. Italia continues to explain,

And then my mom came around sooner than my partner's family did. When I graduated, my family came from Mexico to see me graduate and had a strong influence on how my mom was seeing the situation . . . Now she's like best friends with my partner because of her . . . After four and a half years, things are better. I think it's hard a lot of time to understand, you want it to be better sooner because it's been four and a half years but you know every parent or family has their own time to cope with things.

Even once their families came to terms with their relationship, the process in which that took place was painful for Italia and her partner. Like Kassandra, Italia experienced various nonlinear stages of coming out. While both Kassandra and Italia experienced similar obstacles in coming out to family, they had different outcomes. This speaks to the rhizomatic nature of coming out as undocumented and queer because their experiences were different but also connected in the sense that they lived through intimate wounds.

Other families were more receptive of the coming-out moment. Monica's[5] coming out to her family was influenced by the fear she felt after the Orlando shooting.[6] She explains,

I thought that I had always tried to be really studious, always tried to follow the rules, do the best that I could in everything. It made me think is this the one thing that is going to make people not want to reach out to me or not respect me as much for the stuff that I have accomplished . . . I told my dad recently, because I came out to DC this summer which

Beyond Identity 157

> was really exciting but I was coming out here a week after the Orlando shooting. He was confused that I was feeling uncomfortable and then I told him that . . . you know I'm gay and this is who I am . . . and then he was like it doesn't matter.

The moments before coming out to her father were filled with anxiety and fear as she thought of the possible outcomes. Her main concern was that if her family was not receptive, her valued status as a good student would be tarnished. She feared that a negative reaction about her sexual orientation would override anything else they thought about her. The Orlando shooting further increased her anxiety levels since it created a sense of urgency to come out to her family. Although her father's response could be read as neutral, in the context of coming out this neutrality functioned as a positive reaction that alleviated some of the fears and trauma she was feeling from the impact of the Orlando shooting. The positive coming-out experience created a safe space to be out within her family. Similarly, Juan's[7] coming out was influenced by deaths caused by a mass shooting:

> I was dating someone that I thought was going to be a serious thing of course on the down low when we were dating. You know what I think I want to tell my mom, and then the Charleston shooting happened that summer and I was like these folks were so young and some of them might have not been able to tell people the things they wanted to tell them, so it was in that spur. I went to a Black Lives Matter action and got home and called my mom. I said "mom, by the way ughh" and I came out to her.

The Charleston shooting[8] became a pivot point for Juan to make the decision to come out to his family. Although coming out was already on his mind, the concept of death that the Charleston shooting presented gave urgency to coming out. The concept of death reminded him of the heavy baggage he carried at the time in closeted sexuality. At that moment, he realized he would not be at peace without being out as queer to his family. He recognized how important his sexual orientation was to him, particularly in thinking about the future. Further, that moment of realization was not only tied to the Charleston shooting but also connected to the Black Lives Matter action he went to, because together they reflected the reality Juan lived in, that is: an undocumented gay man whose existence is constantly under attack by the state. In this context, coming out then becomes an act of resistance and protest since it declares strength even when the surrounding environment is violent. Monica's and

Juan's coming-out stories show that the intimacy of coming out is not only connected to desire but also to more violent notions of intimacy. Violent intimacies such as the mass shootings of queer populations create a point of departure for coming out.

The rhizome along with intimacies opens an abstract space where resistance can take place. Fear of death and trauma is manifested through the intimate wound that is then connected with a reflection of the self. To resist and to confront those fears of death, it became crucial for Juan to come out to his family since only then will he be able to be completely honest about his sexual orientation. As the following shows, Juan's coming-out story took a positive path:

> My mom is too supportive, she's like beyond a PFLAG mom. She's like, "If you fall in love with a man and you want a child with both of your blood I will carry his baby." I'm like mom that is GROSS. And like "I won't have sex with him" and I'm like I know it's still gross! . . . I know the concept is cute [laughs]. The intention behind it is cute but I'm like mom that's kind of gross but she's like, "well the offer is there whenever you want." Then my dad too. I think my siblings yeah of course they were super supportive. My sister cried and was like, why didn't you tell me before? And I'm like girl this isn't about you. My dad was the hardest to tell. I was on the phone with him for two hours before I came out and he was like oh shoot alright then. He's like I'm going to look at you differently but in a good way. He's like you just look stronger to me now because you have had to deal with bigger things and all this other stuff. I was just crying! I'm like, stop dad!

His coming out story is not completely unmarked by pain; he initially feels pain when imagining the possible negative outcomes, but after coming out, the narrative takes a very optimistic path that even has some comical tone to it. An intimate wound was starting to manifest during the pre-coming-out stages through feelings of fear and pain, but the welcoming reaction of his family allowed for that intimate wound to not be fully formed.

Equally important to the experience of coming out to family is the decision to not come out. Relationships with family members influence the readiness of the individual to come out. Reading the family's attitude toward LGBTQ+ topics also proves crucial in predicting the level of acceptance of the family and, in turn, whether to come out. But each case is unique. A close relationship with family, for example, might intuitively suggest that coming out is feasible, but in some cases can discourage coming out due to fears of losing that relationship. For instance, Lara[9] decided not to be out with her family because she still lives with her mother. Her mother's stand on LGBTQ+ issues makes Lara worry about the possible changes in the household if she were to come out. She explains:

> If I do let my mom know that I am gay, that I like girls, because I kind of know how she thinks already about it, it would be kind of awkward going home. We have a really good relationship so I don't want that to jeopardize our relationship in any way. She is the best thing for me, so it is hard. I am pretty sure she will be a little bit open to it, but it will take time for her to understand it completely. I am pretty sure she is going to understand it. I am her daughter. She says I am her favorite, so hopefully.

As Lara reveals, coming out holds the possibility of undoing current positive relationships and adding tension to them. Although she concludes by hoping her position as the favorite daughter will help her mom be more accepting, she also feels unsure and opts not to come out to avoid any negative consequences to their otherwise close relationship. Her fear of losing close ties with her mother also elicits conflicting feelings of having to choose between family and being out. Even when Lara can imagine the possibility of being out and maintaining a good relationship with her mother, she does not imagine that experience as being a smooth process. Instead, in her pre-coming-out stage, she imagines it being a process of adjustment, pain and compromise for her mother.

Similarly, Susy[10] shared why she did not come out to her parents. In particular, she focused on describing her father's attitudes on LGBT+ topics:

> But, for it to be public like that, it's not. I've been thinking about it but I don't know when. I don't know; it was hard when I told my friends, and my brother took it all right. He didn't tell me anything. He hugged me and said he supported me, but I have a very strict father, so I don't know. He is very hard-headed and I don't know how well he is going to take it, he has always said that if any of his children were like that or that were not how they should be, they would stop being his children.

Susy begins by explaining that although she is out to friends and her brother, she is not publicly out. This association of being "publicly out" refers to being out with everyone, and for Susy this specifically refers to being out to all her family members. Even after having had a positive experience coming out to her brother, she does not expect that from her father. Her father's open homophobia has prevented Susy from coming out to him since she predicts that he will not be accepting of her. Despite the fact, she is considering the possibility of coming out; she is hesitant to do so since she believes it will disrupt her relationship with her father and therefore unsettle the family dynamics. In contrast to Lara, Susy does not think her status as a daughter gives her any leverage in the possible outcome of her father's reaction. Even as his daughter, she remains exposed to her father's homophobia. The inability to imagine being out while maintaining family ties and emotional well-being are the strongest setbacks in coming out.

Coming-out experiences are manifested in various forms, which represent the rhizomatic nature of the coming out. For each of them, coming out was influenced by different factors, the reactions of their family were different, and most importantly the emotions they experienced took a different course. Coming out or not coming out takes place through multiple planes allowing for multiple separate-yet-connected experiences. The rhizome is navigated through the concrete and nonlinear process of coming out, which includes the formation of intimacies.

The abstract nature of the rhizome in relation to coming out is grounded in the real-life experiences of queer undocumented coming-out stories. While individuals process coming out as either undocumented and/or queer as separate experiences, they must reconsolidate both experiences because they are connected. Even when some individuals are out as queer, they face separate barriers when disclosing their undocumented status. Similarly, those who are out as undocumented face obstacles in disclosing their sexual orientation. Thinking of coming out as undocumented and queer as a rhizomatic process proves helpful in highlighting that there is no one universal narrative when coming out as both undocumented and queer.

UndocuQueer as an Assemblage

The concept of UndocuQueer attempts to fuse two fragmented identities to create a whole, but falls short in creating a complete identity. While categories such as UndocuQueer fail to convey the entire experience in being, I borrow Deleuze and Guattari's (1987) image of the rhizome to liberate the infinite ways in which identity can be expressed through the queer undocumented individual. In this section I argue that UndocuQueer as an identity politics is restricted by a linear and binary identity formation that proposes a fixed identity by piecing together an individual's undocumented status and sexual orientation. The rejection of UndocuQueer highlights the impossibilities of identity politics but also shows a potential to view UndocuQueer as something other than identity. In this section, I propose to view UndocuQueer as an assemblage outside of linguistic essentialism that treats the categorization of "undocumented" and "queer" as events in constant motion.

Most, but not all, of the individuals I interviewed were familiar with the UndocuQueer movement. Monica, for example, explained that her appreciation for the UndocuQueer movement was more about the visibility and political possibilities it creates. She explained:

> I think there's some that I do identify with, I think I really appreciate the work that shows the diversity even in being UndocuQueer. I think that's why I like it, not exactly because I identify with everything but it shows visibility. . . . I don't think I say it but if I post something on social media I'll tag it like UndocuQueer, or like UndocuQueer woman of color, but I think when I am speaking to someone often as an undocumented queer woman of color, I'll say it. UndocuQueer looks cooler as a hashtag.

While Monica values the work done by the UndocuQueer movement because of the space it creates, for her, using the term is mostly relevant only through social media. UndocuQueer is not a term that she uses to introduce her identity to someone with whom she is speaking in person; instead, when the opportunity comes to disclose both identities, she prefers to state both "undocumented" and "queer" as two separate words.

In this instance, Monica states both identities to introduce herself as an undocumented queer woman of color instead of using the term UndocuQueer, which she uses on social media. The inability to reduce her identities to one, or even two, reflects the complexities of categorizing the self. Similarly, Christian also said he did not use the word UndocuQueer and instead introduced himself as both undocumented and queer because it feels more natural. However, his justifications for why he did that are slightly different than Monica's. He explained:

> UndocuQueer still sounds weird for me to say just because it sounds like alphabet soup, it sounds like too much to say. For me I'm just like oh I'm undocumented and I'm queer, which is the same thing. But there is power in that word when you say it out loud and people listen to you when you say it. I've never used that word. It almost sounds like something that the DREAMers or older activists were using when they first were trying to get AB 540 or the DREAM Act out. I have a friend, she did all that activism work and she has friends from that circle who identify

as UndocuQueer, so by the time I got to college they already did all that work for me you know? They set up the DREAM Act they set up AB 540. So for me I had a cushiony spot—I didn't need to have such a political word attached to my identity because that work was already done. I was given that space to be undocumented and queer.

Although UndocuQueer may be a shorthand expression, it does not work that way in the daily lives of these individuals at a personal level, since it feels unnaturally constraining. For Christian, the term is too politically charged to be used as representative of his identity. It is not relevant for him to use it, as the term has connotations of activism in which he did not participate. He is grateful for that work because it has given him the option to not have his personal identity politicized, and it has allowed him to shape his sense of self beyond a list of policies. Although social movements and policies regarding undocumented people are connected to his identity, they do not define his entire identity.

To more effectively think about both the connection and the rejection of UndocuQueer as an identity based on political associations, I turn to Deleuze and Guattari's (1987) concept of "transformational multiplicities" characterizing the rhizome. "Transformational multiplicities" expand the spatial dimension in which identity is formed by its countless connections without depending on one main link. Through "transformational multiplicities" there is no center to understanding the self, instead there are various depths contributing to an expression of the self. "Transformational multiplicities" shape a fluid articulation of the self that is never fixed or linear because it is constantly developing.

Like Monica, Christian, and all the other people I interviewed, Karla[11] did not think of the term UndocuQueer as reflective of her identity. In the following quote she reflects on the function of UndocuQueer:

I don't like the use of it just because of the fact that it's not something people should think of you as. Oh not only are you undocumented but you're queer. Well you're whatever you are, you're documented or came here or queer or straight. I don't personally like labels. That's one of the main reasons why I don't like some people knowing I'm bi because it's like you're this or you're that. One of each, and you can never be whatever you think yourself as. I don't always see myself undocumented and yet I am . . . Growing up it was never a priority for me. Now, yeah I see the difference in it. In either one I never put much importance to it because I never like thinking of myself that I'm

Beyond Identity   163

just this label that they put on me and being UndocuQueer it's nothing more than a label.

Karla's rejection of UndocuQueer is based on its working as an imposed category. Even though the term was created by undocumented queer activists, it still holds the potential to be perceived as an imposed identity. She rejects labels that indicate that she is undocumented and queer because it is more liberating to identify as she pleases, whenever she pleases. The experience of being undocumented and queer lies in what Deleuze and Guattari (1987) call a "plane of consistency" of multiplicities in which various identities are mapped in the same dimension. Karla's refusal to give in to categorization as someone who has been categorized by immigration policies shows an exhaustion with the fixed labeling and categorization in identity politics. By undoing the polarized structure of identity formation, the rhizome also undoes the totalization of imposed categories.

While UndocuQueer intended to create a space of inclusion, as a category, by definition it establishes boundaries that limit fluidity. Interlocutors felt detached and hesitant to use UndocuQueer to describe their identity because it not only spoke to political activism in which they did not participate, but also because the term limits the possibility of fluid understanding of the self. This limitation of UndocuQueer is inevitable since, as David Valentine (2007) demonstrates in *Imagining Transgender: An Ethnography of a Category*, it is impossible for a category to encompass every existing experience that may fall under it. Clearly, an identity category holds both power and limitations. While it adequately creates visibility of an intersectional experience of undocumented queer immigrants, it unavoidably creates a restrictive approach to describing the self. Therefore, approaching UndocuQueer as a rhizomatic assemblage rather than an identity opens up a space for fluidity in which individuals experience being undocumented and queer in relation to other events and encounters. UndocuQueer as an assemblage opens more possibilities of connections that pertain to understanding the self that would otherwise be restricted by the rigid categorization of identity politics.

Conclusion

This study has suggested that UndocuQueer, as a form of identification, is restricting in understanding the self. Instead, interlocutors' coming-out stories suggest that being undocumented and queer are manifested as multiplicities that treat the categories of "undocumented" and "queer" as fluid events and encounters. For these individuals, although their undocumented status and queerness are influential factors in their lives, they reject the term UndocuQueer because to them, that term is restrictive and does not fully express their identities. The depolarized nature of the rhizome demonstrates the existence of various multiplicities and plateaus in which the self actively reconstructs and expands itself in the form of lines connected to each other but not solely to each other. An undocumented status and a queer identity then take the form of lines connected to each other, but also connected to various other lines relevant to understanding an individual's existence. Through this perspective, it is impossible to shape the self as rooted in either simply an undocumented status or simply a queer identity.

The rhizome provides a space in which the embodiment of identity can be drawn as some phenomena that are unstructured, depolarized, and in constant movement. It is through the rhizome that undocumented queer individuals experience coming out as rhizomatic connections of different forms of intimacies. The experience of coming out as undocumented and queer at different times, to different people, and in different locations is reminiscent of Anzaldúa's own depiction of a geographical border as an open wound that scars but bleeds again and again.

The rhizome and the globalized identity show the messiness of constructing the self and of being undocumented. The rhizomatic coming outs as undocumented and queer speak against the linear way in which academics have written about the experience of being undocumented. Being undocumented alone is not as structured as previous research suggests. Instead, being undocumented is a complex and diverse experience. Including the experiences of undocumented queer youth will disrupt and inform the current heterosexual scholarship on undocumented youth. Given the lack of research focused on queer undocumented individuals, I insist that further research is needed across disciplines to reshape the current body of literature on undocumented youth to be more representative of the undocumented experience.

NOTES

1. The name Kassandra credited in the epigraph is a pseudonym.
2. Pseudonym.
3. Pseudonym.
4. Real name.
5. Pseudonym.
6. The Orlando Shooting: on June 12, 2016, a shooting occurred at the Pulse nightclub in Orlando, Florida. There were forty-nine victims and dozens of people injured. The nightclub was known to be a gay and Latino club, but many of the victims were

not out to their families and it was that night of their deaths that the families found out about their sexual orientation.

7. Real name.

8. The Charleston shooting: on June 17, 2015, a white man conducted a mass shooting against black people at a church in South Carolina.

9. Real name.

10. Real name.

11. Real name.

REFERENCES

Abrego, Leisy. 2008. "Legitimacy, Social Identity, and the Mobilization of Law: The Effects of Assembly Bill 540 on Undocumented Students in California." *Law and Social Inquiry* 3(3): 709–34. https://doi.org/10.1111/j.1747-4469.2008.00119.x.

Anzaldua, Gloria. 1987. *Borderlands/La Frontera: The New Mestiza*. San Francisco: Aunt Lute.

Boellstorff, Tom. 2003. "Dubbing Culture: Indonesian Gay and Lesbi Subjectivities and Ethnography in an Already Globalized World." *American Ethnologist* 30(2): 225–42. https://doi.org/10.1525/ae.2003.30.2.225.

Boellstorff, Tom. 2007. "Queer Studies in the House of Anthropology." *Annual Review of Anthropology* 36: 17–35. https://doi.org/10.1146/annurev.anthro.36.081406.094421.

Deleuze, Gilles, and Felix Guattari. 1987. *A Thousand Plateaus: Capitalism and Schizophrenia*. Minneapolis: University of Minnesota.

García Peña, Lorgia. 2012. "New Freedom Fights: The Creation of Freedom University Georgia." *Latino Studies* 10(1–2): 246–50. https://doi.org/10.1057/lst.2012.2.

Gonzales, Roberto G. 2016. *Lives in Limbo: Undocumented and Coming of Age in America*. Oakland: University of California Press.

Lewin, Ellen, and William L. Leap, eds. 2002. *Out in Theory: The Emergence of Gay and Lesbian Anthropology*. Urbana: University of Illinois Press.

Lopez, Janet K. 2010. *Undocumented Students and the Policies of Wasted Potential*. El Paso, TX: LFB Scholarly Publishing.

Luibhéid, Eithne. 2008. "Sexuality, Migration, and the Shifting Line between Legal and Illegal Status." *GLQ: A Journal of Lesbian and Gay Studies* 14(2–3): 289–315. https://doi.org/10.1215/10642684-2007-034.

Manalansan, Martin F., IV. 2003. *Global Divas: Filipino Gay Men in the Diaspora*. Durham, NC: Duke University Press.

Negrón-Gonzales, Genevieve. 2014. "Undocumented, Unafraid and Unapologetic: Rearticulatory Practices and Migrant Youth 'Illegality.'" *Latino Studies* 12(2): 259–78. https://doi.org/10.1057/lst.2014.20.

Nicholls, Walter J. 2013. *The Dreamers: How the Undocumented Youth Movement Transformed the Immigrant Rights Debate*. Stanford, CA: Stanford University Press.

Patel, Lisa (Leigh). 2013. *Youth Held at the Border: Immigration, Education, and the Politics of Inclusion*. New York: Teachers College Press.

Perez, William. 2009. *We Are Americans: Undocumented Students Pursuing the American Dream*. Sterling, VA: Stylus Publishing.

Puar, Jasbir. 2005. "Queer Times, Queer Assemblages." *Social Text* 23(3–4): 121–39. http://jasbirkpuar.com/wp-content/uploads/2018/08/Queer-Times-Queer-Assemblages-1.pdf.

Puar, Jasbir. 2013. "'I Would Rather Be a Cyborg Than a Goddess': Intersectionality, Assemblage, and Affective Politics." *Meritum, Revista de Direito da Universidade FUMEC* 8(2): 371–90. http://fumec.br/revistas/meritum/article/viewFile/2172/1332.

Soltis, Laura Emiko. 2015. "From Freedom Schools to Freedom University: Liberatory Education, Interracial and Intergenerational Dialogue, and the Undocumented Student Movement in the U.S. South." *Souls* 17(1–2): 20–53. https://doi.org/10.1080/10999949.2015.998578.

Suárez-Orozco, Carola, Dalal Katsiaficas, Olivia Birchall, Cynthia M. Alcantar, Edwin Hernandez, Yuliana Garcia, Minas Michikyan, Janet Cerda, and Robert T. Teranishi. 2015. "Undocumented Undergraduates on College Campuses: Understanding Their Challenges, Assets, and What It Takes to Make an UndocuFriendly Campus." *Harvard Education Review* 85(3): 427–63. https://doi.org/10.17763/0017-8055.85.3.427.

Terriquez, Veronica. 2015. "Intersectional Mobilization, Social Movement Spillover, and Queer Youth Leadership in the Immigrant Rights Movement." *Social Problems* 62(3): 343–62. https://doi.org/10.1093/socpro/spv010.

Valentine, David. 2007. *Imagining Transgender: An Ethnography of Category*. Durham, NC: Duke University Press.

Weston, Kath. 1996. *Render Me, Gender Me: Lesbians Talk Sex, Class, Color, Nation, Studmuffins*. New York: Columbia University Press

White, Melissa Autumn. 2014. "Documenting the Undocumented: Toward a Queer Politics of No Borders." *Sexualities* 17(8): 976. https://doi.org/10.1177/1363460714552263.

AUDREY SILVESTRE

8

Me Vestí De Reina

Trans and Queer Sonic Spatial Entitlement

In May 2014 *Time* magazine, drawing mainly on the experiences and increased visibility of white and wealthy celebrities, declared that we had arrived at the "trans tipping point." They suggested that conditions had improved so significantly for transgender people, that their existence was no longer considered a problem in our society. That same month and year, transgender immigrant rights activist, Zoraida Reyes, took to the streets of Santa Ana, California, protesting and calling for an end to a contract between the city and Immigration and Customs Enforcement (ICE). As she did at many protests she had organized, Zoraida took hold of the megaphone, leading chants of "Not 1 More!" A month later, on June 12, 2014, Zoraida Reyes's passion for justice and her giving energy were violently taken. Her lifeless body was found in a dumpster outside of a fast-food restaurant.[1] The tragic incident was a painful reminder that while trans visibility has increased, so has the murder rate of trans women (Hauser 2018). Clearly, we have not reached the tipping point, as violence against trans women and men continues.

Part of the problem is that mainstream media sources that cover the lives of transgender people often focus on narratives of trans women like Caitlyn Jenner, centering white and wealthy experiences while marginalizing narratives of poor or working class trans women of color.[2] Trans women of color, on the other hand, are often depicted through a hegemonic optic that categorizes them in a binary opposition of exceptional or tragic, thereby neglecting quotidian moments filled with nuances, silences, rebellions, resistance, sorrow, anger, and joy—everything that makes transgender people fully human. To counter such limited mainstream representations, in this chapter I center both the vigil organized to commemorate Zoraida's life in June 2014 and the May 8, 2015, civil disobedience in Santa Ana, California, and I trace the impact and contributions of undocumented trans women to the immigrant rights movement. My analysis underscores the everyday experiences of undocumented trans women who in small but significant ways experience joy outside the discourse of the nation-state through space, sound, and the visual.

Zoraida Reyes

I first met Zoraida after an event organized by De Colores Orange County in 2011. Many of us gathered for an after-party at the apartment where Zoraida and other organizers lived. I remember Zoraida being excited and preoccupied about a date she had that night and we all playfully teased her about it. My interactions with Zoraida were informal and it was only after her death that I learned about her many accomplishments—including what an amazing friend and person she was.

Zoraida Reyes was born in Michoacán, Mexico, and migrated to the United States when she was young. She graduated from Century High School in Santa Ana, briefly attended the University of California Santa Barbara (UCSB), where she was majoring in gender studies. Without access to financial aid, however, she left without her degree. When Zoraida was at UCSB, awareness about the needs of undocumented students was limited and there were few resources for undocumented and trans students. The California Dream Act had not passed and Deferred Action for Childhood Arrivals (DACA) was nonexistent. The structural barriers affected her ability to complete her education at UCSB but also informed Zoraida's activism. Zoraida returned to Santa Ana where she lived with her chosen family. She attended Santa Ana Community College where she received an associate degree. While there, she began organizing with El Movimiento Estudiantil Chicano de Aztlan (MEChA), on behalf of the DREAM Act with Orange County Dream Team, and De Colores Queer Orange County.

Zoraida's impact on her community is traceable through the various political actions that have placed Santa Ana, California, on the map for mobilizing and fighting for the rights of their community centering queer, trans, and undocumented folks.[3] Zoraida organized with Orange County Dream Team; she was a key figure in the annual De Colores OC[4] conference; performed in fundraisers for the organization; and conducted online campaigns such as the

#Not1More. Zoraida's greatest impact, however, was her presence in queer and immigrant rights spaces. Despite her generally shy disposition, she was charismatic and learned to become outspoken, often sharing her struggles to offer and demand a critical lens for all participants in these movements.

Zoraida's murder was deeply hurtful to many. This was true, in part, because the contributions of undocumented trans women to the immigrant rights movement often go unnoticed—both in the immigrant rights movement and in the scholarship on undocumented migrants in the United States. Zoraida's chosen family planned two important events to remember and honor her life. Sonic memory ties the two events—the vigil and the civil disobedience. Indeed, both events were marked by pain, suffering, and joy—all emotions that were simultaneously expressed in the face of white heteropatriarchal supremacy, which with impunity harms undocumented trans women of color. I argue that considering the contributions of undocumented trans women is not simply a move to include their stories, but rather, it serves to inform new theories and ways of organizing that lend themselves to transformative moments.

Who Is Deserving? Whose Life Is Irrecuperable?

To understand the process of devaluation of lives I turn to the work of Ethnic Studies scholar Lisa Cacho (2012), who argues that under the mainstream media's process of racialized criminalization the legibility of Black people and communities of color is irrecuperable to the wider U.S. public. That is, most people do not see or fully recognize the value of these marginalized people's lives. This, in turn, subjects them to a continual state of rightlessness—a kind of devaluation of people deemed to be different, or labeled as the *other*. Considered less-than-human, marginalized people may live as though they have no rights because the various forms of violence they experience usually take place with impunity. In the case of Zoraida, the mainstream media coverage of her death was only recoverable to the wider public and to the community of Santa Ana, California, through the organizing efforts of her chosen family and community. As part of their grieving process, they drew on the skills and resources they learned alongside Zoraida to organize a vigil calling for justice for her. It was her own history of organizing with De Colores OC that moved activists to organize and demand justice in a way that challenged narratives of rightlessness that otherwise make undocumented trans lives irrecuperable.

Centering marginalized communities' everyday struggles shifts our understanding of trans narratives presented in mainstream media. In a neoliberal context it becomes difficult to separate success and respectability from each other. For marginalized communities, this often creates a binary narrative of deserving versus undeserving. Cacho's (2012) emphasis on the racialized criminalization that renders people of color ineligible for personhood is crucial to understanding how instances of integration are always conditional and highly dependent on the devaluation of the other. For instance, the concept of the DREAMer exemplifies a neoliberal subject that is productive through educational achievements and who is then the threshold for determining deservingness for all undocumented migrants. This logic requires that the DREAMer be valued but only through the simultaneous criminalization of other undocumented migrants, such as undocumented trans people who under these parameters might not fit the mold of a DREAMer.

In this context of deservingness, framed by a neoliberal logic that prioritizes economic gains over the wellness of people, the mainstream immigrant rights movement has largely ignored the specific issues facing undocumented trans people.[5] This is especially harmful for the trans community because it represents yet another level of exclusion. Indeed, the inability of the immigrant rights movement to center the unique experiences of undocumented trans women is in part due to the overall systemic marginalization of the trans community. The ordinary lives of undocumented trans women do not usually come to our attention. We only hear about their stories when tragedy strikes. Problematically, this leaves out nuances and gestures of joy that better center their humanity.

The erasure through omission of trans women is supported through a white supremacist heteropatriarchal hegemonic lens that operates linearly where anything that does not follow the "norm" automatically falls outside of our visibility, resulting in the marginalization of their narratives. I argue that centering undocumented trans women in the analysis of immigrant rights provides us with a map that teaches us different ways of being, forcing us to reexamine what we know and how we know it but also how we listen and how we see. We must contend with what we do not know, see, or hear as a challenge to epistemologies informed by a white supremacist heteropatriarchal society. The challenge to register these narratives and acknowledge the nuanced moments of bliss requires a multilayered set of tools to get at the multidimensional experiences of undocumented trans women of color—this uplifts their stories and their voices.

Gaye T. Johnson's notion of sonic spatial entitlement is helpful in understanding how marginalized communities "situate themselves within particular spatial histories and when they express a spatial claim to change the stakes of an existing space and to remake its meaning in relation to themselves and their communities" (2013, 124). In this way, the May 28, 2015, civil disobedience that this chapter centers offers a unique opportunity to see how queer and trans undocumented sonic spatial entitlement contests normalized ideas about gender, sexuality, class, nationality, and belonging.

Understanding Rightlessness through Multiple Lenses

Cacho's (2012) theory of rightlessness, based on Orlando Patterson's (1982) theory of social death, serves as a theoretical framework to consider how white supremacy continually works to uphold itself through the devaluation of the other. Patterson articulated social death as that which during slavery, produced conditions in which Black people were socially dead given that their ties to society and kin were severed through the process of enslavement. It was through that process that Black people were removed from the category of human. In today's context, I draw on Cacho and Patterson's work to use rightlessness as a frame to underscore the precarious condition in which undocumented trans women find themselves because not only are they under continuous threat of deportation, but they are also under continuous threat of social and literal death as informed by transphobia that results from white supremacist heteropatriarchy.

QUEER TEMPORALITY

Cacho also wrestles with the process of reckoning irrecuperable and devalued lives by drawing from Jack Halberstam's (2005) analysis on queer temporality as a way of existing beyond mainstream ideas of family as an institution and reproduction, making room for radical formations on kinship. Queer temporality is also shaped by the struggles of queer communities against afflictions that cut lives short, such as HIV/AIDS. Trans women already operate under queer temporalities but for undocumented trans women this is much more pronounced due to the lack of opportunities available to them as determined by their immigration status. Undocumented trans women, therefore, must contend not only with their sexuality, gender expression, class, and race, but also with their immigration status, because this plays a role in delaying Western ideas of adulthood. For example, undocumented immigrants are generally unable to obtain a driver's license at age sixteen, attend college, achieve homeownership, enter into marriage, have children, or attain steady employment in the moments when it is socially expected. The instability created by xenophobic laws combined with heteropatriarchy place undocumented trans women into a temporal uncertainty as deportation and detention continually loom over them. Falling outside of time can be reason enough to be deemed as irrecuperable and undeserving.

QUEER OF COLOR CRITIQUE

Queer theory is helpful in unpacking heteronormativity, but it does not account for the experiences of queer people of color, undocumented queer people of color, or undocumented trans women. Queer of color critique—an area of scholarship produced by queer scholars of color—is important because it offers an interrogation of white supremacy and heteropatriarchy within queer theory. Political scientist Cathy Cohen explains that, "one of the great failings of queer theory and especially queer politics has been their inability to incorporate into analysis of *the world* and strategies for political mobilization the roles that race, class, and gender play in defining people's differing relations to dominant normalizing power" (1997, 457). Cohen offers an intersectional analysis of white heteropatriarchy of "the world" but leaves out immigration status as it relates to "dominant normalizing power."

Roderick A. Ferguson (2003), following the work of feminists of color, is interested in "how intersecting racial, gender and sexual practices antagonize and/or conspire with the normative investments of nation-states and capital" (4). Ferguson's analysis is important to considering how different identities subvert or reinforce normative ideas about race, class, gender, and sexuality. For example, the category of "UndocuQueer" participated in asserting the limitations of mainstream LGBTQ concerns that did not consider undocumented queers and also risked their lives by publicly declaring their immigration status. In this way, UndocuQueers participated in "antagonizing" the state by declaring their immigration status through the coming-out mainstream LGBTQ narrative.

Queer temporality challenges the bounds of capital production and heteronormativity, interrupting both heteronormative and homonormative[6] ideas of productivity. But as demonstrated by the work of Cohen (1997) and Ferguson (2003), feminists and queers of colors have always questioned the bounds of Western productivity and normativity. The Combahee River Collective serves as an example of the genealogy of queers and feminists of color who have called into question the limitations of single-issue analysis and activism because it is, "difficult to separate race from class from sex oppression because in our lives they are most often experienced simultaneously" (Combahee River Collective, 1978). To extend this analysis to undocumented trans women and undocumented queer people, I examine the civil disobedience and vigil for Zoraida. My analysis exposes the blind spot of queer theory and the shortcoming of queer of color critique as these fail to grapple with the "unfinished project of freedom"[7] for those who, in this case, lack legal status to reside in the United States.

Understanding the inextricable connection between gender, sexuality, class, race, and immigration status inherently calls for an intersectional method to read the narratives of undocumented trans women of color that traverse social life, rightlessness, and queer temporality. This requires applying an intersectional analysis to immigration to consider how policies and their implementation produce categories of inequality that reinforce white hegemonic heteropatriarchal ideas. Because their gender and sexuality is continually questioned, the lives and experiences of undocumented trans women bring into sharp relief these consequences of immigration policy. This is especially important as current immigration laws have become much more insidious by curtailing a path to legalization, while criminalizing broader swaths of the immigrant population.

Gender, Sexuality, and Immigration Laws

Immigration law reveals how normative expressions of gender and sexuality inform ideas about U.S. citizenship. The Page Law of 1875, for example, prohibited the entry of undesirable immigrants, targeting Chinese women who were under suspicion of engaging in sex work—demonstrating how immigration and the desire to control immigration are intimately tied with notions of sexuality and gender throughout different historical periods. For instance, in 1917, under the category of "constitutional psychopathic inferiors," gay men and lesbians were not allowed to enter the United States. This bar was formally institutionalized in 1952 with the Nationality Act (more widely known as the McCarran-Walter Act). Again, in 1965 entry was denied on the basis of "sexual deviancy" (Luibheid and Cantu 2005). The 1980s Refugee Act allowed people who feared returning to their home country to petition for asylum based on fear of persecution, but it excluded LGBTQ migrants. In 1990, the immigration ban on gays and lesbians was lifted and the number of asylum petitions based on sexual orientation increased notably (de la maza perez tamayo 2013).

The criminalization of undocumented migrants is also tied to how we understand race, gender, and sexuality. For example, explicit criminalization of undocumented migrants dates back to the liberal Immigration Act of 1965 that removed quotas and created restrictive conditions for Mexicans to obtain visas, forcing many Mexican migrants to cross the border illegally for employment opportunities (De Genova 2010). In 1986, the Immigration Reform and Control Act (IRCA) passed, providing amnesty to undocumented migrants for the first time but also militarizing the border. Ten years later in 1996, the Illegal Immigration Reform and Immigrant Responsibility Act (IIRIRA) criminalized undocumented and documented migrants by reclassifying minor offenses into aggravated felonies, including past offenses (Coutin 2010; Golash-Boza 2013). Through a queer of color critique, Reddy offers a reading of IIRIRA where asylum petitions based on sexuality were only possible within the context of "neoliberal restructuring of state power" that contradicts sexual freedom as brown relationships are propelled into heteronormativity (2005, 103); meaning that immigration laws create the conditions that force people into heterosexual relationships, which results in the reinforcement of heteronormativity that defaults into homophobia. In addition, Section 287(g) of IIRIRA allowed local and state police to act as immigration enforcement, creating hostile environments for communities of color including undocumented migrants. These laws were presented as an attempt to deter migration but what they accomplished was increased criminalization accompanied by rightless migrants and an increased death toll at the border (Bhartia 2010).

Turning to the field of queer migrations, scholars such as Lionel Cantu (2002), Eithne Luibheid (2002), Horacio Roque-Ramirez (2003), and Carlos Decena (2008) intervened by applying a critical queer lens to interrogating how sexuality is informed by immigration laws and how undocumented queers have negotiated their sexuality in the United States. Cantu developed what he called a "queer political economy of migration" (Luibheid and Cantu 2005, 2) to understand how "sexuality shapes and organizes processes of migration and modes of incorporation" (Luibheid and Cantu 2005, 21). Drawing from Cantu, Luibheid (2008) expanded and defined queer migration, "to theorize how sexuality constitutes a 'dense transfer point from relations of power' that structure all aspects of international migration . . . Queer migration scholarship, which explores the multiple conjunctions between sexuality and migration, has drawn from and enriched these bodies of research—as well as feminist, racial, ethnic, postcolonial, public health, and globalization studies among other fields" (Luibehid 2008, 169). In this way, nonheterosexual migrants were influenced to shape their identity based on their understanding of U.S. sexuality informed by "structural variables, institutional policies, cultural influences, social relations, and the dynamics of migration" (Luibheid and Cantu 2005, 21). In effect, immigration laws forced migrants into performing gendered racialized categories in order to be legible to the state, particularly around asylum cases based on sexuality. For undocumented trans people of color the surveillance of gender, sexuality, class, and race creates a precarious situation leaving them vulnerable to multiple forms of state-sanctioned violence. Such processes of surveillance also help replicate gender binaries when undocumented trans migrants must identify with either a hyperfeminine or hypermasculine gender identity, leaving little to no room to identify as gender queer because doing so would jeopardize their asylum case.

The intervention by queer scholars has disrupted the heteronormative paradigm that excludes a feminist and queer analysis. However, little attention has been paid to the experiences of undocumented gender nonbinary, undocumented gender queer, and undocumented trans migrants unless related to asylum cases. Immigration research on asylum cases mentions the importance of demonstrating desirability to the U.S. government, constructed around the redeployment of Western hegemonic values. De la maza perez tamayo (2013) writes, "Trans asylum seekers, lacking access to asylum by virtue of their gender identity, are thus compelled to navigate the terrains intelligible to the state (in this case, sexual orientation), regardless of whether those particular topographies are hospitable to their bodily ontologies" (240).

The systematic marginalization of the trans community affects how researchers approach immigration studies and what questions are asked. On the one hand, there are the legal limitations such as those mentioned by de la maza perez tamayo; on the other hand are the experiences of undocumented trans women living in the United States. Both activists and scholars have largely ignored the issues facing undocumented trans people.

It is in conversation with these literatures that I circle back now to Zoraida, whose death makes visible the material consequences of living in a white heteropatriarchal society forcing us to deal with the lasting effects of structural forms of violence. Zoraida haunts us through the sounds from her vigil and those heard at the civil disobedience. Despite social death, hauntings bring us back to explore the humanity of those who are deemed outside of the category of human. Zoraida's death forces us to grapple with the state's multiple forms of violence such as immigration laws, heteronormativity, heteronormative research, and transphobia that produce death. For example, the state has sanctioned the panic defense by allowing defendants to claim "gay panic" as an acceptable reason for murdering trans women.[8,9] These practices reproduce cis-gender binary and heterosexuality as the norms and anything outside of that is subject to both social death and literal death. However, Zoraida's lasting energy and spirit captivated many who have expressed an intense sense of loss after her death. Understanding Zoraida's haunting as "producing a something-to-be-done" (Gordon 2008, xvi) marked a shift in my analysis to focus on potential moments of joy that are not always visible, audible, or decipherable. This type of analysis, however, requires tools not typically used in research on undocumented immigrants.

The narratives of undocumented trans women of color require a willingness to listen. Gloria Anzaldúa (2007) in *Borderlands/La Frontera: The New Mestiza*, asked us to "listen to what your jotería is saying" (107). Following the steps of Anzaldúa (2007), Francisco J. Galarte (2014) invites queers, jotxs, and us to listen differently: "Jotería, listen to what your trans* brothers and sisters are saying, and remember those long forgotten" (229). In this provocation, Galarte is asking jotxs and queers to listen to what goes unregistered, to what is considered indecipherable: "considering new reading practices means exploring what is announced, listening for the iterations of silences within the analytic boundaries between race and sexuality, which can push us to think of gender as much more dynamic and as spatially and temporally contingent" (Galarte 2014, 233).

In 2002, Gwen Amber Rose Araujo, a trans Latina teenager, was murdered in Newark, California by four men. Gwen was a young teenager who unapologetically lived her true authentic life and named herself Gwen after the pop-rock singer Gwen Stefani. Gwen's murder was significant because it brought into attention the horrific details and frequency of violence experienced by trans people. More so, in 2006, her murder influenced then California Governor Arnold Schwarzenegger to sign the "Gwen Araujo Justice for Victims Act" (AB 1160) into law. The assembly bill limited the use of the "gay panic defense" by defendants. That same year, *Lifetime* aired the TV movie, *A Girl Like Me: The Gwen Araujo Story* about the life and death of Gwen.

Drawing from the film, Galarte arrives at the importance of listening by evoking Gwen's last words, "Please don't. I have a family." Galarte seems to feel the haunting through his inability to forget Gwen's last words. The hauntings of Gwen and Zoraida disrupting space and time, "is one way in which abusive systems of power make themselves known and their impacts felt in everyday life, especially when they are supposedly over and done with (slavery, for instance) or when their oppressive nature is denied (as in free labor or national security)" (Gordon 2008, xvi). Their haunting forces us to reckon with the loss of both Gwen and Zoraida, who do not let us forget the tragedy and structural circumstances that made such violence possible. They also powerfully force us to imagine different possibilities and ways of existing that disrupt our understandings of joy, happiness, and love.

Media Presentations and Misrepresentations

On the morning of May 28, 2015, within a year of Zoraida's premature death, I attended an action organized by community members and organizers from GetEQUAL,[10] Familia: Trans Queer Liberation Movement,[11] and #NOT-1MORE[12] who staged a civil disobedience calling for the release of undocumented trans detainees by blocking the intersection of Flower Street and Civic Center Drive in Santa Ana, California. The protestors targeted the Santa Ana police department because at the time it held a space inside the jail that housed LGBTQ undocumented migrants. They were specifically targeting reports that trans women were placed in solitary confinement and sexually assaulted.[13] The organizers did not secure a permit for the civil action, resulting in the Santa Ana police arriving in full riot gear and declaring that the civil disobedience was an unlawful assembly. The police then proceeded to arrest Isa Noyola, Sandra Jarariveros, Mariela Martinez, Jiselle Onell, and Jorge Hernandez,[14] who were sitting in the center of the intersection. The civil disobedience drew attention from local mainstream media as reporters interviewed participants and gathered footage. The organizers of the action announced that they would not leave until all detainees were released. Yet, many of the local mainstream media news reporters left while activists were still detained.

ABC 7,[15] one of the local mainstream media news outlets that covered the protest at the time it was happening and throughout the day, broadcasted clips of the civil disobedience in the daily news hour shows. In the minute and a half clip they briefly described that around seventy protestors attended the civil disobedience and were "calling for an end to the detention and deportation of undocumented immigrants, particularly those who are part of the LGBTQ community." The news report included the names and mug shots of the five protestors who were arrested. They were described as "suspects" who were charged with obstruction and failure to disperse. The mug shots were accompanied by their "legal" names, thereby misgendering trans and gender-non-conforming protestors. While the practice of releasing legal names and mug shots appears to be following standard police and media procedures, it reproduces administrative violence (Spade 2015) toward the trans community by continually dismissing their gender identities.

The mug shots and legal names were placed alongside the same report in which Jorge Gutierrez, organizer at Familia: Trans Queer Liberation Movement,[16] was quoted as stating that, "trans women are being thrown in solitary confinement. They're still being sexually abused, physically abused. They're not being respected for their gender identity." Additionally, the ABC 7 news report included a statement from ICE saying that, "ICE has a strict zero tolerance policy for any kind of abuse or inappropriate behavior in its facilities and takes any allegations of such mistreatment seriously . . . committed to upholding an immigration detention system that prioritizes the health, safety, and welfare of all those in our care in custody, including lesbian, bisexual, and trans (LGBT) individuals." The news report ended by stating that protesters would wait for all five detainees to be released. While the news report aired footage of the protest, it did not include any footage of the protesters waiting outside of the police department. Although this news report may seem like a generic news report, in a minute and a half it reinscribes limited narratives of the trans and the LGBTQ community.[17] Media and visual representations play a key role in ascribing unequal levels of value to different groups of people, thereby placing communities of color at odds with each other while always maintaining Black as the disavowed category.

In much more holistic coverage, the local newspaper, the *Orange County Register*, also reported the protest on their website.[18] They began their article by centering the story of Luna Rivas, an undocumented trans woman from Honduras, who had been recently released from the Santa Ana jail. Rivas was detained for six months in the special designated area for the LGBTQ undocumented people and had been transferred across different detention centers after she was detained when she reentered the United States. The article mentioned that protesters would remain waiting outside the Santa Ana police department until everyone arrested was released. Rivas wrote, "They rallied and sometimes danced awaiting the release of those arrested." The news reporter connected the protest to the national movement working to end the detention of undocumented people who are detained while awaiting their immigration hearings. Unlike the local news station coverage, the article did not include mug shots of the arrested protesters. Instead, it included images of the protest and the dancing that took place. Cacho points to the importance of cultural production that opens up moments of possibility that speak against rightlessness, "When the story about the value of lives cannot be told, the visual can be an alternative mode of expression" (2012, 155). Thus, the visual serves to disrupt the normalization of irrecuperable bodies such as trans undocumented women. In this case, the written article resulted in a much more informed, humanizing, and nuanced piece. ABC 7 also published an online version of the story on their website, simply reiterating what was in the clip.

In 2015, ABC 7 was ranked as generating the highest rating for their evening newscast reaching about 250,000 viewers.[19] In contrast, the *Orange County Register* operates at a much smaller scale through paid subscribers that have access to exclusive content. What is starkly distinct between the coverage of

ABC 7 news and the article in the *Orange County Register* is the treatment of the stories of undocumented trans and LGBTQ communities. The news reporter for the *Orange County Register*, Roxana Kopetman (2015) did not reinforce gender binaries and did not correlate criminality through the use of mug shots. In this way, Kopetman (2015) was disrupting the process and maintenance of who is deemed valuable and who is irrecuperable. Feminist scholar Gayatri Gopinath (2005) also explains how the logic of patriarchy operates in the visual, through silences and omissions that exclude and police queer diasporic narratives. Gopinath (2005) writes that a queer reading recovers the "desires, practices, and subjectivities rendered impossible and unimaginable" (11). By drawing on both Cacho (2012) and Gopinath (2005), I provide visual, sonic, and spatial possibilities and insight into the civil disobedience and the vigil that demanded justice for the brutal murder of trans immigrant rights activist, Zoraida Reyes. This approach makes visible what may be unimaginable or missed by a white heteropatriarchal normative framework.

Reclaiming Spaces and Joy: Recognizing the Full Humanity of Transgender Undocumented Immigrants

In the civil disobedience that took place in Santa Ana, California, protesters marched from Flower Street to the Santa Ana police station for about an hour and waited for the release of all five detainees. About twenty minutes after standing in front of the police station, a group of undocumented trans women from Central America and Mexico began to share their stories about the violent and inhumane conditions they experienced inside the detention centers.[20] Some of these women had been detained for two months, others six months, and others had been shuffled from center to center for over sixteen months. They came from different detention centers from all over the country. Rivas, for example had only been released two days prior to the civil disobedience from a detention center in Santa Ana. Others had made their way from Arizona detention centers to Santa Ana and San Francisco for other scheduled actions. As was the case for many undocumented trans migrants, the guards had misgendered and humiliated them inside the detention center. Their testimonies were powerful in voicing the multiple abuses they experienced inside immigration detention centers based on their gender and sexual identity.

The testimonies were followed by a period of awkward silence and many of the community members and activists took this silence as a cue to leave. Suddenly, an organizer connected their iPhone to a speaker and pop music began to play. Immediately the mood shifted, and people began to dance. This important and moving moment of resistance was not captured by the mainstream media but is exemplary in showing the ways that mainstream practices of sharing information, such as ABC 7 in this case, miss opportune moments that shift existing paradigms of how race and gender are understood within the discourse of immigration.

The importance of sound cannot be underestimated in the aftermath of the civil disobedience because it immediately transformed the ambiance of the space. Sound has the power to inform us of what we know and how we understand the visual and space. Gaye Theresa Johnson's (2013) notion of "sonic expressions of spatial entitlement" is useful in understanding how sound can transform and reclaim space. Spatial entitlement is helpful for those who are systematically marginalized because technology serves as the medium to build communities when people are able to reclaim both physical and imaginary spaces. Johnson describes that sonic spatial entitlement can "constitute some of the most eloquent articulations of the right to space. Sounds have shared meanings that are informed by and give inspiration to the social, political, and economic power relations experienced by their products" (2013, 85). Indeed, sonic spatial entitlement has the power to suspend time and space, just as dancing and music have the power to erupt into moments of joy and empowerment.

Forms of spatial entitlement often go unnoticed because they happen every day and are not extraordinary moments. For example, the aftermath of the protest may seem inconsequential, but to those of us present in that space, it felt humanizing, joyful, and empowering. Perhaps it is no coincidence that the first song played was "Todos Me Miran" (Everyone Looks at Me),[21] that also happened to be one of Zoraida's favorite songs. "Todos Me Miran" has been regarded as a queer Latinx anthem[22] that confronts issues of gender performance while also contesting heteronormative romantic relationships. The song starts up slowly and then builds momentum. The lyrics and music video emphasize the ways in which heteropatriarchy weighs down on women, trans, and queer people. Some of the lyrics read, "Tú me hiciste sentir que no valía / Y mis lágrimas calleron a tus pies / Me miraba en el espejo y no me hallaba" (You made me feel unworthy / My tears fell at your feet / I couldn't find myself in my own reflection [Trevi 2006]). The lyrics could be applied to a tumultuous relationship but are also applicable to the ways that society devalues the lives of queer and trans people, including those that are undocumented. But as the beat picks up, it signals a shift toward empowerment and agency. Trevi responds with, "Y me solté el cabello, me vestí de reina / me puse tacones, me pinté bien bella" (I let my hair down, I dressed like a queen / I put my heels on, and my make-up made me look beautiful [Trevi 2006]). The song moves the listener toward sentiments of empowerment fueled by the power of femininity. Considering the sterile Santa Ana police department in which the action took place, the sounds emerging from a small speaker transformed the moment by allowing us to imagine the radical possibilities of a just world sparked by happiness.

The song title and chorus "Todos me miran" speaks to queer, trans, and undocumented visibility. Through the sonic and participation in the civil disobedience and the aftermath, undocumented trans and queer people intentionally declared themselves visible as queer, as trans, as gender nonconforming, as undocumented by taking control of the gaze and objectification that are enacted onto racialized bodies. This reclamation of the gaze achieved through the sonic is connected to a queer of color politic that does not necessarily align with what has become the "normative" coming-out narrative by the mainstream LGBTQ movement, the "coming out of the shadows," and UndocuQueer. The experiences of joy outside the police stations are also important because they demonstrate happiness that is dependent on their community and not recognition by the nation-state.

Through most analytical lenses, these moments of dancing and joking around by marginalized communities such as undocumented trans women of color are likely to go unregistered, dismissed as frivolous and inconsequential. Sound may seem as though it is neutral, heard and understood in the same way. However, the way we listen and understand sound is framed within white heteropatriarchal supremacist auditory. Sound, so often connected through the volume of our voices and the music associated with different groups of people, is closely tied to racial ways of knowing (Cacho 2012, 2) and racialized assumptions (Stoever 2016) and I would add gendered assumptions. In this context, it is important that the first song played by the undocumented trans women was a Spanish pop song. This is meaningful because it creates a register of familiarity through language and also produces a sense of belonging and freedom that queer dance parties or clubs create for queer people of color. Additionally, the empowering message of the song and the sense of freedom create moments of joy. Said differently, this joy resists and ruptures the heteropatriarchal supremacist logics operating in this public space, outside this police station.

Organizers specifically selected the location where the civil disobedience took place because of the multiple state agencies located within the same vicinity. This area of the city houses the city court, the sheriff's department, immigration detention center, coroner, and the police department. The concentration of state surveillance and power point to the significance and importance of the organic transformation that took place through the music that was played. Music and dancing, then, allowed these activists to momentarily reclaim space, giving it a new meaning, and to replace the violence of state surveillance, the source of so much of their suffering.

As other people were leaving the Santa Ana police department, they were confused by what was happening. This interruption of meaning of space creates moments of confusion and illegibility that speak to the possibilities of imagining alternate ways of living and existing. This parallels the experience of the trans community and how so-called gender transgression halts the gender binary. Furthermore, Santa Ana is an important place of inquiry due to the current struggle to claim the right to space as the city is undergoing gentrification.[23] Therefore, the sounds of Spanish pop music combined with the presence of trans and queer bodies of color further attest to the contestation over space that happened there. Alluding to the mom and pop shops that play music loudly in attempts to draw in customers, creating a lively shopping experience, Spanish music serves as a *haunting* and reminder of the displaced Latinx community that lived in Santa Ana.

From a distance, the festive mood, the dancing and music, would suggest that we were taking part in a celebration. As undocumented and documented trans women waved the gay pride and trans pride flags, time was momentarily suspended, allowing spectators and participants to briefly forget that the gathering was an immigrant rights rally. The banners demanding the end to all deportations mark the important reason of the gathering but also their colorful aesthetic added to the festive mood. The gay pride and trans pride flags also serve as important visual signifiers. The use of the flags as props to claim space by undocumented and documented queer trans women exemplifies a temporary claim to space, accompanied by their dance adding an element of camp, the feminine, and glamor. The flags were waved and served as an accessory to the lip synching. Additionally, undocumented and documented trans women disrupt the perceptions of what a flag represents, such as national pride or even imperialist claims of space.

These undocumented and documented trans women shift the meaning by laying claim to space by smudging the boundaries of who belongs and who does not belong against the narrative of racist, sexist, transphobic immigration laws, detention centers, and police departments. Johnson (2013, xi) speaks to this method of spatial entitlement and claiming space that "requires an alternative understanding and construction of the meaning of citizenship."

In this way, the undocumented and documented trans women are directly challenging the arbitrary construction of citizenship as designed by the state, through the use of flags that represent marginalized communities. Their actions serve as claims of inclusion that traverse the imperial logic of borders.

Some of the undocumented trans women who were recently released escaped transphobic and sexist violence in their hometowns, and upon arrival in the United States were faced with white supremacist, transphobic, and racist violence at the hands of the state when they were detained in immigration detention centers. Yet, through their perseverance and continuous fight to share their stories of horrific violence, these women were still able to feel empowered again by temporarily unsettling the intended use of the police department by changing it into a dance floor. In this way, undocumented trans women shift how we measure a successful action or protest. While the detainees were released later that day, the action and aftermath was successful in providing space to share stories and also to dance and celebrate life. The harsh conditions they experienced did not block them from also experiencing joy. While journalists, activists, and scholars may want to focus on defining the success of an action by the number of attendees or the successful closure of an intersection, I argue that we should instead redirect our attention to the ways that trans and queer people disrupt space. This is a small but important victory because through dance, music, and laughter dignity was reclaimed.

The second song to play was "Run the World" by Beyoncé. Run the World offers an empowering feminist anthem through lyrics such as "Get on your grind / To the other men / That respect what I do / Please accept my shine" and the repetitive chorus "Who run the world? / Girls" offers a call and response with a fast beat. The assertion of spatial entitlement through the use of popular culture created space, as Johnson (2013, 198) theorizes, for the possibility of coalitional and solidarity politics to form. My intent is not to center the English language as a universal language that unites everyone regardless of country of origin, but instead I would like to shift our focus to the ways that sonic spatial entitlement operates across popular culture and music. José Esteban Muñoz argued that queers of color continually shift through what he called disidentifications as, "the third mode of dealing with dominant ideology, one that neither opts to assimilate within such a structure nor strictly opposes it. . . . This 'working on and against' is a strategy that tries to transform a cultural logic from within, always laboring to enact permanent structural change while at the same time valuing the importance of local everyday struggles of resistance" (1991, 11–12).

The language and lyrics become secondary as dancers are moved by the sound and what the artist, in this case Beyoncé, represents. Furthermore, Muñoz would argue that queer people of color also create a "counterpolitics that contests the hegemonic supremacy of the majoritarian public sphere" and offer "the minoritarian subject a space to situate itself in history and thus seize social agency" (Muñoz 1999, 1). Beyoncé's image and sound provide the sonic space for such an assemblage of solidarity to take place. In particular, Black women and women of color are often denied space and silenced. The music video provides space to reclaim and take up space through sound and the movements of their bodies.

Conclusion

These minute performances and actions are often ignored or viewed as superficial movements that do not count as "real" political actions in the way that getting arrested or giving a profound speech count. Yet precisely because of the superficial attributes of pop culture and music, when people hear the music, they feel more relaxed and that adds to the creation of a space that unites people through music. This creates a space of comfort that enables people to connect on a different level and this connection has the possibility to create moments of solidarities across differences. Moreover, it all stands in opposition to the idea that protest should be carried out in a masculine and militant manner that is politically aggressive. Instead, dancing challenges gendered ideas about organizing and social movements, centering femme aesthetics through a refusal of the hypermasculine attitude of detention centers and police departments.

My focus on the dancing that took place after the civil disobedience is not to deflect the importance of the events and sacrifice of those who were arrested, but rather I shine a light on nuanced moments that can inform political subjectivity and challenge hegemony in different ways. The undocumented and documented trans women engaged in a trans immigrant spatial entitlement, where they challenged multiple notions of space and right to space by contesting ideas about belonging, gender, race, class, nationality, citizenship. Through music and the waving of flags they also inspired creative community formations.

In taking up Galarte's (2014) challenge to listen to what our trans community is telling us, this chapter suggests different ways of listening that allow for a distinctive register of joy. Doing so creates the time and space to listen to what may at first appear to be trivial moments. But the civil disobedience demonstrates these moments offer the possibility of reclaiming space and our joy. In intense political moments it becomes much more so important to stop and intentionally listen to our queer and trans gestures of joy.

NOTES

1. "Trans Woman's Mother, 'Other Family' Mourn Her Death." http://www.latimes.com/local/la-me-0625-zoraida-20140625-story.html.

2. See, for example, https://www.huffingtonpost.com/2014/12/16/transgender-women-candy_n_6335864.html.

3. "De Colores Welcomes Entire Spectrum." https://www.ocregister.com/2014/07/10/decolores-queer-welcomes-entire-spectrum/.

4. Founded in 2009, De Colores OC is an organization in Orange County that creates opportunities for social engagement, community visibility, and political activism by organizing cultural events, support groups, civic actions, and an annual conference. https://www.facebook.com/pg/Lafamilialgbtq/about/?ref=page_internal.

5. For example, Victoria Arellano, an undocumented trans woman, was detained for driving without a license and driving under the influence of alcohol. Specific to her experience as a trans woman, she died shackled to a hospital bed after being denied adequate HIV treatment in an immigration detention center in San Pedro, California (Potts 2011; Contreras 2012).

6. Heteronormativity works to normalize behaviors and expectations from society that are tied to heterosexuality and gender binaries of man and woman.

7. Sadiya Hartman, "Venus in Two Acts."

8. "'Gay Panic' Defense Still Used in Violence Cases May Be Banned by New Federal Bill." https://abcnews.go.com/US/gay-panic-defense-violence-cases-banned-federal-bill/story?id=56662902.

9. "Banning the 'Trans Panic' Defense." http://bilerico.lgbtqnation.com/2008/09/banning_the_trans_panic_defense.php.

10. http://www.getequal.org/.

11. http://familiatqlm.org/.

12. http://www.notonemoredeportation.com/.

13. "Dozens Protest Incarceration of LGBTQ Immigrants in Santa Ana; 5 Activists Arrested." http://abc7.com/news/dozens-protest-incarceration-of-lgbtq-immigrants-in-santa-ana/746801/.

14. http://www.advocate.com/politics/trans/2015/05/28/five-arrested-california-rally-end-trans-immigration-detention.

15. http://abc7.com/news/dozens-protest-incarceration-of-lgbtq-immigrants-in-santa-ana/746801/.

16. Familia: Trans Queer Liberation Movement was founded at the beginning of 2014 by trans and queer immigrants, undocumented and allies, youth leaders and parents.

17. Zoraida, who experienced limited access to higher education as an undocumented trans woman of color, organized around the DREAM Act and access to higher education for undocumented youth. Notably, many of the articles written after her

death emphasized her trans identity but ignored her immigration status. In particular, the article in the *Los Angeles Times*, "Transgender Woman's Mother, 'Other Family' Mourn her Death," states that she attended UCSB "but dropped out because of tuition costs" (http://www.latimes.com/local/la-me-0625-zoraida-20140625-story.html). Although they note that she was active in multiple immigrant rights organizations, they still ignored her immigration status. This is an example of how trans identities are fetishized and compartmentalized in the media, thereby obscuring the intersectional struggles that they experience.

18. "'There's a Lack of Respect': Immigrant Advocates Rally in Santa Ana for Transgender Detainees." https://www.ocregister.com/2015/05/29/theres-a-lack-of-respect-immigrant-advocates-rally-in-santa-ana-for-transgender-detainees/.

19. "KABC-TV Retains Lead for 6 p.m., 11 p.m. Newscasts in L.A." http://www.latimes.com/entertainment/envelope/cotown/la-et-ct-la-tv-radio-station-ratings-20150303-story.html.

20. I participated in the civil disobedience. After the arrests took place I walked over to the front of the Santa Ana police department. I was present and witnessed when the undocumented trans women shared their testimonies.

21. This song by Mexican pop icon Gloria Trevi was released in her 2006 album, La trayectoria (The Trajectory).

22. http://www.billboard.com/articles/columns/latin/7393394/latin-lgbt-anthems.

23. http://www.nytimes.com/2011/10/31/us/in-santa-ana-new-faces-and-a-contentious-revival.html?ref=us&_r=1.

REFERENCES

Anzaldúa, Gloria. 2007. *Borderlands/La Frontera: The New Mestiza*. San Francisco: Aunt Lute.

Bhartia, Aashti. 2010. "Fictions of Law: The Trial of Sulaiman Oladokun, or Reading of Kafka in an Immigration Court." In *The Deportation Regime: Sovereignty, Space, and the Freedom Movement*, edited by Nicholas De Genova and Nathalie Peutz, 329–50. Durham, NC: Duke University Press.

Cacho, Lisa. 2012. *Social Death: Racialized Rightlessness and the Criminalization of the Unprotected*. New York: New York University Press.

Cantú, Lionel, Jr. 2002. "De Ambiente: Queer Tourism and the Shifting Boundaries of Mexican Male Sexualities." *Gay and Lesbian Quarterly (GLQ): A Journal of Lesbian and Gay Studies* 8(1): 139–66. https://muse.jhu.edu/article/12195.

Cohen, Cathy J. 1997. "Punks, Bulldaggers, and Welfare Queens: The Radical Potential of Queer Politics?" *Gay and Lesbian Quaterly (GLQ): A Journal of Lesbian and Gay Studies* 3(4): 437–65. https://doi.org/10.1215/10642684-3-4-437.

Combahee River Collective. 1978. "The Combahee River Collective Statement." http://circuitous.org/scraps/combahee.html.

Contreras, Irina. 2012. "Descado en Los Angeles: Cycles of Invisible Resistance." In *Beyond Wall and Cages: Prisons, Borders, and Global Crisis*, edited by Jenna M. Loyd, Matt Mitchelson, and Andrew Burridge, 325–36. Athens: University of Georgia Press.

Coutin, Susan B. 2010. "Exiled by Law: Deportation and Inviability of Life." In *The Deportation Regime: Sovereignty, Space, and the Freedom Movement*, edited by Nicholas De Genova and Nathalie Peutz, 351–70. Durham, NC: Duke University Press.

Decena, Carlos Ulises. 2008. "Tacit Subjects." *Gay and Lesbian Quarterly (GLQ): A Journal of Lesbian and Gay Studies* 14(2–3): 339–59. https://doi.org/10.1215/10642684-2007-036.

De Genova, Nicholas. 2010. "The Deportation Regime: Sovereignty, Space, and the Freedom Movement." In *The Deportation Regime: Sovereignty, Space, and the Freedom Movement*, edited by Nicholas De Genova and Nathalie Peutz, 33–68. Durham, NC: Duke University Press.

de la maza perez tamayo, a. 2013. "(Re) Producing Transgender Invisibility in Asylum Law." *Aztlán: A Journal of Chicano Studies* 39(1): 235–51.

Ferguson, Roderick A. 2003. *Aberrations in Black: Toward a Queer of Color Critique*. Minneapolis: University of Minnesota Press.

Galarte, Francisco J. 2014. "On Trans* Chican@s Amor, Justicia, y Dignidad." *Aztlán: A Journal of Chicano Studies*, 39(1): 229–35.

Golash-Boza, Tanya. 2013. "From Legal to 'Illegal': The Deportation of Legal Permanent Residents from the United States." In *Constructing Migrant "Illegality": Critiques, Experiences, and Responses*, edited by Cecilia Menjívar and Daniel Kanstroom, 203–24. New York: Cambridge University Press.

Gopinath, Gayatri. 2005. *Impossible Desires: Queer Diasporas and South Asian Public Culture*. Durham, NC: Duke University Press.

Gordon, Avery. 2008. *Ghostly Matters: Haunting and Sociological Imaginations*. Minneapolis: University of Minnesota Press.

Halberstam, Jack. 2005. *In a Queer Time and Place: Transgender Bodies, Subcultural Lives*. New York: New York University Press.

Hauser, Christine. 2018. "Transgender Woman Shot Dead in Motel Is 7th Killed in U.S. This Year, Rights Advocates Say." *New York Times*, March 30, 2018. https://www.nytimes.com/2018/03/30/us/transgender-woman-killed-baton-rouge.html.

Johnson, Gaye Theresa. 2013. *Spaces of Conflict, Sounds of Solidarity: Music, Race, and Spatial Entitlement*. Berkeley: University of California Press.

Kopetman, Roxana. 2015. "'There's a Lack of Respect': Immigrant Advocates Rally in Santa Ana for Transgender Detainees." *Orange County Register*, May 29, 2015. https://www.ocregister.com/2015/05/29/theres-a-lack-of-respect-immigrant-advocates-rally-in-santa-ana-for-transgender-detainees/.

Luibheid, Eithne. 2002. *Entry Denied: Controlling Sexuality at the Border*. Minneapolis: University of Minnesota Press.

Luibheid, Eithne. 2008. "Queer/Migration: An Unruly Body of Scholarship." *Gay Lesbian Quarterly (GLQ): A Journal of Lesbian and Gay Studies* 14(2–3): 169–90. https://muse.jhu.edu/article/241318.

Luibheid, Eithne, and Lionel Cantu Jr. 2005. *Queer Migrations: Sexuality, U.S. Citizenship, and Border Crossings*, edited by Eithne Luibheid and Lionel Cantu. Minneapolis: University of Minnesota Press.

Muñoz, José Esteban. 1999. *Disidentifications: Queer of Color and the Performance of Politics*. Minneapolis: University of Minnesota Press.

Patterson, Orlando. 1982. *Slavery and Social Death: A Contemporary Study*. Cambridge, MA: Harvard University Press.

Potts, Michelle C. 2011. "Regulatory Sites: Management, Confinement and HIV/AIDS." In *Captive Genders: Trans Embodiment and the Prison Industrial Complex*, edited by Eric A. Stanley and Nat Smith, 99–111. Chico, CA: AK Press.

Reddy, Chandan. 2005. "Asian Diasporas, Neoliberalism, and Family: Reviewing the Case for Homosexual Asylum in the Context of Family Rights." *Social Text* 23(3): 101–19. http://courses.washington.edu/com597j/pdfs/reddy,asiandiasporas.pdf.

Roque-Ramirez, Horacio N. 2003 "'That's my place!': Negotiating Racial, Sexual, and Gender Politics in San Francisco's Gay Latino Alliance, 1975–1983." *Journal of the History of Sexuality* 12(2): 224–58. https://muse.jhu.edu/article/48726.

Spade, Dean. 2015. *Normal Life: Administrative Violence, Critical Trans Politics, and the Limits of the Law*. Durham, NC: Duke University Press.

Stoever, Jennifer Lynn. 2016. *The Sonic Color Line: Race and the Cultural Politics of Listening*. New York: New York University Press.

Trevi, Gloria. 2006. "Todos Me Miran." On *La Trayectoria*. Universal Music Group. https://www.billboard.com/articles/columns/latin/7393394/latin-lgbt-anthems.

LUCÍA LEÓN

9

Legalization through Marriage

When Love and Papers Converge

Leslie entered the United States at the age of seven with her mother and two siblings to reunite with their father in Los Angeles. At the time of our meeting, at the age of twenty-four, she had been undocumented for nearly sixteen years. As we began our conversation about her experience applying for adjustment of legal status through her marital relationship, she placed between us her portfolio containing her application packet for U.S. Citizenship and Immigration Services (USCIS). Looking through the contents of her portfolio, I asked how she felt about the process of putting her application together. After a long pause, Leslie pieced together her thoughts:

> What's the feeling? I guess slightly uncomfortable. It's not really a big deal but the thought of me collecting intimate moments to legitimize our relationship feels a little uncomfortable. Not too much, just because of the importance of it. I guess I didn't think that I was ever really going to get papers. It's not something that, oh, you know, I'm going to be married and fix my papers. I thought I was going to be undocumented for a while, especially with the current administration, so it's kind of like you gotta do what you gotta do even if it feels slightly uncomfortable. I'm going to just lean right in and do my best and try to do a better job at checking in with my partner.

Leslie's understanding of the process as one that involves "collecting intimate moments to legitimize our relationship" made her feel uncomfortable, yet she was also aware that it was a necessary step in a particularly uncertain moment. For Leslie, as for others I will discuss in this chapter, her decision to enter marriage is one based on the convergence of both her romantic relationship with her partner and the circumstances that have led to legalization through marriage as a limited and timely option. After all, much is at stake for Leslie. Although she is a Deferred Action for Childhood Arrivals (DACA) beneficiary, the temporality and precariousness of the program leaves her ability to work and remain in the United States at the whim of the political climate.

Since the 1960s, a series of restrictive and punitive immigration policies have limited pathways to legalization even as the number of undocumented immigrants has grown notably. For example, the 1965 Immigration and Nationality Act placed racially restrictive national caps on the Western Hemisphere, including Mexico (Golash-Boza 2012). These restrictive caps were too low to accommodate the migration waves of Mexicans, resulting in prolonged indeterminate statuses directly linked to this policy change. Moreover, policies like the 1996 Illegal Immigration Reform and Immigrant Responsibility Act (IIRIRA) criminalized migration and led to increased deportations and diminished options for legal immigration into the United States from Mexico. As a result, for many undocumented immigrants, marriage continues to be the only viable option for adjustment of their prolonged immigration status. Not surprisingly, in their long-term experience with illegality, the undocumented young adults I spoke with also shared Leslie's hyperawareness of marriage as their only pathway for legal status, along with their hope that obtaining legal permanent residency will profoundly alter their lives.

Drawing on interviews with twelve heterosexual and queer undocumented Latina and Latino young adults in Los Angeles, California, I consider how they experience and navigate the marriage-based legalization process.[1] I pay particular attention to the ways 1.5-generation undocumented young adults negotiate the social and cultural notions of "marriage for papers" and "marriage for love." I demonstrate that undocumented young adults' decisions to transition into marriage are much more than an entry into family formation or legalization; rather, the process involves a twofold decision caught in the uncomfortable convergence of "marriage for love *and* papers."

In conjunction with social and cultural expectations of marriage I also examine undocumented young adults' legal consciousness, a framework that makes visible how people interpret, experience, and apply the law to their lives (Ewick and Silbey 1998). Through a legal consciousness lens, this chapter demonstrates how young adults' understanding of immigration laws, through prolonged experiences with illegality, intersect with social and cultural norms about marriage to inform their decisions about legalization. This mutually constitutive relationship between law and norms leads undocumented young adults to make decisions about marriage rooted in both love and a need for legalization—placing young adults in a mutually conflicting predicament. They find themselves in a catch-22. The process through which they must prove that their marriages are "marriages for love," not "marriages for papers," places them at risk of being accused of marriage fraud and facing dire consequences, including deportation. Yet, in their efforts to legitimize their marriages in the face of arbitrary immigration laws, the burdens of a bureaucratic and invasive legalization process push their love in directions that feel inauthentic.

The Study of the 1.5-Generation Undocumented Youth

To date, much of the research in the emerging field of *illegality* studies has centered on the 1.5-generation undocumented young adults' daily lives, opportunities, and outcomes within educational and labor sectors (Abrego 2006, 2008, 2011; Abrego and Gonzales 2010; Gonzales 2011, 2016). Researchers are only now pursuing a more holistic approach to undocumented young people's lives as they enter adulthood. For example, there is recent growth in the area of mental health, showing that undocumented immigrants report higher acculturation stress than their documented counterparts (Gonzales, Suarez-Orozco, and Dedios-Sanguineti 2013). Other studies have also found that 1.5-generation undocumented immigrants experience gender differences in the realm of dating and parenthood (Abrego 2014; Enriquez 2015; Pila 2016). Here, I extend these studies to the realm of marriage and legalization.

In a related set of studies, emerging scholarship regarding the adjustment of the legalization process has focused almost exclusively on the perspective of first-generation undocumented immigrants or the experiences of U.S. citizen sponsors married to undocumented migrants (Abrams 2007; Mossaad 2016; Gomberg-Muñoz 2016; Lopez 2015; Dreby 2015; Golash-Boza 2012). Little, however, is known about the nexus of generation and the legalization process among 1.5-generation young adults. For some undocumented young adults, their new family formations, primarily in the form of marital relationships with a U.S. citizen spouse, deem them eligible for a legalization pathway. While marriage to a U.S. citizen is not an automatic pathway to citizenship, some members of this generation are becoming eligible for legalization through marriage due to both their entry into family reunification categories (Pila 2016; Enriquez 2015) and the emergence of new policies that may provide reprieve from previous barriers (Creighton et al. 2013).[2] At this critical moment, as questions are emerging about how 1.5-generation immigrants experience the transition into adulthood, I consider the experiences of undocumented young adults who enter adulthood as they navigate legalization through marriage.

As a point of departure for this study, I want to highlight my own positionality. I vividly remember the interviews, focus groups, and surveys I filled out for graduate students and professors who did not share my undocumented experience. As I, and other undocumented youth, shared our stories with academics, many of us were simultaneously sharing our stories to a broader audience— to journalists, at town halls, during rallies and protests. We did so in efforts to expand an understanding of our daily lives, to claim our humanity, and to seek justice for our fellow undocumented peers and our families. Our generation has not only contributed our stories to the literature about our lives, we have also read, exalted, and critiqued the body of work on undocumented immigrants. Now we, the formerly undocumented, and the many who remain undocumented, find ourselves in the academy. We have our own voice to contribute to the knowledge of our experiences as we grow and bring our whole selves to understanding the ways in which prolonged illegality has affected the more personal aspects of our lives. As such, this work is also guided by the efforts of undocumented youth organizing to demand our rights and to tell our own stories. I bring my own experience as a formerly undocumented Latina who adjusted her immigration status through marriage. Intimately familiar with the nuances of navigating this process, my work is informed by the complexity of what it means to fight for our love and humanity in the midst of a bureaucratic and dehumanizing system.

Immigration Law Changes Limiting Pathways to Legalization

Since its creation in 1965, family reunification privileges nuclear family ties and has become the largest category for legal entry (Abrams 2007; Mossaad 2016), particularly for first-generation immigrant women (Salcido and Menjívar 2012). While other legalization processes (like employment-based, asylum, and refugee) can provide immigrants with a pathway to legal status, marriage continues to be the primary avenue for gaining legal status (Salcido and Menjívar 2012). Family reunification modifications in the 1980s and 1990s have continued to expand state structures and policies that construct, define, (re)produce, (re)unite and divide families, resulting in lasting implications for immigrants and their families (Abrego 2014; Boehm 2012; Fix and Zimmerman 2001; Gomberg-Muñoz 2016; Hagan 1998). Moreover, changes in immigration policies during the 1990s influenced a variety of factors associated with the legalization process: the types of petitions migrants are eligible for, the length and cost of the process, and the level of deportation risk undertaken when applying for legalization; making the obtainment of legal residency increasingly difficult while also leading to higher rates of deportations (Abrego 2014). Consequently, although in theory family reunification claims to reunite families, scholars argue that in practice we need these policies because immigration laws separate families to begin with (Abrego 2014; Boehm 2012; Hagan 1998; Menjívar, Abrego, and Schmalzbauer 2016; Salcido and Menjívar 2012).

The undocumented young adult participants I interviewed experience their immigration statuses and legalization processes within the context of these restrictive and punitive immigration laws. Indeed, many of our conversations centered on the ways that immigration law changes and the legalization process itself have restricted their entry into legality and affected their personal decisions about marriage. While the legalization process can vary across applicants, the legal permanent residency process presented below provides an overview of the restrictive and bureaucratic nature of the process.

Legal Permanent Residency Process for Undocumented Young Adults

There are two main pathways to apply for lawful permanent residency or a "green card," contingent on where the migrant is living at the time of application. One such pathway is for an individual to apply as a status adjuster when living in the United States at the time of application (Mossaad 2016). To apply as a status adjuster, migrants are required to demonstrate that they are admissible under the Immigration and Nationality Act of 1965.[3] First, they must fit one of the three categories of admissibility: through family reunification, an employer petition, or a refugee/asylum petition. The women and men I interviewed were all undocumented immigrants already living in the United States and adjusting their status from undocumented/unauthorized[4] to lawful permanent residence via family reunification policies. As such, their family reunification eligibility to adjust their immigration status was legally determined by their connection as immediate relatives of United States citizens or residents. Their only eligibility would be as spouses, parents, or unmarried children younger than twenty-one years of age. However, because many undocumented young adults aged out of being eligible for legalization as children of U.S. residents or citizens, their only remaining avenue for legalization is through marital relationship to a U.S. citizen or resident.

An undocumented person's status as an immediate relative to their U.S. citizen spouse is not an automatic qualifier. The immigrant's type of entry into the United States plays a critical role in their eligibility. Undocumented youth who entered the country with a visa are eligible to apply when they become spouses of U.S. citizens. For immigrants who entered the country without authorization—typically by crossing the border without inspection—their unlawful entry into the United States is punished with significant barriers to legalization. Importantly, the sanctions against unlawful entry have blocked many undocumented young adults from legalizing their status through marriage to a U.S. citizen. However, the passage of DACA and consequently, DACA recipients' ability to exit and reenter the country legally through Advanced Parole has opened the door for some undocumented young adults to become eligible to apply through marriage-based Adjustment of Status (AOS) petitions.[5]

Upon meeting the eligibility requirements to apply for marital-based adjustment of status, undocumented young adults may begin the bureaucratic application process (Boehm 2012; Lopez 2015; Gomberg-Muñoz 2016). There are a number of components to the application, which includes three main parts: (1) official documents to prove eligibility and identities, (2) USCIS application forms,[6] and (3) supportive evidence to substantiate marriage. The third component, supportive evidence, holds most variability, as it has no set standard guidelines on what constitutes sufficient evidence to legitimize a marriage. Consequently, this third component makes couples most vulnerable when they face the discretionary power written into seemingly arbitrary immigration policies. The USCIS guideline to these documents reads: "Supporting evidence of your relationship, such as copies of any documentation regarding joint assets or liabilities you and your spouse may have together."[7] Furthermore, USCIS documents state, "If your eligibility is based on your marriage, supportive evidence of the relationship must be presented." "Supportive evidence" can include: "photos, correspondence or any other documents you feel may substantiate your relationship." Following USCIS's guidelines, applicants' understanding of supportive evidence mainly translates to: joint tax returns, joint bank/credit card statements, joint utility bills and rental agreements, photos, correspondence, letters of support, and any other documents that "substantiate your relationship."

Following the gathering of these documents, in Los Angeles the process can take approximately six months before an interview is set. The interview requires the married couple to attend an interview with a USCIS officer who reviews their application and original documents and may request additional information about the applicant's admissibility requirements and the marital relationship. If the AOS application is a success, a conditional legal permanent residency or "green card" is granted for a conditional two-year period. Contrary to the "permanent" language, this green card is a provisional two-year legal status that requires applicants to maintain eligibility. Moreover, because they legalized through a marital petition, applicants must also prove to be "married in good faith," primarily by remaining married for the conditional period in order to be eligible to remove the conditional status. At the two-year mark, conditional residents must apply to remove conditions and become legal permanent residents (LPRS). Removing the conditional status of their residency is mandatory and critical in maintaining lawful status. Applicants who fail to remove conditions risk having their legal status terminated and being placed in removal proceedings. After the removal of conditional status, applicants' legal permanent residency becomes renewable every ten years. LPRS who reside continuously in the United States for a minimum of three years (five years for all other LPR categories), can then choose to either renew their legal permanent residency every ten years or apply for naturalization.[8] If they decide to naturalize, applicants undertake a new petition that requires them to demonstrate good moral character, ability to read, write, and speak English, and pass a U.S. history and government test. Taking the process for its totality, for those who obtain citizenship through a marriage-based application, this process requires them to undertake three distinct applications: conditional residency, renewal of residency, and naturalization. Given the high stakes for young adults who undertake this rare opportunity to adjust their long-term undocumented status, their ability to navigate this legalization pathway requires an understanding of immigration law for each distinct immigration application, its requirements and consequences.

Legal Consciousness Framework

Developed within the field of law and society in the 1980s and 1990s, the framework of legal consciousness makes visible how people interpret, experience, and apply the law to their lives (Ewick and Silbey 1998). Migrants' legal consciousness is a complex nexus of law and social life, developed through formal and informal channels, such as interactions with legal institutions and actors and everyday activities (Menjívar and Lakhani 2016). A formal application of law can control behavior; however, in practice, people's interpretation, mediated by their social locations and norms, can affect how they understand

and apply the law. Thus, legal consciousness intersects with and is mutually constitutive of social norms. Moreover, since legal consciousness is socially constructed, individuals' interpretations and application of the law can shift and change over time (Ewick and Silbey 1998; Abrego 2008).

Among undocumented young adults, legal consciousness has been found to have developed as a result of their migration experiences and the social context and norms surrounding them (Abrego 2011). Scholars have also demonstrated that the legal consciousness of undocumented youth stems from their experiences with the educational system (Abrego 2006, 2008, 2011; Gonzales 2011, 2016; Gleeson and Gonzales 2012) and as they experience changes in immigration law that make them hyperaware of the consequences of law, such as the implementation and rescindment of DACA (Nicholls 2013; Mena and Gomberg-Muñoz 2016). I employ a legal consciousness framework to examine how undocumented young adults understand immigration laws in conjunction with social and cultural expectations of marriage to make decisions rooted in both love and a need for legalization. Through this lens, I demonstrate the ways social and cultural norms about marriage are shaped by immigration law.

Undocumented Young Adult Participants

The undocumented young adults I interviewed entered the United States as children and form part of the 1.5 generation of Latin American immigrants residing across the nation (Rumbaut 2004). They all migrated before the age of eight and are now in between their twenties and early thirties. They have navigated most of their lives with an undocumented status, in some cases for as long as twenty-five years. Most were born in Mexico, with the exception of two women who migrated from Guatemala. Few, however, hold memories of their native countries. Rather, they vividly recall their early childhood memories as rooted in the United States upon their arrival. For many, their earliest memories were of reuniting with parents who had migrated before them. The stories they share about their countries of origin are memories passed down by parents, older siblings, or extended family. At the time of our meeting, all twelve participants were married to their U.S. citizen partners; some had recently married within the last year while others had been married for two to three years. Nevertheless, at the time of writing this piece only two participants had received provisional legal permanent residency, three were scheduled for their immigration interview, and the remaining seven had recently submitted their applications and were awaiting a response on their cases.

Social and Cultural Expectations of "Marriage for Papers" and "Marriage for Love"

Much like their U.S.-born counterparts, undocumented young adults enter romantic relationships and after some time, when the relationship is successful, they contemplate the next steps in their relationships—mainly engagement and marriage. However, for undocumented young adults, their decisions to get engaged and to marry are mediated by a complex negotiation between their personal decisions about their relationships, the social/cultural expectations of marriage, and the role of marriage as the only medium for a legalization pathway. While the young people I spoke to expressed views of marriage ranging from a desired next step in their relationship to something they never considered, the majority shared that they never thought they would adjust their immigration status through marriage. Nonetheless, they also had to negotiate a critical understanding that many had aged out of their family-sponsored petitions and had no other legal pathway for legalization beyond a marital-based petition.

When discussing marriage, undocumented young adults immediately shared the multiple instances in which family, friends, coworkers, and even strangers advised them to fix their "immigration problem" through "marriage for papers." As one participant, Felix, recounts: "Ever since right after high school everyone was like, 'just get married so you can get the papers.' Even if they were just kidding it happens. Unfortunately, it's a conversation they've [family and friends] had with me." Indeed, "marriage for papers" is a popular social and cultural notion that many undocumented young people confront from well-meaning people (Mercer 2008; Pila 2016; Enriquez 2015). Precisely because of the primacy of legalization through marriage, marital-based processes have been conflated with the "green card myth"—a common myth about immigration law which falsely assumes that marriage to a U.S. citizen will allow all undocumented immigrants to regularize their status (Mercer 2008). Despite the prevalence of the idea of "marriage for papers" as a practical solution to their long-term undocumented status, participants' decision-making process about when and how to marry point to the complexity of the meaning of marriage that goes beyond "marrying for papers."

Despite the pressures to marry for papers, having been socialized within cultural norms and scripts of dating and marriage (Pila 2016), undocumented young adults also express the importance of love and commitment as motivators for entry into marriage. As Leslie explains, her distinction between marriage for love and marriage for the purposes of obtaining legality was an important conversation with her partner.

A lot of people were telling me 'oh you should get married now, get married before January 20th' but I didn't want to rush it,[9] which I had told her [spouse] before because before when we had talked about marriage she said "Why don't we get married right now? Let's do it, I would marry today." And I told her so many times I don't want to rush this at all. I want it to be special, I want to have a special proposal. But I mean, we had been talking about marriage for the longest time, but nothing to do with immigration, just, you know, love.

Despite being advised to consider marriage during a time of political uncertainty, Leslie made clear distinctions that her discussions with her partner centered on the idea that marriage is for love and not for immigration. Like Leslie, other undocumented young adults point to conversations they've had with romantic partners in which they discuss marriage as a decision that should be about love and a special celebration; however, alongside that conversation they cannot ignore the added complication of marriage as a dual entry into a rite of passage for their relationships and a potential fix to their immigration status. Thus, their decisions about marriage are much more nuanced negotiations about the norms of marriage as the next stage in their relationships, their romantic partners, and pressures to take a rare opportunity to adjust their immigration status during an anti-immigrant climate.

The Uncomfortable Convergence of "Love and Papers"
Regardless of the fact that people throughout society may marry for various practical reasons, including access to healthcare and other social and economic benefits (Oppenheimer 1988), for undocumented young people, their inability to follow the social expectations of a purely uninterested marriage weighs heavily on them when they have had to deal with being undocumented for so many years. The undocumented young adults I spoke to were acutely aware that their only feasible pathway toward legalization was through marriage to a U.S. citizen. While many had discussed the topic of how to regularize their undocumented statuses with their families and partners, others went further and sought information from community groups or legal counsel on their legalization options. They all heard the resounding message that the only way to regularize their legal status was through marriage. Along with the popular narrative that legalization is mainly achieved through marriage to a U.S. citizen, it is also popularly believed to be one of the fastest legalization processes, but one that involves an element of peering into the personal and

romantic relationships, which must be legitimized in the eyes of those who represent the law. While all participants distinguished between "marriage for papers" and "marriage for love," ten of the participants state having made an affirmative decision to marry once these two seemingly mutually exclusive motives converged—love and papers.

Informed by these prevalent narratives of legalization through marriage, a few study participants expressed their unease and discomfort in adjusting their status through marriage. As Diana shared:

> I never really thought I was going to get married. I thought I was just not going to do anything like that. But the older I get it's hard to imagine how else am I going to change my circumstances and those of my family. So, I'm going to go through this process. I feel uneasy about it, but I have a very loving partner. He thinks the process is a pretty [straight]forward process so we are just going to push forward, get married, and get started on this.

Like Diana, all of the participants in this study described being in relationships with loving partners, yet they all expressed unease and discomfort in adjusting their status through marriage. Feeling cornered by a lack of other viable options for legalization, marriage becomes the only answer, but this path exists counter to a powerful social discourse that upholds marriage as an institution that is only reserved for partners in love. The reality that marriage can lead to benefits outside of uninterested love and companionship does not fit within the mainstream narrative on marriage. These migrants, therefore, must grapple with the ways their marriage decisions fall outside of socially accepted norms for marriage. It is in that process that Diana underscores the "pretty forward process" to minimize the part of her marriage that is not strictly and only about a union based on love.

In another example of these types of justifications, Christina shared that her decision to marry was based on the uncomfortable convergence of love and opportunity:

> This is an important opportunity for me and my family to really radically change our lives and I am going to take it even if it's not a comfortable way. Now we're trying to be fine with the process, we'll just blame the immigration system, but also that I don't want to struggle to find secret doors anymore.

Christina's description of adjusting her legal status through marriage as "not a comfortable way" was balanced by her affirmation that it is also a life-altering "opportunity" for her and her family. She only felt comfortable with the decision to move forward with marriage after she and her spouse came to a mutual understanding that this makes sense in a broader context of an unfair immigration system. Christina's reference to "secret doors" is indicative of alternative routes undocumented people have to find or create in order to navigate institutions that were not meant to be accessible to them. In the face of these vast structural barriers that constantly had her struggling to find "secret doors" in search of access and stability, marriage becomes an acceptable option, but given the powerful narrative of marriage only for love, they still have to work together to "be fine with the process."

Having experienced being undocumented for sixteen years, Christina recounted in other parts of the interview the limitations of her undocumented status and the burden of finding "secret doors" to access a four-year institution and pay her tuition. Prior to DACA, during her years in high school and college, her lack of a social security number required her to struggle to find alternative internships with minimal stipends or unpaid volunteer work to build her resume. After receiving her bachelor's degree, she applied for DACA and gained employment with a nonprofit organization in Los Angeles. DACA also allowed her to obtain a state ID, driver's license, and a car loan, while also providing her an opportunity to travel for work. Upon the rescinding of DACA, she faced having to continue finding "secret doors" to obtain employment, state documents, and participate in social events freely. Fearing the imminent loss of DACA's conditional levels of inclusion and protection from deportation, Christina became intensely aware of her vulnerability to immigration law changes. Her continued trajectory within precarious legal situations informed Christina's awareness about the limitations of her undocumented status and the critical role of marriage in facilitating her claim to a potential avenue for legal permanent residence. It was only in recognizing these constant and long-term hardships created by the legal system that the couple could come to terms with their decision to marry for both love and legalization.

Both women and men in the study expressed similar ethical challenges with the process. Like Diana and Christina, Luis shared his frustrations with his realization that marriage and legalization would have to be experienced hand in hand. As he spoke about the pressures to find a solution to his undocumented status, he shared:

> I guess we thought if only we solved this problem, we could both start our lives together and I wouldn't be undocumented anymore and I wouldn't have those barriers anymore. But then that meant that we

> had to get married then instead of doing it like everyone else, like we wanted. And that's, I don't know, infuriating I guess because then our marriage is about that [immigration process] when I just wanted to love this person and be able to get my papers on my own.

Luis's reflection underscores what he and most study participants understand as a clear distinction between a decision to marry solely because of love and a decision to enter marriage as a strategy for legalization. After exhausting all other possibilities, he is unable to follow the socially promoted steps to marriage. He deeply regrets not being able to do it "like everyone else" and is forced to face what he describes as the "infuriating" reality of the duality of marriage as a process of love and simultaneously for papers.

Some of the study participants discussed their attempts to stick to the socially prescribed timelines toward marriage to avoid their discomfort in transgressing the expectation that marriage should only be based in uninterested love. Many, for example, had turned down a few proposals before deciding to move forward with marrying their partners. Hugo, a bioengineering undergraduate student, expresses this most clearly when discussing having turned down a few proposals from his girlfriend before deciding to marry.

> Everything was going well and because she saw me struggling with not being able to get loans, not being able to do a lot of stuff, she told me 'Why don't we get married? Because you'll have all those benefits if you become a resident.' At that point it was a little too early so I told her 'I don't think that's a good idea just because we are barely getting to know each other.' We had barely moved in together and I just didn't think it was a good idea and I didn't think it was fair to her because I thought we shouldn't just get married because I need my residency. I wanted it to be something special for her too, special for the both of us. She brought it up again and it just felt different because of all the time we had spent together and I thought maybe it was a good idea and we decided to get married.

Although Hugo and his partner's relationship was going well, and she seemed particularly aware of the difficulties he faced due to his undocumented status, he reasoned his initial rejection of her proposal on the grounds that "we shouldn't just get married because I need my residency." A year later, when she proposed marriage again, he decided that their relationship had progressed significantly and that marriage was a good step forward for both.

Marriage decisions, as difficult as they are for these study participants, are often also informed by greater family contexts. While marriage decisions for all people can be generally difficult and often include family pressures, for these young adults these added family burdens are heightened because marriage is a pathway to legalization. In other parts of the interview, for example, Hugo relayed the role that his family's situation also played in his decision. Hugo's parents had undergone prior unsuccessful legalization pathways. In the last year, his mother had applied through employment-sponsored petition; however, the company shut down and her petition was terminated. Additionally, Hugo has a U.S.-born little sister who, through her citizenship, will be able to adjust the family's legal status. However, as is true in all cases like theirs, this will not be possible until the U.S. citizen child turns twenty-one years of age—at the time of interview Hugo's sister was only two years old. It is in this context, too, that Hugo moved from being opposed to marriage to accepting that it was a practical and acceptable solution for him and his family. Within the span of a year from his girlfriend's original proposal, Hugo felt that his relationship had progressed to a stage that was more appropriate for entering marriage. Coupled with his realization that his family has no feasible legalization pathways, Hugo came to rationalize that he is not entering marriage simply because "I need my residency"; rather, his decision to marry would also likely benefit other relatives, as well. Similarly to Hugo, other participants shared that their decisions to marry involved some aspects of family pressures that were directly linked to an understanding that marriage was a critical opportunity for the family to have at least one member of the immediate family obtain legal status.

In effect, immigration law and the social and cultural notions of marriage shaped undocumented young adults' personal decisions about their private lives, their romantic relationships, and their precarious immigration statuses. Like Diana, Christina, Luis, and Hugo, participants in this study began to conceptualize the uncomfortable paradox of marriage for love and marriage for legality. In the convergence of these seemingly competing expectations of marriage, they adjusted their beliefs about marriage in the face of the immigration regime that produces their legal instability. Moreover, they contextualize the benefits at the individual, couple, and extended family levels to underscore the practical nature of their decision, especially when paired with being in a loving relationship. In explaining these contradictions, undocumented young adults challenge the notion that adjusting one's immigration status through marriage is an easy pathway. On the contrary, they exemplify the negotiations and difficulties in deciding to apply for legalization through their romantic relationships.

Navigating the Legalization Process

While the convergence of love and papers allowed undocumented young adults to move forward with their decisions to marry their partners, they nonetheless had to mediate these competing ideologies—the paradox of marriage as both for love and for legality. They faced the question of how, in practice, to navigate this paradox in the daily lives of their romantic relationships. This section reveals some of the various lengths that couples go through to distinguish between the practical aspects of legalization through marriage and the emotional or romantic aspects of their relationships. Christina and her husband are a case in point. They met while they were both undergraduate students. After a two-year relationship, they moved in together before deciding to get married. Four months after their wedding, she began to put together their application, with the aid of a friend who had undergone the legalization process a year before. At the time of our meeting, she and her husband were preparing for their interview with the immigration official. As she showed me the archive of documents she had organized to take with her to the interview, I asked her how she felt about attending the interview. She shared:

> It just feels so scary to feel that you are trying to legitimize your love for someone, that you care about someone. That's a horrible feeling that we have to go through. I feel that it's very dehumanizing and very invading. But I love my husband, so I guess it's ok to go through this process of documenting our love. To go through having to share these private moments to show them [USCIS] that it's a legit marriage.

Notwithstanding her concerns about the interview, Christina cites her love for her husband as a foundation to shoulder her fears about her upcoming interview with an immigration official. Having heard many stories about the invasiveness of the immigration interview, Christina like the other women in the study, shared anxieties about the personal questions they will be asked and the burden they will have to endure in convincing an immigration agent, who holds great discretionary power, that their marriages are legitimate. They were aware that their successful application relied on being able to "document our love" and in their willingness to "share intimate moments" with immigration officials who would ultimately decide if their marriages were in "good faith." As a result, while Christina struggles with feeling the constant burden of having to legitimize her love, she also shares some strategies in finding ways to combat the negative effects of what she views as a dehumanizing and invasive process. She, like other young adults, centers her courage to endure the process on the very thing they are trying to legitimize—the love for their partners. They find ways to reclaim intimate moments with their partners. This often involved, when possible, seeking ways to separate their love and relationships from the procedural parts of the application.

Within the burdensome and bureaucratic process of legalization, some participants shared specific approaches to finding moments to fully center the love they shared with their spouses. Close to a year ago, after Diana and her husband were informed at a DACA clinic that Diana's only pathway to citizenship was to obtain residency through marriage, they mutually decided that marriage was their next logical step. They went to the courthouse and obtained their marriage license, alone. When I asked why they decided to go alone, she responded:

> I guess we sort of eloped. But I don't think about it that way although I guess technically that's what we did. We got married before we told our families. But it was important for us to go through the [immigration] process and then to plan a normal wedding with an engagement and a big family party and then potentially, we had hoped, we could go on a honeymoon. But it didn't quite work out that way. We had to tell our parents eventually, we needed their help in the process but it wasn't easy, but here we still are, still in the process of planning our wedding.

Diana and her husband were in a committed relationship and despite their decision to marry as the next step in their relationship, they made an attempt to keep their marriage for papers separate from their marriage for love through these different ceremonies. The couple focused on the fact that obtaining their marriage license was part of a bureaucratic process that would deem Diana eligible to apply for legalization. So, they obtained their marriage license and began the immigration application without informing their families. In their understanding, they would certainly include family in the "real" celebration that would come later, after their bureaucratic process was over.

Like Diana, in practice, nine other participants separated the obtainment of their marriage license as part of the bureaucratic process and made plans for a separate wedding party where family and friends would celebrate their entry into marriage. However, because of the invasive nature of the process, most couples were forced to tell their families about their secret marriages eventually. As part of the legalization through marriage process, couples needed their parents' information for parts of the application or required letters of support from family and friends confirming that the couple's marriage was legitimate. This, in turn, prevented them from truly being able to separate the legalization process from their "real" wedding and added a new burden—that of having to disclose to families that they had already effectively eloped.

Parents, siblings, and friends were often hurt to learn that they had been excluded from the couple's wedding. Based on the undocumented young adults' decisions to distance the bureaucracy of legalization from their planning of future weddings, however, they expressed no regret in their initial decisions. They felt that they had made the best decision under the circumstances to make sense of the uncomfortableness of documenting their love. They and their spouses negotiated ways to first tackle the legalization process as a means to obtain their work permits, to save for future weddings, and to obtain the ability to travel for eventual honeymoons. Their strategy of creating separate plans for their marriages and weddings points to the ways these couples are still finding to participate in the social and cultural expectations of traditional weddings centered on love. While love and legality became an uncomfortable convergence during the legalization process, they ameliorate these feelings of discomfort by centering their love and making concrete plans to re-center their love once they are done undergoing the immigration process.

Although not all participants shared plans of separating love and legalization through different ceremonies, all participants expressed their conscientious decisions to center their love during the legalization process. As they shared with me their application packets, they also shared their intentional, and as I observed sometimes *unconscious* ways, of centering their love for their partners. As part of the "supplemental documents to substantiate their relationship" they described why they chose certain photos as "proof of their relationship." While certainly some were guided by legal aid about which photos are best to include for a successful application, in my conversations with participants I heard them fondly describing the context of every photo. The Disneyland trip for their anniversary—she remembers the Mickey Mouse matching ears they bought. The pictures of them at birthday parties—he remembers it as the first time he thought he would propose to her. The pictures of them on their trip up the California coast—she remembers it as the first time they risked a long-distance trip together. The pictures of their "secret wedding" from the date they went to the courthouse—something which only they have seen. These pictures represent the types of evidence immigration requires—anniversaries, birthdays, trips, a wedding—yet in sharing these formalized photos, undocumented young adults also recount the intimacy of the moments captured, an intimacy that only they continue to be privy to. In some ways, these are the precise moments and emotions that help them counter the invasiveness and practical side of their decision to marry.

Moving Forward: "We Did the Best We Could"

Although undocumented young adults' practices in negotiating the uncomfortable convergence of marriage for "love and papers" were helpful during the arduous tasks of having to document their relationships, participants also held concerns about the possible long-term effects on their marital relationships. They wonder if they have done enough to combat the oxymoron of love and papers. In their concerns, it is evident that the weight is especially heavy on the undocumented spouse. As Alex so poignantly explains "I don't want her to ever think that I married her just because she is a citizen. But I think I'll always have that." In their candid words, I am reminded of the difficult balance undocumented young adults face in navigating the legalization process and protecting our marriages, all while also claiming our humanity against a system that deems us eligible for legal recognition only upon the bureaucratization of our most intimate relationship. In facing the daunting question about long-term effects, some shared phrases like: "We did the best we could," "We did what was best for us at that time," and "Under my circumstances, I made a decision to protect myself and my family." Thus, the discomfort we are left with in having to converge our love and our legality leads us to remediate the decisions we've made while also wondering about what it means to enter legality through our love.

Most of the undocumented young adults I interviewed also expressed curiosity about my legalization process, particularly those who were the first in their networks to have entered the legalization through marriage process. Together we discussed what kind of support would be helpful in ameliorating the consequences of a complex and deeply intimate process. Many shared that long-term care for them means a variety of things, whether it be through formal channels like seeking individual and couples counseling, or informally forming friendships and networks of support among those who've also endured the process. While our strategies vary, many of us agree that as the undocumented spouse, finding support amongst each other is pivotal in our healing, as we too need gentle reminders that we did the best we could under the circumstances of illegality.

As I have shown, the marriage-based legalization process for undocumented young adults illuminates how their understanding of immigration law shapes their decisions to enter marriage despite the uncomfortable convergence of both their romantic love and the circumstances that have led to legalization through marriage as a limited and opportune option. Like their documented counterparts, they too negotiate decisions about marriage based on their intimate relationships, family pressures, personal, academic, or career goals, and their own perceptions about marriage. However, given the increasing immigration laws that limit options for legalization and because of their prolonged undocumented experiences, marriage is not solely about these common factors; rather it involves an additional layer that forces them to consider the implications of immigration law changes on their livelihoods and their families. In my conversations with undocumented young adults, it is clear that they made difficult negotiations about a complex process that fuses their intimate relationships with a life-altering legal process, forcing them to employ strategies to manage what they describe as an invasive process. However, as our conversations underscore, their entry into legalization is not an easy pathway; rather, it often leaves undocumented young adults with feelings of ambivalence and fears of immigration laws' long-term effects on their intimate lives. Much like our parting words to each other, their legalization process also doesn't end neatly tied with a happily ever after ending; rather, we are all left with reservations about the decisions we made under the double-bind conditions when our lives converged for love and papers.

NOTES

1. The focus on sexuality to examine differential experiences between same-sex and heterosexual couples is something I'm exploring further in ongoing projects.

2. Not all undocumented young adults are eligible to apply for adjustment of status (AOS) when they marry U.S. citizens. To be eligible, applicants must demonstrate legal entry and hold no criminal record or health impediments.

3. The Immigration and Nationality Act of 1965 provides the categories of admissibility, outlines the immigration process and its requirements.

4. I utilize the terms undocumented and unauthorized to denote a category of migrants who do not have legal immigration status and are residing in the United States without legal permission. Participants in this study utilized the term "undocumented" to describe their legal status.

5. In some cases, additional documents have allowed some immigrants with unlawful entry to gain eligibility, such as provision 245(i)—allowing undocumented applicants to adjust within the United States without facing a bar to readmission (Golash-Boza 2012).

6. All USCIS forms can be found online at https://www.uscis.gov/forms.

7. USCIS guidelines are stated in participants' applications from USCIS, which they shared with me during my interviews and fieldwork.

8. Although LPRs apply for the removal of "conditional" status, their permanent LPR status still carries certain conditions such as carrying "green cards" at all times (not doing so can lead to a misdemeanor offense), no felony offense, and renewing every ten years.

9. January 20, 2017 was the inauguration date of U.S. President Donald Trump. Many organizations released statements advising of potentially drastic legal or procedural changes with the change of administrations.

REFERENCES

Abrams, Kerry. 2007. "Immigration Law and the Regulation of Marriage." *Minnesota Law Review* 91: 1625–1709. https://heinonline.org/HOL/P?h=hein.journals/mnlr91&i=1637.

Abrego, Leisy. 2006. "'I Can't Go to College Because I Don't Have Papers': Incorporation Patterns of Latino Undocumented Youth." *Latino Studies* 4(3): 212–31. https://doi.org/10.1057/palgrave.lst.8600200.

Abrego, Leisy. 2008. "Legitimacy, Social Identity, and the Mobilization of Law: The Effects of Assembly Bill 540 on Undocumented Students in California." *Law and Social Inquiry* 33(3): 709–34. https://doi.org/10.1111/j.1747-4469.2008.00119.x.

Abrego, Leisy. 2011. "Legal Consciousness of Undocumented Latinos: Fear and Stigma as Barriers to Claims Making for First and 1.5 Generation Immigrants." *Law and Society Review* 45(2): 337–70. https://doi.org/10.1111/j.1540-5893.2011.00435.x.

Abrego, Leisy. 2014. *Sacrificing Families: Navigating Laws, Labor, and Love Across Borders*. Stanford, CA: Stanford University Press.

Abrego, Leisy J., and Roberto G. Gonzales. 2010. "Blocked Paths, Uncertain Futures: The Postsecondary Education and Labor Market Prospects of Undocumented Latino Youth." *Journal of Education of Students Placed at Risk (JESPAR)* 15(1): 144–57. https://doi.org/10.1080/10824661003635168.

Boehm, Deborah. 2012. "Family 'Reunification.'" In *Intimate Migrations: Gender, Family, and Illegality among Transnationals*, 53–67. New York: New York University Press.

Creighton, Emily, Mary Kenney, Patrick Taurel, Susan Schreiber, and Tatyana Delgado. 2013. "Advance Parole for DACA Recipients." Silver Spring, MD: Catholic Legal Immigration Network. https://cliniclegal.org/resources/articles-clinic/advance-parole-daca-recipients.

Dreby, Joanna. 2015. *Everyday Illegal: When Policies Undermine Immigrant Families*. Oakland: University of California Press.

Enriquez, Laura. 2015. "Multigenerational Punishment: Shared Experiences of Undocumented Immigration Status within Mixed-Status Families." *Journal of Marriage and Family* 77(4): 939–53. https://doi.org/10.1111/jomf.12196.

Ewick, Patricia, and Susan S. Silbey. 1998. *The Common Place of Law: Stories from Everyday Life*. Chicago: University of Chicago Press.

Fix, Michael, and Wendy Zimmerman. 2001. "All Under One Roof: Mixed-Status Families in an Era of Reform." *International Migration Review* 35(2): 397–419. https://doi.org/10.1111/j.1747-7379.2001.tb00023.x.

Gleeson, Shannon, and Roberto G. Gonzales. 2012. "When Do Papers Matter? An Institutional Analysis of Undocumented Life in the United States." *International Migration* 50(4): 1–19. https://doi.org/10.1111/j.1468-2435.2011.00726.x.

Golash-Boza, Tanya. 2012. *Due Process Denied: Detentions and Deportations in the United States*. New York: Routledge.

Gomberg-Muñoz, Ruth. 2016. "The Juárez Wives Club: Gendered Citizenship and U.S. Immigration Law." *American Ethnologist* 43(2): 339–52. https://doi.org/10.1111/amet.12309.

Gonzales, Roberto G. 2011. "Learning to be Illegal: Undocumented Youth and Shifting Legal Contexts in the Transition to Adulthood." *American Sociological Review* 76(4): 602–19. https://doi.org/10.1177/0003122411411901.

Gonzales, Roberto G. 2016. *Lives in Limbo: Undocumented and Coming of Age in America*. Berkeley: University of California Press.

Gonzales, Roberto G., Carola Suárez-Orozco, and Maria Cecilia Dedios-Sanguineti. 2013. "No Place to Belong: Contextualizing Concepts of Mental Health among Undocumented Immigrant Youth in the United States." *American Behavioral Scientist* 57(8): 1174–99. https://doi.org/10.1177/0002764213487349.

Hagan, Jacqueline M. 1998. "Social Networks, Gender, and Immigrant Incorporation: Resources and Constraints." *American Sociological Review* 63(1): 55–67. https://www.jstor.org/stable/2657477.

López, Jane Lilly. 2015. "'Impossible Families': Mixed-Citizenship Status Couples and the Law." *Law and Policy* 37(1–2): 93–118. https://doi.org/10.1111/lapo.12032.

Mena Robles, Jorge, and Ruth Gomberg-Muñoz. 2016. "Activism after DACA: Lessons from Chicago's Immigrant Youth Justice League." *North American Dialogue* 19(1): 46–54. https://doi.org/10.1111/nad.12036.

Menjívar, Cecilia, Leisy Abrego, and Leah Schmalzbauer. 2016. *Immigrant Families*. Cambridge: Polity Press.

Menjívar, Cecilia, and Sarah M. Lakhani. 2016. "Transformative Effects of Immigration Law: Immigrants' Personal and Social Metamorphoses through Regularization." *American Journal of Sociology* 121(6): 1818–55. https://doi.org/10.1086/685103.

Mercer, Julie. 2008. "The Marriage Myth: Why Mixed-Status Marriages Need an Immigration Remedy." *Golden Gate University Law Review* 38(2): 293–325. https://heinonline.org/HOL/P?h=hein.journals/ggulr38&i=297.

Mossaad, Nodwa. 2016. *U.S. Lawful Permanent Residents: 2014 Annual Report*. Office of Immigration Statistics. https://www.dhs.gov/immigration-statistics/lawful-permanent-residents.

Nicholls, Walter. 2013. *The DREAMers: How the Undocumented Youth Movement Transformed the Immigrant Rights Debate*. Stanford, CA: Stanford University Press.

Oppenheimer, Valerie K. 1988. "A Theory of Marriage Timing: Assortative Mating Under Varying Degrees of Uncertainty." *American Journal of Sociology* 94(3): 563–91. https://www.jstor.org/stable/2780254.

Pila, Daniela. 2016 "'I'm Not Good Enough for Anyone': Legal Status and the Dating Lives of Undocumented Young Adults." *Sociological Forum* 31(1): 138–57. https://doi.org/10.1111/socf.12237.

Rumbaut, Rubén G. 2004. "Ages, Life Stages, and Generational Cohorts: Decomposing the Immigrant First and Second Generations in the United States." *International Migration Review* 38(3): 1160–1205. https://doi.org/10.1111/j.1747-7379.2004.tb00232.x.

Salcido, Olivia, and Cecilia Menjívar. 2012. "Gendered Paths to Legal Citizenship: The Case of Latin-American Immigrants in Phoenix." *Law and Society Review* 46(2): 335–68. https://doi.org/10.1111/j.1540-5893.2012.00491.x.

KATY JOSELINE MALDONADO DOMINGUEZ

10

Undocumented Queer Parenting

Navigating External and Internal Threats to Family

Sergio and Cecil met in the 1990s during their early twenties when they both worked in the same factory in Honduras. After dating for a few months, they had their first child, Kasandra. Unable to make ends meet despite their full-time work and double income, in 2000 Sergio decided to migrate to the United States to better support their three-year-old daughter. Overcome by loneliness, two years after Sergio first migrated, he returned to Honduras only to realize that jobs were scarce and he would not be able to provide for his family there. He was forced to migrate once more. This time, however, the couple planned to reunite the family in the United States. After two years of saving, Sergio managed to raise the $11,000 he needed to hire a coyote (smuggler) to bring his wife and daughter across the U.S.–Mexico border. By the time the family finally reunited, Kasandra was seven. The couple had more children, for a total of four: Kasandra (who, like her parents, was undocumented), and Daniela, Antonio, and Sandra (all of whom were U.S. citizens by birth).

Like many migrant families, Sergio and Cecil sought to improve their children's lives. For them this required difficult negotiations that included being separated at different moments. Once they were finally together in the United States, however, they had to work low-wage jobs that took most of their days and energy. When Sergio and Cecil were expecting their second daughter, Daniela, unable to dedicate much time to family, they opted to help Cecil's younger sister, Ana, migrate to the United States to care for their children while they worked. At the time, Ana was twenty-six and desperate. Her father, Julio, had just kicked her out of their home over an argument about her sexual identity as a lesbian woman. Though undocumented, Ana was happy to help and reunite with her older sister who she had been very close to throughout their childhood; and she felt safe moving in with the only family who seemed to accept her. Years went by and Ana cared lovingly for every new child, growing closer and closer to her nieces and nephew. This arrangement, however, would eventually be ruptured. After seventeen years of marriage and ten years of living together in the United States, Sergio came out to Cecil as a gay man. The couple divorced, and Cecil remarried to Andres, a homophobic man who kicked Ana out. The family dynamics changed for everyone, and Ana was once again cut out from her family.

As this family's history and dynamics demonstrate, family life is complex, often including moments of vulnerability, empowerment, love, and pain. While migration scholars demonstrate that undocumented families struggle to simply be together, make ends meet, and cope with constant fear in a country that criminalizes them (Dreby 2010, 2015; Menjívar, Abrego, and Schmalzbauer 2016; Zavella 2011), queer scholars reveal that queer families must navigate the rejection and invalidation of their mere existence (Acosta 2010; Bernstein and Reimann 2001; Moore 2011). Few researchers examine the intersections between these two realities, and even then, they typically focus only on queer children in immigrant families (Acosta 2010; Ocampo 2012). In this chapter, I examine the experiences of queer and undocumented parents in mixed-status families through the experiences of Sergio, Cecil, Ana, and their children.

This study sheds light on how these parents create and navigate family, but more specifically, how their experiences as both undocumented and queer have informed their parenting and relationships within their families. For these parents, family is a process that consists of reshaping and negotiating idealized expectations of family, as determined by their sexuality, gender, and legal status. I argue that these parents endure two forms of threat to their family formations: as undocumented parents they face the external threat of a xenophobic country that deports and separates families, and as queer parents they must navigate the internal threats of homophobia and heteronormativity that similarly and more immediately disrupt their families. Despite these threats, these parents resist homophobia and xenophobia by creating new spaces of vulnerability and empowerment within their families to discuss sexuality and legal status together which, in the case that I examine, ultimately fortifies their parent-child relationships. I find that the intersection between queer and undocumented identities creates a unique but vulnerable parental position that offers new ways to reconfigure families. In a research field and immigrant rights movement that overlook queer families, my work centers nonnormative parental experiences to be more inclusive in our fight for the rights of all immigrants.

Challenging the Heteronormative Nuclear Family

Families are not uniform, but society assumes that they all fall under one hegemonic mold—that of the self-sufficient, middle-class heteronormative nuclear household (Bernstein and Reimann 2001; Cantu 2009; Moore 2011; Zavella 2011). This model is defined as a family that consists of children and two married parents, a male husband and female wife who follow traditional gender roles with the husband as the main breadwinner and the wife as the homemaker (Bernstein and Reimann 2001). Because this outline of a family is ingrained in most social and legal institutions, it carries significant consequences for those who challenge it, including working-class families, families of color, families without children, queer families, undocumented families, single-parent families, and families of choice (Bernstein and Reimann 2001; Menjívar, Abrego, and Schmalzbauer 2016; Moore 2011; Weston 1991; Zavella 2011).

In this chapter, I draw on Reimann and Bernstein's (2001) more fluid and open definition of family as "groups of individuals who . . . share a strong emotional and/or financial commitment to each other, whether or not they cohabit, are related by blood . . . or are recognized by the law" (3). In the following sections, I review the literature on how undocumented families challenge the idealized heteronormative and nuclear family ideal; how queer families contest this model; and how families navigate the intersections between undocumented and queer.

Legal Status, Deportability, and Family Separation

Undocumented legal status and deportability powerfully shape migrant families (Dreby 2010, 2015; Menjívar, Abrego, and Schmalzbauer 2016; Zavella 2011). Legal violence, or the normalized structural and symbolic effects of the law on immigrant families, blocks their access to resources and institutions thereby thwarting their incorporation into the United States (Menjívar and Abrego 2012). Because legal violence is legitimated by the law, it authorizes the harm perpetuated on these families and makes their everyday lives a constant struggle. For example, as undocumented workers, these family members are confined to low-wage jobs that take advantage of the way the law criminalizes them to deny them livable wages. These conditions result in economic insecurity and harm the well-being of the entire family (Dreby 2010; Menjívar, Abrego, and Schmalzbauer 2016; Zavella 2011). Clearly, the idealized notion of a self-sufficient nuclear unit is inaccessible for undocumented immigrant families.

Undocumented and mixed-status families also contest ideals of the physical nuclear model. For example, transnational immigrant families must learn to navigate their family dynamics separately across different countries (Abrego 2014). Even when they are together in the United States, undocumented immigrant families must endure the threat of deportation and fears of separation, revealing the unfortunate reality that not all nuclear families can be or will be together, putting even more strain on already fragile family formations (Abrego 2016; Dreby 2010, 2015; Menjívar and Abrego 2012; Zavella 2011).

In fact, deportation rates have skyrocketed over the past ten years. Most deportees are men (Golash-Boza and Hondagneu-Sotelo 2013). When husbands are deported, migrant mothers become "suddenly single mothers" who must transgress gendered expectations to fend for themselves and lead a family that does not meet idealized notions of the heteronormative nuclear unit (Dreby 2015, 175). Additionally, the deported parent is no longer able to play an active role in their children's lives (Dreby 2015). In all of these instances, the realities of undocumented and immigrant families block them from embodying the heteronormative nuclear unit.

Queer Family Making

Queer families also challenge the heteronormative nuclear model. Although some queer parents may have children from previous heterosexual relationships, other queer individuals must become parents through insemination, surrogacy, or adoption, thereby challenging notions of how a family can be formed (Boggis 2001). Importantly, these alternative methods are not economically feasible for all queer parents (Boggis 2001). As a result, queer parents who cannot afford these processes might resort to uncomfortable and unsafe situations to create a family, including heterosexual contact or insemination with an unchecked donor (Boggis 2001). Queer parents who engage in these agreements not only risk their own health but also the ability to control the formation of their families (Boggis 2001). This is mainly because the donor may choose to claim their parental rights and seize the rights of the other nonbiological partner, a risk that queer parents who can afford insemination or surrogacy do not undergo (Boggis 2001).

Much like undocumented and immigrant families, queer families are forced to be flexible in determining what their family looks like. Additionally, like undocumented immigrant families, queer families must navigate legal systems that invalidate their families. For example, if queer parents with children were to separate and each parent wanted custody, courts would prioritize the biological parent and essentially force both the nonbiological parent and child to undergo the emotional trauma of separation (Dalton 2001). Among migrant families, even biological ties can be severed by legal systems. For instance, when parents get deported, their biological children may be put into the foster care system and then placed into adoption without parental consent and at the expense of the child (Rodriguez 2017). Regardless, queer and undocumented parents engage in family structures with or without the support of the legal system (Bernstein 2001; Boggis 2001).

Creating Undocumented Queer Families

For undocumented queer individuals, such as gay migrant Mexican men, sexuality is one axis of power that shapes their lives, relationships, and families (Cantu 2009; also see Ramirez's chapter in this volume). Already on the margins of mainstream white society, Latino communities, and queer communities, these gay migrant men must navigate sexuality, legal status, and race. In such vulnerable positions, they initially seek support from biological family networks or migrant "landing pads." However, these landing pads often fail to support their sexual identities and as a result, they create "chosen families" that allow them to further develop as queer undocumented migrants, and Latino men (Cantu 2009, 121; Weston 1991).

Gender performativity is another factor that shapes queer families. Because notions of gendered femininity and masculinity are socially constructed, and because these gendered ideals are assumed to carry heterosexual roles, one can perform these gender expectations to an extent and navigate a heteronormative society (Butler 1990; Salih 2007). By gender performance, I am referring to the act of performing a preexisting gendered role which, depending on the performance, may embody or challenge mainstream notions of gender (Butler 1990; Salih 2007). Gender performativity moves beyond the expression of a gendered role to highlight how the continued repetition of that gender performance constructs and reconstructs gender in ways that result in specific consequences or effects (Butler 1990; Salih 2007). For instance, Latina lesbian daughters in migrant families perform specific gendered notions of femininity in order to silence, erase, or avoid their sexual identities and mitigate familial and societal rejection, revealing how queer individuals enact specific forms of gender performativity to navigate the material and familial consequences that may arise as a queer family member (Acosta 2010).

Thus, gender performativity is an ongoing process that is shaped by how continued gender performance is read and understood. This, in turn, results in the privileging of gender performances that exemplify normative notions of gender and the disparaging of those who challenge these gendered ideals (Butler 1990; Rosenfeld 2009; Salih 2007; Stryker 2008). In fact, the LGB movement has historically kept queer individuals who transgress these gender norms in the shadows. Transgender, minorities, or low-income people are eclipsed in the movement by those who are able to perform and maintain a homonormativity that privileges the "construction of an acceptable homosexuality" (Bernstein and Reimann 2001; Rosenfeld 2009, 621).

These studies convincingly argue that sexuality and gender function as sites of unequal power that queer migrants must navigate, often reshaping their understanding of biological and chosen families in unique ways. This chapter extends this line of research by examining the experiences of parents who are both queer and undocumented to understand how they create and shape family and establish parenting with their children.

Methods

I ground this chapter's findings in a case study and three interviews with the father, aunt, and eldest daughter of one family. Pseudonyms are used throughout the chapter to protect the confidentiality of participants. Sergio, the father of the family, was forty-two years old at the time of the interview. Ana, the biological maternal aunt with a strong maternal role in the family, was thirty-six years old. Kasandra, the oldest of Sergio's four children, was twenty years old and the only child over eighteen (see Figure 10.1). The project began as a class assignment through Kasandra's participation. She introduced me to her father and aunt who also agreed to participate as a family in the project. However, due to the family's current dynamics, Kasandra, Sergio, and Ana preferred that I not request an interview with Cecil, the mother of the family, or her new husband. Sergio and Ana were concerned that discussing the topic of their sexual orientation with either Cecil or her

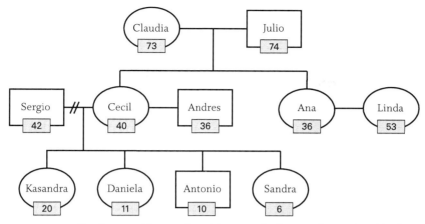

FIGURE 10.1. Family tree with ages of participants and other people mentioned in this case study.

husband could potentially exacerbate tensions within the family. To respect their wishes, this study only centers the narratives and experiences of Sergio, Ana, and Kasandra.

Sergio identifies as a gay man; Ana identifies as a lesbian woman; and Kasandra, their daughter/niece, identifies as a heterosexual woman. Both Ana and Sergio are undocumented and work in the service industry as cooks, while Kasandra is a Deferred Action for Childhood Arrivals (DACA) recipient and a full-time college student. The participants have all migrated from Honduras and have lived together in the greater Los Angeles area for ten years. Ana has no biological children but cared for her nieces and nephew for the ten years when they all lived together. The interviews each lasted two hours and were conducted separately in 2016, a few weeks after Trump's election and both Sergio and Ana expressed heightened fears of deportation in the new political climate. Our discussions broadly focused on their experiences with migration, sexuality, parenting, and family. Ana and Sergio's responses allow me to capture the gendered ways in which the acceptance of their sexuality within their working-class migrant Latina/o/x family unfolds, while Kasandra's responses reveal how children experience undocumented queer parenting. Although some of the broken emotional bonds within this family are common in divorces in which friends, children, and family choose sides, this chapter specifically focuses on how homophobia and xenophobia have distinctly shaped the dynamics of this family (Barumandzadeh et al. 2016; Emery 2002).

Immigration Laws as Threats to Family

For millions of mixed-status families, deportation is a constant looming threat (Dreby 2015; Menjívar, Abrego, and Schmalzbauer 2016). For Sergio, this fear of deportation was especially heightened amid Donald Trump's election. Sergio expressed his fear as an undocumented parent and the possible dismantling of his family in such an explicitly xenophobic environment:

> It is difficult for me to live with the fear that we are all living right now, all the parents that don't have papers. If they send me over there [to Honduras] what am I going to do? What are my children going to do? Who will help them? . . . Because right now, the truth is that I am really scared . . . if it was before, and they sent me back, I would just come back. But right now, . . . if they send you back they give you ten years . . . and then what about the children? What are you going to do? . . . I've never been as afraid of being undocumented as I am right now.

Deportation then becomes an external threat to family, as it undermines undocumented parents by creating a constant state of anxiety and becomes more immediately damaging when deportation actually occurs and tears these families apart (Dreby 2015).

Being an undocumented parent in the United States also carries other structural obstacles that further undermine and threaten these families. For instance, without proper documentation, undocumented immigrant parents have to work long hours in low-wage, physically draining jobs to be able to financially provide for their family (Dreby 2010; Menjívar, Abrego, and Schmalzbauer 2016). This means being away from their family most of the day, and though not guaranteed, if the parents had more time, they might spend it with their children instead (Menjívar, Abrego, and Schmalzbauer 2016; Zavella 2011). Kasandra explains how this reality harms parent-child relationships. In particular, she explains that the family's step-migration process physically distanced her from her father, which informs the way she initially developed her relationship with him upon being reunited in the United States. The realities of an undocumented legal status aggravate this physical distance to create an emotional rift between them:

> I feel like migrating really had a toll on our family . . . I remember when I first got here to the U.S. I didn't think that my dad was my dad, I just thought he was a stranger. I mean I knew we were coming to see my dad, but I don't think I even fully understood what the concept of a dad

was. I had been with my mom for the first seven years of my life without my dad for most of the time . . . Even later, when I finally understood he was my dad after living with him for a few years I never really got to know him. He's been working several jobs ever since he got here so we never really had time to get to know each other.

Kasandra's reflection reveals that the separation between families that occurs while immigrating may create disconnected relationships between parent and child, while the structural obstacles of an undocumented legal status in the United States, including being confined to low-wage work, may inhibit the full potential of these relationships.

Middlewomen as Strategy and Threat

These family dynamics are further complicated when undocumented parents extend their immediate families to also include other relatives, such as "middlewomen" (Dreby 2010). Middlewomen are female relatives who enact the role of caregiver for children whose parents have migrated to the United States (Dreby 2010). However, I argue that middlewomen are also essential once in the United States because migrant parents rely on extended family members to assist with childcare when working long hours. The role of middlewomen can be considered as a "substitute parent of sorts" but is never meant to usurp the actual role of a biological parent (Dreby 2010,175). This was the responsibility that Ana took on when she arrived at Sergio and Cecil's home. As she explains:

> I have always lived very closely to Sergio and Cecil . . . to the point that I have done things thinking about what is best for the family. For example, when I first arrived [in the United States], I opted to work during the night shift and they worked during the day . . . because I could take care of the kids and I could take Kasandra to school and Sergio and Cecil would not have to worry.

Ana clearly played an active role in the everyday lives of her nieces and nephew. Kasandra, her eldest niece, confirms this as she recalls:

> I was always really close to my aunt, I mean she was just always there. I remember doing little school projects about her. You know how they always ask you who your role model is, and everyone always says their parents are but for a while I always said it was my aunt.

Ana and Kasandra's love for one another underscores the point that familial arrangements within undocumented migrant Latina/o/x families are often reshaped when other relatives must provide childcare and take on parental roles while migrant parents work. Such experiences ultimately call into question our assumptions about who can be considered a parent and who children value as crucial loved ones in their lives.

However, these family formations may also include new tensions. For example, biological parents may feel threatened by the role that middlewomen play in their families. Ana explains that her sister often argued with her over her discomfort with the way Ana spoke to her nieces and nephew:

> I always call [the kids], "baby." I always tell Daniela "Hi baby" and she told me "Don't call me that anymore because it bothers mom" and I don't understand why it bothers her . . . so now I only tell her "Hi niece." I think that what Cecil has is fear. Fear that the kids won't like her if I'm there . . . so I asked her "what do you want me to do?" and she said, "When they throw themselves on you, you should scold them and tell them to leave you alone" and I ask her "Why if it doesn't bother me? On the contrary that's why I go see them."

Such negotiations are not surprising within migrant families when undocumented parents are limited to low-wage jobs that consume their days. Although these families need the care that middlewomen provide, tensions may arise when children develop intimate relationships with middlewomen. This results in parents wanting to establish emotional distance between middlewomen and the children they care for, which ultimately harms both caregiver and child.

Thus, the external threat of a nation-state that criminalizes undocumented individuals undermines these parents and their families in numerous ways. Not only must they risk their lives as they migrate to the United States, but once in the country, as undocumented individuals they must take on time-consuming, low-wage jobs that separate them from their family yet again. This leads to the need for middlewomen to take care of their children, but this only results in more tension as these parents must negotiate the normative roles of a heteronormative, middle-class family when they extend the boundaries of their nuclear unit to include other family members to aid with the care of their household (Dreby 2010; Zavella 2011). And now, in this political climate, these parents are in "a constant state of emergency" as they try to evaluate their possibilities and their children's future if they happen to be separated (Menjívar, Abrego, and Schmalzbauer 2016).

Homophobia as Threat to Family

While navigating the external threats of a xenophobic nation-state, these undocumented queer parents must also overcome the internal threats of homophobia within their families. Just as Sergio described his fear of losing his family due to his undocumented status, he expresses a similar fear of losing his family as a queer parent:

> The fear that your family won't accept you or the fear of losing your family . . . I've met so many people in a situation like that . . . At least for me, my first wish was to have kids. If I had felt that [coming out] would have put that at risk, that it would have risked me having kids then I would have continued like I was [married to Cecil], because I was in that situation because I wanted kids. That was the first thing I wanted in my life, to have kids, to have a family.

Family acceptance as a queer parent is clearly tremendously important. However, familial acceptance is not always guaranteed, especially when homophobic ideologies engulf the families that queer individuals are a part of.

Ana experienced a similar fear of family rejection due to her sexual orientation. She explains that it was never her dream to migrate to the United States but when her father discovered her sexuality, she was barred from ever coming back home. As a result, when Sergio offered to loan her money for the trip to the United States, she took the chance:

> I thought I was finally recovering part of what I had lost because it was Sergio, Cecil and Kasandra, it was a family. I always considered Sergio and Cecil almost like parents because I always went to their house [in Honduras] for the holidays, and when I went back to school they bought me notebooks. I still consider them like my parents . . . they were the only people who I really shared many things with . . . Well, since I was sad, I could not even see my mom, or anyone. It was just a chaos I was in, so I said yes.

Ana's migration to the United States was rooted in a search for family. She initially relied on Cecil and Sergio financially but once in the United States, looked to her new nieces and nephew, to her sister, and to Sergio to provide safety, love, and a sense of belonging. Ana's relationship with Sergio and Cecil was intimately shaped by both emotional interconnection and economic interdependence, thus making her experience with familial acceptance as a queer individual much more challenging.

For these reasons, it was a shattering experience for Ana when she was once again faced with familial rejection and rupture due to the homophobic beliefs of Cecil's new husband. When Cecil remarried, and her new partner learned about Ana's sexuality, he refused to allow Ana to care for Cecil's newborn daughter, Vanessa, and soon dismantled the relationships she had already established with her nieces and nephew. With tears in her eyes and her voice breaking, Ana describes the emotional toll of this familial rupture:

> I would like everything to be fixed, that everything went back to like it was before. That I could see them and take them to the movies and everyone would say "yes" . . . right now I'm missing a lot of their moments . . . I would like to go back to sharing almost everything, practically everything. It is really difficult for me, it is very difficult to know what I had and then all of a sudden, it's gone. And I know that it's not because of the kids, I mean it's not because they do not feel comfortable with me. And at the end of the day they are the ones that are hurt . . . The children need things that I did for them . . . like with the awards they give children at school . . . [the kids] look to see if someone is there, to see someone they know who really went to see them, it makes them feel very good . . . I know this because many times I was there and sometimes I came almost to the very end and I would see Daniela and Antonio searching through the crowd. That's what they need. I guess every kid likes someone to be there.

Although immigration policies and the threat of deportation are thought to be the most fundamentally disrupting threats to immigrant families (Dreby 2015; Menjívar and Abrego 2012), Ana's experience demonstrates the devastating ways in which homophobia also breaks families apart for undocumented queer parents.

The ways in which homophobia intrudes and destabilizes undocumented queer families are further evident when analyzing the coercive forces that pushed Cecil to cut her own sister out of her family. Ana herself explains, "I never imagined that Cecil would change to such an extreme." Sergio further clarifies this by describing the situation Cecil was in, as she was forced to choose between her sister and her new husband and father of her newborn child:

> This happened because he was pushing her. She came to me and told me "estoy entre la espada y la pared [I'm between a rock and a hard place], what do I do?" . . . Cecil was one of the few people that always

fought for Ana, she was always fighting for her . . . when she found out about me [Sergio coming out], she said "I won't let anyone treat you the way they treated Ana her whole life" . . . It's not that she doesn't want her [Ana] there, it's that he won't let her.

Although Cecil had an intimate bond with Ana, Andres's homophobia and his new position in the family granted him the power to control who would be involved in his child's life and in the lives of his stepchildren. Additionally, although Sergio provides for his children's financial needs, he no longer lives with Cecil, so she now relies on Andres for other expenses that Sergio previously helped with. After forcing Ana to leave, Andres also provided Cecil with money to find childcare for Vanessa, making it more difficult for Cecil to argue for Ana's position in the family as the children's caretaker. In this context, the threats of homophobia, as well as the gendered and economic dynamics of Cecil's new marriage, shattered the intimate bond between Cecil and her younger sister, but also dismantled the ties that Ana had with her nieces and nephew.

Gender Performativity and Gendered Familial Acceptance

This familial rift also provides a look into ways gender manifests itself within undocumented queer families, specifically regarding familial acceptance. As Sergio reveals, if coming out as a gay man would have meant losing his kids, he would have chosen to continue hiding his sexuality to protect his relationship with his children. In fact, queer individuals sometimes must adopt strategies that allow them to perform gender in specific ways to minimize familial rejection (Acosta 2010; Ocampo 2012). Consequently, gender performativity—the ongoing performance of gender and its consequences—may determine both familial and societal acceptance (Bernstein and Reimann 2001).

For Ana, gender performativity shaped her relationship with family in various ways. In particular, Ana explains that the way she presents herself is not within a traditional form of femininity, but in Honduras she might adopt such a traditional gender performance for the sake of protecting her mother, Claudia:

> If I were in Honduras . . . maybe I would even be dressed as a woman . . . maybe I would not have the freedom to dress as I dress. I'm not saying I'm dressing like a man, I dress like I feel. But when I say dressed as a woman I mean that I would wear dresses, be very feminine . . . and

> I would not do it for me but for the respect and for the "el qué dirán" [what will they say]. I would do it for my mother.

In order to ease both societal and familial acceptance, Ana feels that she would have to perform a hegemonic notion of femininity if she were still in Honduras. However, in the U.S. she does not feel the same pressures to perform gender in that manner. Her gender performativity also intersects with her role as a middlewoman as she explains that "I never told them [her nieces and nephew] to call me dad, although Antonio and Daniela always got confused like that. Because they get excited when they talk to me, so they just say 'Daddy, oh no, Ana.'" Thus, not only do her nieces and nephew see Ana as a parent but also read her gender performance as one related to a father figure.

Despite being a crucial presence in her nieces' and nephew's lives, Ana's role in the family was stripped from her due to the homophobia that Cecil's husband imposed. As Ana explains, "people think that this is a sickness and that it is going to stick to people who live with me . . . and that's what [Cecil's husband] told me, he did not want his daughter near me because I am like this." In a heterosexist and heteronormative society, and in the face of homophobia, Ana's sexuality and gender performativity challenged hegemonic femininity and was seen as morally deviant, to the extent that she was deemed unacceptable for children to be around. In fact, in her study on lesbian Black mothers, Mignon Moore (2011) explains that "society tells women that good mothers are responsible not only for nurturing their children and protecting them from harm, but also for representing a particular standard of heterosexuality . . ." (116). Although Ana fulfilled the gendered role of a nurturing parent, her open lesbian identity and relatively masculine gender performativity simultaneously contradicted good motherhood or parenthood as it challenged heterosexuality and mainstream notions of gendered femininity, ultimately resulting in familial separation.

Moreover, as an undocumented migrant who relied on her family for emotional support and shelter, she suddenly found herself without either. Fortunately, at the time Ana had just entered into a relationship with her partner, Linda, who was open to letting her stay in her two-bedroom apartment. Ana explains how she came to the housing arrangement she now lives in after this familial rupture:

> What came to mind was to live with Linda in her home. I already had a relationship with her but it was new and we barely knew each other . . . but at that time I had no other option and Linda had said yes, so I opted for that because it would have been much more difficult to find a room

for myself . . . when I was living with Cecil and Sergio I only paid around $300 for rent, just to help out and with Linda, I would be paying almost the same, around $350 for rent, but I'm not living in a room by myself, I'm just paying to live in a little space in the living room because Linda lives with her two daughters in one room and it would have been too uncomfortable to stay there with them . . . and she was renting out the other room to some of her friends.

The effects of familial rejection are then not solely emotionally devastating but as an undocumented migrant, being rejected and kicked out by her family meant living without a stable home and in crowded and uncomfortable conditions. Family rejection is thus extremely destabilizing both emotionally and materially. Therefore, we see how the intersecting struggles of being queer and an undocumented immigrant makes navigating family in the United States a complex process. As Lionel Cantu (2009) discusses, the United States may provide somewhat more freedom for undocumented queer immigrants because Ana initially felt that the United States would be an escape from the homophobia within her family in Honduras, but ultimately the safety of undocumented queer immigrants is never guaranteed, and they may experience the same risk and exploitation they were fleeing from to begin with, evident in Ana's experiences once settled in the United States.

Family life for any immigrant is complex and full of unexpected changes. For someone like Ana, whose sexuality and gender performativity has so powerfully determined her family situation, changes can also have long-term impacts. For example, a few months before she was forced to leave Cecil's home, Ana's father died. Although this was emotionally devastating, it also meant she had to work even more to cover his funeral expenses. Ana's relationship with her mother had always been very close, and in Latin America it is not unusual for children to send remittances to their parents (Abrego 2014). However, in the face of her father's death Ana felt even more responsible to ensure that her mother had the necessary funds to survive in Honduras now that there was no primary economic provider. In this context, finding a fast, convenient, and cheap home was urgent for Ana. At the time of the interview, Ana held three different jobs to stay afloat and to send her mother the funds she needed. Ana works as a cook in three different fast-food restaurants, being paid around $10 to $12 an hour in each job. She explains:

Right now, I'm working 82 hours a week. One, to distract myself from the whole situation with Cecil and the other because I have to send my mom $500 a month . . . I always sent her $350 a month but since my dad died I have to send her more money and since Cecil and my other brothers have families of their own and it's already expensive to live here, I'm the only one that usually sends her anything.

Therefore, in a time when Ana needed the most financial and emotional support, she was left alone, forcing her to work herself to such an extreme to both numb herself from the emotional pain but also to make ends meet and support her mother.

Yet, as harmful as this gendered acceptance was for Ana, these gendered norms ease familial acceptance for individuals like Sergio who can fulfill some heteronormative expectations. For example, although Cecil's partner opposed Ana's sexuality, even after he learned of Sergio's gay identity, he did not confront him as he did with Ana. These differences can be explained through a gendered lens. For example, when women are seen solely as individuals entrusted with the responsibility of teaching children moral and cultural knowledge, it becomes extremely difficult to legitimize their motherhood or parental role when a significant part of their identity challenges the societal norm (Acosta 2010; Moore 2011; Menjívar, Abrego, and Schmalzbauer 2016). Men, on the other hand, have different spaces to legitimize their masculinity, whether it be through physical strength, economic mobility, or sexual prowess (Dreby 2010; Menjívar, Abrego, and Schmalzbauer 2016; Zavella 2011). Therefore, queer men can gain familial acceptance if they fulfill some form of masculinity (Cantu 2009). This is evident in Sergio's experience as he explains his current economic situation working in two fast-food restaurants and an adjunct car wash to one of those restaurants. He tends to work sixty hours a week and gets paid around $12 an hour in each job. He explains how this economic situation influences his role as a parent:

> Right now, I'm working well . . . I'm making around twenty dollars an hour between the three jobs.[1] It doesn't bother me when my kids ask "oh, I want this," I mean that's why I work right? . . . I mean it is a lot of money every time we go out, but now I can maybe save $1,500 a month.

Due to this economic situation, Sergio is able to fulfill the hegemonic ideal of masculinity in which he can financially provide for his family, even when he does not fulfill the expectations for heterosexuality (Cantu 2009; Menjívar, Abrego, and Schmalzbauer 2016). Sergio expresses this sentiment clearly when he says, "The family I have is a small family, and they know me and know that regardless of what I do in my private life I will try to be responsible. They know I will comply with what I have to fulfill." Consequently, because

Sergio is able to fulfill different forms of masculinity, as an economic provider, as a responsible individual, and as an independent father, his gay identity is not meticulously examined (Ocampo 2012). As Acosta (2011) and Cantu (2009) explain, "financial and other resources can help facilitate acceptance as the individual receives a prominent role within family or loses the need for acceptance" (Acosta 2011, 68).

Sergio, moreover, is also the biological father of his children. His parental role is not questioned in the same way it was for Ana, who in contrast holds a nonbiological middlewoman status. Much like other queer families with children in which queer individuals lack legal parental rights, Ana's middlewoman status allowed her to create emotional attachment to the children she cared for but at the same time this nonbiological status allowed her parental role to be removed, resulting in a traumatic separation for both Ana and her nieces and nephew (Dreby 2010; Menjívar, Abrego, and Schmalzbauer 2016).

Therefore, just as the external threats of a xenophobic nation-state present challenges for undocumented queer parents, we see that the internal threats of homophobia present similar but somewhat more immediate threats to family. Although immigration laws are destabilizing, they seem to have more structural consequences that are ongoing in a family's trajectory, such as restrictions to low-wage work and the harms of such economic instability on a family's well-being in the long-run. On the other hand, homophobia creates immediate rifts between families as certain queer family members are rejected and stripped of their roles in the family. This internal threat of homophobia is also shaped by unequal gendered dynamics, evident in the ways Ana was immediately rejected while Sergio was able to fulfill other gendered norms and maintain his role in the family.

Potential Spaces of Resistance: Undocumented Queer Parent-Child Relationships

Despite these immense challenges, undocumented queer parents also create spaces of vulnerability that allow them to explore creative solutions and combat the threats of xenophobia and homophobia. In particular, within the context of working-class masculinities, I am arguing that the possibility of being vulnerable and open is a positive and powerful tool to strengthen family relationships and heal from structural systems of oppression (Cantu 2009; Ocampo 2012). The responses that Sergio and Ana provided regarding how they see their sexual and undocumented identities interplay with their parenting reveal the potential for resistance within their families. They both emphasized that being in the United States compared to Honduras, provided more freedom to speak about their sexuality within their parent-child relationships. Sergio expands on how he sees his sexuality unfold within his parenting:

> I feel that [my sexuality] helps because I can talk freely with [my children] and teach them that people's worth is about what they can accomplish, and that living your private life the way you want to is not going to hurt anyone . . . [Also] I feel that [my sexuality] helps because if one of them feels like this . . . they won't have to hide or live [through] depression because they can't do what they want to do. That's why I feel [my sexuality] helps because they will have more freedom to live their lives the way they want to.

Although these parents may experience the harsh realities of being undocumented, they find that they can discuss their sexuality with their children in a safer environment and provide valuable lessons of resistance, while normalizing discussions around the topic. Ana provides another look into these discussions as she describes her conversation with her nieces and nephew when they asked her if she knew about Sergio's new living arrangement with his partner:

> Well I've always been honest . . . [so] when Daniela asked me last year, "Ana, did you know that dad was living with his friend?," I told her "yes" . . . and then Antonio said "it's like you and Linda" . . . [so] they ask me, and I answer, I mean why would I say, "I don't know" . . . when I would be the right person to talk about it?

The fact that these discussions are happening and that both children and parents are comfortable asking and answering questions is a step toward a more inclusive family experience. In these instances, these parents are creating new spaces to normalize and comprehend the challenges they face as a family and establish stronger ties with each other despite the external and internal threats they face.

Parent-child relationships within undocumented queer families also disrupt traditional power dynamics and reveal the potential for emotional growth and healing within their families. Migration sometimes creates an environment in which the power dynamics between parent and child are renegotiated. For instance, children in immigrant families sometimes hold relative power to exert their interests (Dreby 2010). As undocumented migrants in the United States, these parents must often rely on their U.S.-born or acculturated children to function as language brokers and help them navigate through institutions

(Dreby 2010). Similarly, as queer individuals, when these parents come out to their children, they undergo a process in which power is inverted as a parent's role in the family may depend on children's acceptance or rejection. But it is precisely because power dynamics have been inverted that undocumented queer families create spaces to potentially heal from the challenges of migration, xenophobia, and homophobia, as Kasandra reveals that:

> I didn't get to finally know my dad until he came out to me. I remember that day. It was in eighth grade I think, and we were driving to Universal Studios, just me and my dad . . . And then on the way there in the middle of traffic he told me he was gay and started to cry. That was the first time I ever saw my dad cry. I mean I didn't care that he was gay . . . But what was really painful . . . was just the fact that he was so scared that I wouldn't love him anymore because he was gay. Ever since then our relationship has definitely grown a lot more. We talk about everything and he tries to be as open and honest with me as he can.

Kasandra reveals that the imbalance in power in these parent-child relationships may be untraditional because power dynamics have been inverted and parents are placed in positions in which they must be vulnerable with their children. In those moments, in the best-case scenario, children begin to comprehend their parents' experiences in a different perspective. More importantly, because parents have been vulnerable with their children, the parent-child relationship that was once harmed by other obstacles such as migration and undocumented status begin to heal as there is now a greater commitment to each other. In other words, because undocumented queer families are placed in positions that force them to be flexible and negotiate traditional power dynamics, they have the potential to create unique spaces of vulnerability that allow parents and children to heal the wounds of being an undocumented queer parent in a xenophobic, homophobic, and heteronormative society.

Kasandra goes on to suggest that the growth that occurred within her own family after her father expressed vulnerability also created a new space to interact with his children differently:

> I can see the difference even now when I see how my dad treats my siblings. He's still working a lot of jobs, but he actively makes time to play with them and talk to them . . . he's always telling them that he's there for them and that they can tell him anything . . . I am really happy that he's in a better place and that my siblings get to enjoy that with him.

Such interactions demonstrate the valuable and transformative ways in which these undocumented and queer parents learn to navigate simultaneous systems of oppression to create powerful spaces of resilience, growth, and resistance.

In particular, I find that for this family, sexuality was a defining factor that shaped these parent-child relationships. For instance, it was Sergio's act of coming out that first destabilized the traditional power dynamics between parent and child and allowed for a space of vulnerability to occur between both Kasandra and Sergio, to see each other through a lens in a way that they had not done so before. In doing so, Kasandra and Sergio also began to heal other wounds created by the external threat of xenophobia. For example, they minimized the distance and emotional rift that existed between father and daughter due to Sergio's need to consistently be confined to low-wage labor as an undocumented worker. Kasandra describes this reality in the following way:

> I mean, we can't change what happens outside our family. We can't immediately change laws, we can't immediately change homophobic people. But we can change how we go about doing family and if we have that, if we at least have that, then what the outside world throws at you seems less difficult to confront.

In this sense, when there are already so many threats to undocumented queer families, including deportation and homophobia, it is meaningful and consequential for these parents and families to transform their family unit in such a way that they can support each other. For this family, this was done through discussions of sexuality which proved to function as a source of solidarity and strength that then allowed them to establish stronger family foundations and tackle other wounds brought about by other systems of oppression in an anti-immigrant context. I find that this is the case because although immigration laws are detrimental to undocumented families, for queer undocumented families the threat of homophobia may have more immediate consequences and thus they are more likely to deal with the immediate internal threat as a family unit.

Conclusion

Sergio, Ana, and Kasandra's experiences with family have been confusing, painful, but also fruitful, revealing just how crucial it is to delve deeper into the realities of undocumented queer parents and their families. These experiences have not only demonstrated the unique and innovative ways these individuals reshape their family but have also exposed some of the ways in which they experience family in unequal ways, specifically through gendered acceptance as queer parents. The external threat of xenophobia and internal threat of homophobia have manifested in their households, at times separating and dismantling relationships. Yet the family has been able to navigate these threats by allowing children and parents to reshape their relationships in such a way that the act of being vulnerable, open, and honest creates a potential path to heal from these oppressive experiences.

As research on undocumented and mixed-status Latina/o/x families grows, it is important to keep in mind that this community is complex and heterogeneous. Moreover, as social movements continue to fight for both queer and undocumented immigrant rights, we must ensure that in these fights we do not overlook the most vulnerable of our communities by glorifying narratives and depictions of deserving and proper groups for the sake of social acceptance and legal protection. Instead, we must actively work to transform public consciousness and dismantle hegemonic cultural norms that harm and exclude our families (Bernstein and Reimann 2001; Dreby 2015; Menjívar, Abrego, and Schmalzbauer 2016). Thus, as individuals with the resources to educate, we must make our lived experiences heard. As undocumented scholars, immigration scholars, and family scholars, we have a responsibility to expose inequalities, highlight forms of resistance, and work to eliminate oppression within our families.

NOTE

1. Sergio does not actually earn $20 an hour in a single job, he means that if he were to combine his hourly wage between his three jobs, he would make around $20 an hour. His official hourly wage is $12 an hour in each job.

REFERENCES

Abrego, Leisy J. 2014. *Sacrificing Families: Navigating Laws, Labor, and Love across Borders*. Stanford, CA: Stanford University Press.

Abrego, Leisy J. 2016. "Illegality as a Source of Solidarity and Tension in Latino Families." *Journal of Latino/Latin American Studies* 8(1): 5–21. https://doi.org/10.18085/1549-9502-8.1.5.

Acosta, Katie. 2010. "'How Could You Do This to Me?': How Lesbian, Bisexual, and Queer Latinas Negotiate Sexual Identity with Their Families." *Black Women, Gender Families* 4(1): 63–85. https://www.jstor.org/stable/10.5406/blacwomegendfami.4.1.0063.

Barumandzadeh, Rozita, Elisabeth Martin-Lebrun, Taghi Barumandzadeh, and Gerard Poussin. 2016. "The Impact of Parental Conflict and the Mitigating Effect of Joint

Custody after Divorce or Separation." *Journal of Divorce and Remarriage* 57(3): 212–23. https://doi.org/10.1080/10502556.2016.1150150.

Bernstein, Mary. 2001. "Gender, Queer Family Politics, and the Limits of Law." In *Queer Families, Queer Politics: Challenging Culture and the State*, edited by Mary Bernstein and Renate Reimann, 420–46. New York: Columbia University Press.

Bernstein, Mary, and Renate Reimann. 2001. "Queer Families and the Politics of Visibility." In *Queer Families, Queer Politics: Challenging Culture and the State*, edited by Mary Bernstein and Renate Reimann, 1–17. New York: Columbia University Press.

Boggis, Terry. 2001. "Affording Our Families: Class Issues in Family Formation." In *Queer Families, Queer Politics: Challenging Culture and the State*, edited by Mary Bernstein and Renate Reimann, 175–81. New York: Columbia University Press.

Butler, Judith. 1990. *Gender Trouble: Feminism and the Subversion of Identity*. New York: Routledge.

Cantu, Lionel. 2009. *The Sexuality of Migration: Border Crossing and Mexican Immigrant Men*. Edited by Nancy A. Naples and Salvador Vidal-Ortiz. New York: New York University Press.

Dalton, Susan E. 2001. "Protecting Our Parent-Child Relationships: Understanding the Strengths and Weaknesses of Second-Parent Adoption." In *Queer Families, Queer Politics: Challenging Culture and the State*, edited by Mary Bernstein and Renate Reimann, 201–20. New York: Columbia University Press.

Dreby, Joanna. 2010. *Divided by Borders: Mexican Migrants and Their Children*. Berkeley: University of California Press.

Dreby, Joanna. 2015. *Everyday Illegal: When Policies Undermine Immigrant Families*. Oakland: University of California Press.

Emery, Robert E. 2002. "Easing the Pain of Divorce for Children: Children's Voices, Causes of Conflict, and Mediation-Comments on Kelly's Resolving Child Custody Disputes." *Virginia Journal of Social Policy and the Law* 10(1): 164–78. https://heinonline.org/HOL/P?h=hein.journals/vajsplw10&i=174.

Golash-Boza, Tanya, and Pierrette Hondagneu-Sotelo. 2013. "Latino Immigrant Men and the Deportation Crisis: A Gendered Racial Removal Program." *Latino Studies* 11(3): 271–92. https://doi.org/10.1057/lst.2013.14.

Menjívar, Cecilia, and Leisy J. Abrego. 2012. "Legal Violence: Immigration Law and the Lives of Central American Immigrants." *American Journal of Sociology* 117(5): 1380–421. https://doi.org/10.1086/663575.

Menjívar, Cecilia, Leisy Abrego, and Leah Schmalzbauer. 2016. *Immigrant Families*. Cambridge: Polity Press.

Moore, Mignon R. 2011. "Lesbian Motherhood and Discourses of Respectability." In *Invisible Families: Gay Identities, Relationships, and Motherhood among Black Women*, 113–52. Berkeley: University of California Press.

Ocampo, Anthony C. 2012. "Making Masculinity: Negotiations of Gender Presentation among Latino Gay Men." *Latino Studies* 10(4): 448–72. https://doi.org/10.1057/lst.2012.37.

Rodriguez, Naomi Glenn-Levin. 2017. *Fragile Families: Foster Care, Immigration, and Citizenship*. Philadelphia: University of Pennsylvania Press.

Rosenfeld, Dana. 2009. "Heteronormativity and Homonormativity as Practical and Moral Resources: The Case of Lesbian and Gay Elders." *Gender and Society* 23(5): 617–38. https://doi.org/10.1177/0891243209341357.

Salih, Sara. 2007. "On Judith Butler and Performativity." In *Sexualities and Communication in Everyday Life: A Reader*, edited by Karen E. Lovaas and Mercilee Jenkins, 55–68. Thousand Oaks, CA: Sage Publications.

Stryker, Susan. 2008. "Transgender History, Homonormativity, and Disciplinarity." *Radical History Review* (100):145–57. https://doi.org/10.1215/01636545-2007-026.

Weston, Kath. 1991. *Families We Choose: Lesbians, Gays, Kinship*. New York: Columbia University Press.

Zavella, Patricia. 2011. *I'm Neither Here nor There: Mexicans' Quotidian Struggles with Migration and Poverty*. Durham, NC: Duke University Press.

Appendix

Keywords

1.5-Generation Immigrant

Individuals who migrate at a young age and have had most of their social, cultural, and educational development in the country they migrated to (Abrego 2011; Gonzales and Chavez 2012). 1.5-generation immigrants have different experiences from first-generation immigrants who migrate to a country as adults, typically enter the workforce rather than educational institutions, and have already developed their social and cultural perspectives in their country of origin (Abrego 2011; Gonzales and Chavez 2012).

Assembly Bill 540 (AB 540)

A 2001 assembly bill that allows California residents to pay in-state tuition at public colleges and universities regardless of their legal status in the United States (Abrego 2008; Gonzales and Chavez 2012). This legislation has made higher education more accessible to undocumented students who would otherwise have to pay out-of-state tuition (Abrego 2008; Gonzales and Chavez 2012). To be eligible for AB 540, individuals must have either three years of full-time attendance at a California high school, adult school, or community college or three years of completed California high school coursework and three years of attendance at a California elementary school, secondary school, or a combination of both (Abrego 2008; UC Admissions 2019). Additionally, individuals must have a high school diploma, GED, associate degree, or have fulfilled the requirements to transfer from a California community college to a UC or CSU campus (UC Admissions 2019). Lastly, individuals who are undocumented must state that they are in the process of adjusting their legal status or will do so when possible (UC Admissions 2019).

Assimilation/Integration/Incorporation
Assimilation is commonly thought of as the process by which minority or immigrant groups adopt the culture, values, and ideologies of a dominant group over time in order to be successfully incorporated or integrated into that society (Gordon 1964). Assimilation is rooted in the notion of minimizing ethnic/racial, cultural, and social differences that shape both that specific ethnic/racial group and society as a whole (Alba and Nee 1997).

California Dream Act
The California Dream Act was passed in 2011 and provides undocumented students with private and state financial aid to attend public colleges and universities in California. In order to qualify for financial aid, undocumented students must graduate from a California high school, have at least three years of attendance in a California school, and be in the process of adjusting their legal status (Gonzales and Chavez 2012).

DREAM Act
The federal Development, Relief, and Education for Alien Minors (DREAM) Act was first introduced in 2001 and was meant to provide a path to citizenship for undocumented migrants who arrived in the United States as children (Gonzales and Chavez 2012; Abrego 2011). The proposed legislation has been under debate for nearly two decades. This legislation would provide conditional access to legal permanent residency and eventually citizenship, if individuals can prove that they arrived in the United States before they were sixteen years old, have at least five years of residence in the United States, have graduated from a two-year college or have studied for at least two years toward a higher degree and/or have served in the U.S. Army for at least two years (Gonzales and Chaves 2012). Recently, the American Dream and Promise Act of 2019 was introduced, and would expand legal status to a much larger group than solely DREAMers, specifically Temporary Protected Status (TPS) and Deferred Enforced Departure (DED) recipients (Gelatt 2019).

DREAMer

The term DREAMer draws from the narratives that were used to challenge the negative depictions of undocumented immigrants in order to justify the federal DREAM Act (Lauby 2016). DREAMer refers to an undocumented individual who arrived in the United States as a child, has been raised and educated in the United States, and is often depicted as a high-achieving student deserving of legal status (Lauby 2016). Authors in this book challenge the DREAMer narrative, which only upholds a few "deserving" undocumented immigrants while excluding and further marginalizing the rest of the undocumented community.

The DREAMer narrative is rooted in notions of "achievement, innocence, meritocracy, individualism, and injustice, which together create the story of the ideal, high-achieving undocumented youth who is unfairly prevented from gaining access to college and pursuing his or her dreams" (Lauby 2016, 376).

NOTE

Joel Sati defines DREAMer in his chapter as:

> The DREAMer, in discourse on immigration, denotes someone who entered this country at a young age, achieves impeccable grades or is otherwise high-achieving professionally, has a lack of accent or otherwise accepts various aspects of American culture, and wholeheartedly believes in the American Dream and its attendant myth of meritocracy. Despite their undocumented status, DREAMers consider themselves part of the American community in every relevant way save papers. In making a claim for immigration reform or for a more piecemeal policy, DREAMers mark themselves as deserving of residency and citizenship.

Illegality

Illegality is commonly thought of as a "juridical status" or a status determined by the state that places an individual outside the law. However, migration scholars have problematized this definition and argued that we should examine illegality as both a product and a condition (De Genova 2002; De Genova 2004; Chavez 2007; Menjívar and Kanstroom 2013). The production of illegality includes the underlying, ongoing processes, laws, and ideologies that exclude or include particular bodies in the state (De

Genova 2002). The condition of illegality is centered on the everyday lived experiences of individuals who are deemed to be outside the law and contend with a sense of deportability or "the possibility of deportation" (De Genova 2002; De Genova 2007, 161).

NOTE

Carolina Valdivia's definition of "illegality" in the literature review section of her chapter in this book is particularly insightful: "As a theoretical concept, illegality moves beyond a purely juridical understanding of an individual's lack of legal immigration status to one that encapsulates both (1) the production of illegality (i.e. the mechanisms and policies that make individuals undocumented and that regulate their movement) and (2) its condition (i.e. migrants' lived experiences) (Abrego 2014, 71; Chavez 2007, 192–95; De Genova 2002, 423; Menjívar and Kanstroom 2013, 5–13)."

Intersectionality

Intersectionality, a term coined by legal scholar Kimberlé Crenshaw, refers to an analytical tool that allows one to examine the complex ways in which the various social identities (race, gender, sexuality, class, age, etc.) of an individual or group are woven together to create overlapping and interconnected systems of oppression for that particular individual or group (Crenshaw 1989, 1991; Collins and Bilge 2016).

Latinx/Chicanx

Latinx and Chicanx are used as gender-neutral terms for Latina/o and Chicana/o. Latinx refers to individuals with Latin American ancestry and first appeared on internet and social media sites in 2014 but is known to have been used by queer communities as early as 2004 (Salinas Jr. and Lozano 2017). Although there are various definitions of who is considered Chicana/o/x, these terms generally refer to U.S.-born individuals with Mexican ancestry. Latinx and Chicanx are meant to be more inclusive by disrupting dominant notions of gender and highlighting the intersectional nature of these communities (Salinas Jr. and Lozano 2017; de Onís 2017). However, the use of "x" in Latinx or Chicanx has been critiqued as potentially symbols of linguistic imperialism because it is argued that it is a U.S.-born Latina/o/x creation that is imposed on recent Latina/o/x migrants, who may not identify with the terms (de Onís 2017).

LGBTQ

LGBTQ is often used to refer to Lesbian, Gay, Bisexual, Transgender, and Queer identities and experiences. However, there are several critiques regarding the depiction of Lesbian, Gay, Bisexual, Transgender, and Queer as a collection of equal, distinct, and "cohesive" identities (Murib 2014, 118). These critiques are rooted in the history of excluding Transgender identities and the issue of conflating sexual identity with gender identity (Murib 2014).

Queer

Queer is a reclamation of a homophobic slur and is often understood to function as an umbrella term for marginalized sexual and gender identities (e.g., lesbian, gay, bisexual, asexual, intersex, transgender) (Mallan 2011). As a theoretical concept, queer opens up discussions to a "wider spectrum of sexual [and gender] nonnormativity" by highlighting the violence experienced by individuals who challenge the binaries of sexuality and gender (Love 2014, 172; Mallan 2011).

REFERENCES

Abrego, Leisy. 2008. "Legitimacy, Social Identity, and the Mobilization of Law: The Effects of Assembly Bill 540 on Undocumented Students in California." *Law and Social Inquiry* 33(3): 709–34. https://www.jstor.org/stable/20108779.

Abrego, Leisy. 2011. "Legal Consciousness of Undocumented Latinos: Fear and Stigma as Barriers to Claims Making for First and 1.5 Generation Immigrants." *Law and Society Review* 45(2): 337–70. https://doi.org/10.1111/j.1540-5893.2011.00435.x.

Alba, Richard, and Victor Nee. 1997. "Rethinking Assimilation Theory for a New Era of Immigration." *International Migration Review* 31 (4): 826–74. Accessed April 22, 2019. http://dx.doi.org/10.1177/019791839703100403.

Chavez, Leo R. 2007. "The Condition of Illegality." *International Migration* 45(3): 192–96. https://escholarship.org/uc/item/6zh533s6.

Collins, Patricia Hill, and Sirma Bilge. 2016. *Intersectionality*. Cambridge: Polity Press.

Crenshaw, Kimberlé Williams. 1989. "Demarginalizing the Intersection of Race and Sex: A Black Feminist Critique of Antidiscrimination Doctrine, Feminist Theory and Antiracist Politics." *University of Chicago Legal Forum* 1989(8): 139–67. https://chicagounbound.uchicago.edu/uclf/vol1989/iss1/8.

Crenshaw, Kimberlé. 1991. "Mapping the Margins: Intersectionality, Identity Politics, and Violence against Women of Color." *Stanford Law Review* 43(6): 1241–1300. https://heinonline.org/HOL/P?h=hein.journals/stflr43&i=1257.

De Genova, Nicholas P. 2002. "Migrant 'Illegality' and Deportability in Everyday Life." *Annual Review of Anthropology* 31: 419–47. https://doi.org/10.1146/annurev.anthro.31.040402.085432.

De Genova, Nicholas. 2004. "The Legal Production of Mexican/Migrant 'Illegality.'" *Latino Studies* 2: 160–85. https://doi.org/10.1057/palgrave.lst.8600085.

de Onís, Catalina (Kathleen). 2017. "What's in an 'x'?: An Exchange about the Politics of 'Latinx.'" *Chiricú Journal: Latina/o Literatures, Arts, and Cultures* 1(2): 78–91. https://muse.jhu.edu/article/664597.

Gelatt, Julia. 2019. "More Than a DREAM (Act), Less Than a Promise." *Migration Policy Institute*, March 2019. https://www.migrationpolicy.org/news/more-dream-act-less-promise.

Gonzales, Roberto G., and Leo R. Chavez. "'Awakening to a Nightmare:' Abjectivity and Illegality in the Lives of Undocumented 1.5-Generation Latino Immigrants in the United States." *Current Anthropology* 53(3): 255–81. https://doi.org/10.1086/665414.

Gordon, Milton. 1964. *Assimilation in American Life*. New York: Oxford University Press.

Lauby, Fanny. 2016. "Leaving the 'Perfect DREAMer' Behind? Narratives and Mobilization in Immigration Reform." *Social Movement Studies* 15(4): 374–87. https://doi.org/10.1080/14742837.2016.1149461.

Love, Heather. 2014. "Queer." In *Postposttranssexual: Key Concepts for a Twenty-First Century Transgender Studies*, edited by Paisley Currah and Susan Stryker. *Transgender Studies Quarterly* 1(1–2): 172–76. https://doi.org/10.1215/23289252-2399938.

Mallan, Kerry M. 2011. "Queer." In *Keywords for Children's Literature*, edited by Philip Nel and Lissa Paul, 186–89. New York: New York University Press.

Menjívar, Cecilia, and Daniel Kanstroom, eds. 2013. *Constructing Illegality in America: Immigrant Experiences, Critiques, and Resistance*. New York: Cambridge University Press.

Murib, Zein. 2014. "LGBT." In *Postposttranssexual: Key Concepts for a Twenty-First Century Transgender Studies*, edited by Paisley Currah and Susan Stryker. *Transgender Studies Quarterly* 1(1–2): 118–20. https://doi.org/10.1215/23289252-2399776.

Salinas, Cristobal, Jr., and Adele Lozano. 2017. "Mapping and Recontextualizing the Evolution of the Term Latinx: An Environmental Scanning in Higher Education." *Journal of Latinos and Education* 1–14. https://doi.org/10.1080/15348431.2017.1390464.

UC Admissions. 2019. "AB 540 Nonresident Tuition Exemption." http://admission.universityofcalifornia.edu/paying-for-uc/tuition-and-cost/ab540/index.html.

Contributors

LEISY J. ABREGO is a professor in the Department of Chicana/o and Central American Studies at UCLA. Her work on Latinx families, Central American migration, and the production of "illegality" centers the role of U.S. immigration laws in contextualizing and determining migrants' well-being. Her scholarship analyzing legal violence, legal consciousness, and "illegality" explores how different subsectors of Latinx immigrants, including undocumented 1.5-generation immigrants, internalize, endure, and resist immigration policies in the United States. Drawing on dozens of interviews over two decades, her peer-reviewed articles and books uncover the multiple and multidimensional consequences of various local, state, and federal immigration practices for undocumented young people. She also dedicates much of her time to supporting and advocating for refugees and immigrants by writing editorials and pro bono expert declarations in asylum cases.

GABRIELLE CABRERA is a PhD student in the Department of Anthropology at Rutgers University. Her dissertation project explores how young undocumented women construct their everyday lives and imagine possible futures without citizenship in an era of continuing anti-immigrant sentiment. Specifically, her project focuses on how young undocumented women conceptualize their political subjectivities, their affective labor, and the ways in which they care for each other and their communities.

GABRIELA GARCIA CRUZ was a grassroots advocate in the immigrant rights movement before transitioning to work in tech, in the arena of Trust and Safety. She served as Board Chair for Faith in Action and is a graduate of the University of San Francisco, where she received her Master of Arts in International Studies. Since her migration to the United States, Gabriela has been driven to understand policies that cause the migration of vulnerable individuals. Through her involvement she became politicized and understood that civic engagement was not only necessary but an important part of her liberation.

LUCÍA LEÓN is a doctoral candidate in Chicana/o Studies at the University of California–Los Angeles. She grew up in Orange County, where she began organizing with undocumented families in the mid-2000s. Her research interests include the production of illegality, racialized illegalities, undocumented young adults, legalization, gender, and sexuality. Her dissertation focuses on an intersectional examination of the consequences of immigration law on the lived experiences of undocumented young adults navigating the marriage-based legalization process.

KATY JOSELINE MALDONADO DOMINGUEZ is a graduate of UCLA, with a double major in Chicana/o Studies and Geography. She is currently a doctoral student in the American Studies Program at Yale University. Her research interests include challenging the homogenization of Latina/o/x student experiences by highlighting the lived academic realities of Central American students. She also examines the complex ways in which Queer Undocumented Latina/o/x parents create and navigate family.

GRECIA MONDRAGÓN is a queer immigrant from Morelos, Mexico. She migrated to the United States at the age of nine and lived most of her life in South-Central Los Angeles. Grecia received her BA in Chicana/o Studies from UCLA in June 2016. She currently works as a case manager and helps youth find educational and employment services throughout Los Angeles. Also, she is a member of a grassroots organization that advocates for and works with Central American refugees.

GABRIELA MONICO was born in El Salvador and immigrated to the United States at the age of sixteen. Upon graduating from high school, she became the first person in her family to attend college. Gabriela received undergraduate degrees in Ethnic and Chicano Studies from the University of California–

Berkeley. At Berkeley, Gabriela's passion for social justice led her to become actively involved with organizations that advocate for immigrant rights, which include Rising Immigrant Scholars through Education and Educators for Fair Consideration. She is currently a paralegal at the Law Office of Helen Lawrence, an immigration law practice with a human rights-based approach located in Oakland, California. In the future, Gabriela hopes to attend law school, and to continue her education with the goal of further engaging in immigrant justice work.

GENEVIEVE NEGRÓN-GONZALES is an associate professor in the School of Education at the University of San Francisco, and affiliate faculty in the MA in Migration Studies program. As a first-generation college student who grew up on the U.S./Mexico border, Dr. Negrón-Gonzales has worked on issues related to immigrant rights, social justice, and educational justice since she was a teenager. Her academic, activist, and community work centers on the way undocumented young people are changing the political and legislative terrain around "illegality" and belonging in this country and the racialized experiences of Latina/o/x students in the educational system. Genevieve has been working with, supporting, and researching undocumented youth for the past fifteen years as a student affairs professional, a researcher, and an activist. Her work seeks to bridge political economy, higher education, and immigration in order to highlight the ways in which migrant illegality is (re)produced through the racialized spaces of higher education within the context of neoliberalism. She is a coauthor of *Encountering Poverty: Thinking and Acting in an Unequal World*.

MARIA LILIANA RAMIREZ is a doctoral student in the Department of Anthropology at the University of California–Irvine where she also completed the Law, Society and Culture emphasis. Prior to UC Irvine, Liliana completed her undergraduate degree in anthropology with a minor in Spanish language and literature at the University of California–Riverside (UCR). There, she participated in UCR's Mellon Mays Undergraduate Fellowship (MMUF) and engaged in research for two years. Under this program, she also participated in the University of Chicago's MMUF Summer Research Training Program, where she began to develop personal experiences with immigration and sexuality into a research interest. Chapter 7, "Beyond Identity: Coming Out as UndocuQueer," of this volume is the product of her undergraduate research project.

JOEL SATI is a PhD Candidate in the Jurisprudence and Social Policy Program at UC Berkeley, and a JD candidate at Yale Law School. His research interests are in law and philosophy—in particular analytical jurisprudence, practical reason, moral philosophy, and social epistemology. He focuses on how noncitizens are excluded from epistemic practices in law, political discourse, and the press. His dissertation project explicates the concept of illegalization, which he defines as the legal-institutional processes that render people illegal by positioning those who are illegalized as less-than-capable knowers in the law. In addition to academic writing, he has written or been otherwise featured in publications such as the *Washington Post*, *Huffington Post*, and the Social Epistemology Research and Reply Collective, among others.

AUDREY SILVESTRE grew up in Los Angeles, California. As a doctoral candidate, her research will explore cultural productions and placemaking in Southeast Los Angeles of queer and feminist punk communities.

CAROLINA VALDIVIA is currently finishing her PhD in Education at Harvard University. She is a recipient of the Ford Foundation Pre-Doctoral Fellowship. Her research interests include immigration, education, family life, and social movements. Her work explores the ways in which illegality impacts the lives of immigrant youth and their families, including their educational trajectories, mental health, and political participation. Carolina will soon join the faculty of UC Irvine as an assistant professor in the Department of Criminology, Law and Society.

Index

AB 130 (Assembly Bill 130) (California), 18n1, 83n4
AB 131 (Assembly Bill 131) (California), 83n4
AB 540 (Assembly Bill 540) (California), 11, 45, 55, 149–50, 235–36
academic counseling, 50; mental health services and, 57–63; validation through, 60–61
academic performance: as cry for help, 54–55; emotional challenges and, 58–59; excellence in, 46; expectations for, 46–47; factors influencing, 62; fear influencing, 47
academic probation: experience of, 48–49, 60–61; factors leading to, 50–57, 62–63; stigma of, 35, 45–47, 63
academic resilience, 45
activism, 1, 6, 15, 27, 41, 186n4; connotations of, 162–64; as daring, 1; for DREAM Act, 37; engagement in, 125; excluded by DREAM Act, 15, 102, 104, 111, 121; forefront of, 36; organizing for, 104; strategies for, 150; by students, 61, 72, 93, 105; sustaining of, 35; of women, 110–11, 113–14, 118; by Zoraida Reyes, 169–70
activists, 25–26, 122–24, 162, 164, 170, 176, 178, 180, 183, 184
adjustment of status petitions (AOS), 195–96, 208n2

adulthood: transition to, 95, 193; western ideas of, 172
Advanced Parole, 195
advocacy, 5, 60–61, 91
agency: resistance and, of queer immigrants, 149; retaining, 155; through storytelling, 81; of women, 112
agricultural: sector, 117; workers, 98
alien (term), 25–26, 32, 42n4, 42n6, 55, 69, 70, 79, 82, 84n11, 119, 128
American Dream, 9, 35–36, 93–96, 98–99, 237
analogical transfer, 28
anti-immigrant: climate, 38, 116, 118, 199; context, 34, 63n1, 110, 230; discourse, 24–25, 34–35; enforcement, 111; groups, 23, 119; policies, 7, 87, 125, 128; sentiment, 82, 146, 241
anxiety, 54–55, 134; depression, stress and, 130, 140; due to fear of deportation, 52, 130, 218; fear and, 127, 134; immigration enforcement creating, 139; for queer immigrants, 158; and schoolwork, 57, 60; under Trump administration, 76, 127, 129, 139, 140–42
Anzaldúa, Gloria, 151, 156, 165, 177
AOS (adjustment of status petitions), 195–96, 208n2
Araujo, Gwen Amber Rose, 177

artivism, 106n5
assemblage: queer praxis of, 148; UndocuQueer movement as, 161–65
Assembly Bill 130 (AB 130) (California), 18n1, 83n4
Assembly Bill 131 (AB 131) (California), 83n4
Assembly Bill 540 (AB 540) (California), 11, 45, 55, 149–50, 235–36
assimilation, 147, 236; symbol of, 78

belonging, 1, 37, 147, 172, 221; articulations of, 89, 90, 99–100, 105, 172, 182, 185; citizenship and, 90; claims of, 92–93, 97; communities created through, 112, 121; conceptions of, 17; as determined by market citizenship, 87–88; developing sense of, 121, 124; excluded from, 116; through human dignity, 123; Indigeneity, human rights and, 90, 101–5; reframing of, 114, 125; social citizenship based on, 106n6; women experience of, 110–12, 124–25
Black Alliance for Just Immigration, 37
Black Lives Matter, 37, 158
border: crossing, 96, 195; deaths at, 175; diversity as, 71, 82–83; between Mexico and the United States, 26, 40, 75, 96, 97, 100, 118–20, 141, 142, 174, 211; militarization of, 17, 175; patrol, 119, 135; as political symbol of nation-states, 23, 101, 111–12, 116, 184; wall, 120; as wound, 165
Boroditsky, Lera, 28
BRIDGE Act, 105n2
Brown, Patricia Leigh, 75–77, 81

Cacho, Lisa, 170–72, 179–80
Cal-Grants, 83n4
California: Assembly Bill 130, 18n1, 45, 71, 81, 83n4; Assembly Bill 131, 45, 71, 81, 83n4; Assembly Bill 540, 11, 45, 54–55, 70, 81, 149–50, 152, 162, 173, 235–36
California Dream Act, 45, 83n4, 93, 149, 152, 236; composition of, 18n1; passing of, 1, 11, 49, 88, 236; prior to, 48–49, 54, 57, 71, 169
Campaign for Citizenship, 114, 115, 122, 123
Cantu, Lionel, 175, 225
capitalism, 40, 82, 99, 147
CAPS (Counseling and Psychological Services), 51, 59

CCA (Corrections Corporation of America), 105n5
Charleston shooting, 158, 166n8
Chinese Exclusion Act, 1882, 90, 105n1
citizenship, 1, 4; battle for, 123; belonging and, 90; conforming to normative, 76; construction of, 184; data on, 69; democracy, inclusion and, 78, 80; democratic, 75; deservingness of, 94–97; diversity, race and, 82; experience shaped by, 8; through gendered framework, 110–12; granting of, 24; higher education access enabled by, 153; Indigeneity, belonging and, 101–5; market, 88–92, 95, 97, 104, 106n6; residency and, for DREAMers, 36; right to, 113; social, 106n6; transnational, 90
civic engagement, 2, 61, 110–12, 114, 115, 242
civic participation, 7, 103–4
civil disobedience, 2, 10, 137, 169, 170–72, 173–74, 176; acts of, 2, 10; participation in, 178–86, 187n20
class, 8, 68, 172–76, 185, 238; middle, 93, 220; working, 168, 213, 217, 227
cognitive structures: metaphor, policy deliberation and, 27–34; undocumented immigrant movements and oppositional, 34–41
Cohen, Cathy, 173
The Collective, 89–105
Combahee River Collective, 173
coming out, 148–49; as act of protest and resistance, 158; emotional challenges of, 155–56; to family, 156–61; normative narrative for, 182; by parents, 221, 223, 229; of the shadows, 150–82; UndocuQueer, 149–50, 152, 153–55, 155–65, 173
commodification, 13, 66, 67, 68, 81, 89, 98, 112
community-building, 122, 125–26
community engagement: connection through, 124–25; social transformation through, 121–23
conditional residency, 196, 208n8
copal incense, 101, 106n12
Corrections Corporation of America (CCA), 105n5
Counseling and Psychological Services (CAPS), 51, 59
counselors, 57–61
counterpolitics, 185

246 Index

courage, 2, 4, 204
coyote (smuggler), 211
Crenshaw, Kimberlé, 238
criminality, 39, 40
criminalization, 16, 174–75; dehumanization and, 146; DREAMer narrative and, 72–73; racialized, 170–71
critical pedagogy, 102–4, 106n13
Cunningham-Parmeter, Kenneth, 26, 30–32; economic sanctuary and, 40; opposition to, 41

DACA. *See* Deferred Action for Childhood Arrivals
daily routine: importance of, 129; influenced by Trump administration, 132–38
Decena, Carlos, 175
Declaration of Independence, 1776 (U.S.), 90
De Colores Queer Orange County, 169–70
Deferred Action for Childhood Arrivals (DACA), 4, 6, 88, 91, 131, 143n3, 147; eligibility for, 143n4; Obama administration announcing, 143n1; opportunities created by, 40; passing of, 49, 88, 91, 195; prior to, 57; recipients of, 12, 70, 88–89, 127, 131–33, 139, 150; renewal applications, 38; as result of activism, 93; rights protected by, 36; support for, 147; termination of, 17, 79, 105n3, 129, 138–39, 142, 143n3; Trump administration threatening, 10, 79, 142; uncertainty surrounding, 127, 137, 138
De Genova, Nicholas, 112–13, 121
dehumanization, 35, 39, 98; cost of, 102; criminalization and, 146
Deleuze, Gilles, 148, 161
democracy, 77, 78, 80
Department of Homeland Security (DHS), 16, 38, 120, 128
deportability, 15, 213–14
deportation, 6, 16, 35, 118; aftermath of, 131; experiences of, 99; fear of, 52, 121–22, 130–31, 136; increase in, 128–29, 191; of parents, 214; preventive measures taken surrounding, 135–36; procedural fairness as, 31; protections from, 10; as punishment, 37; ramifications of, 137–38; relief from, 143n1; risk of, 17; threat of, 81, 132; trauma from, 141–42

depression, 2, 46, 50–51; anxiety, stress and, 130; experience of, 140–42; impact of, 62
deservingness, 10, 16, 80, 82, 89, 171; advocacy and, 91; of citizenship, 94–97; claims of, 105; heterosexuality and, 147; immigration status and, 99
Development, Relief, and Education for Alien Minors (DREAM Act), 9, 15, 25, 84n12, 186n17, 236; activism for, 37; market citizenship and, 104; necessary conditions of, 38; as priority, 42n3; proposals for, 81; proposals similar to, 105n2; rise of, 111; support for, 87–89, 94, 147
DHS (Department of Homeland Security), 16, 38, 120, 128
diversity, 8; as capital, 80; initiatives for, 73–75, 76; manifestation of, 70; multiculturalism and, 66–67; race, citizenship and, 82; statistics on, 69; transformation of institutions through, 83
docility, 82
DREAM Act. *See* Development, Relief, and Education for Alien Minors
DREAM and Promise Act, 105n2
DREAMer narrative, 8–14, 37, 67; criminalization and, 72–73; defining of, 45; resistance to, 16; unrealistic standards set by, 46, 56
DREAMers, 150, 237; amenability toward helping, 38; image of, 79–80; as neoliberal subject, 171; residency and citizenship for, 36; standing up for, 42n3
Dream Loan Program, 75
Durbin, Dick, 94

economic sanctuary, 40
emergency plans, creation of, 136
emotional challenges, 226; academic performance and, 58–59; of coming out, 155–56; within writing process, 3–4
empiricism, 41n2
employment: lack of, 51; obstacles in accessing, 148
empowerment, 124, 212
English language, 7, 81
esoteric condition, 42n7
exceptionalism, 111
exclusion: dangers of, 16; experience of, 89, 98; tools of, 31; of trans community, 171

Index 247

Executive Order 13768, 17
exploitation, 89; of bodies, 13; of labor, 97

Familia: Trans Queer Liberation Movement, 178, 186n16
family: coming out to, 156–61; as heteronormative, 147, 213; homophobia influence on, 217, 221–27, 231; immigration enforcement changing dynamics within, 142; immigration law threatening, 218–20, 230; influence of, 62; intimacy and acceptance within, 156–57, 159; Mexico-U.S. border dividing, 142; preventive measures taken by, 134; ramifications of deportation for, 137–38; relationships within, 159–60, 212; reunification of, 53, 147, 192–93, 197; separation of, 17, 29, 46, 52–54, 117–19, 124, 133, 213–14; stressors related to, 51–52
fear, 4; academic performance influenced by, 47; anxiety and, 127, 134; of authorities, 117–19; of cancer, 50–51; of deportation, 52, 121–22, 130–31, 136; of dismissal from college, 56; of going home, homophobia as, 151; justifying, 113; as mechanism of control, 115–18; navigating, 112; of rejection, 156; trauma, love and, 154; Trump administration cultivating, 136–42; women experiencing, 118–20
femininity, 215, 224
Ferguson, Roderick A., 173
Fiat Lux Program (FLP), 75
financial aid, 4; importance of, 54; as state-based, 45
flag: American, 78; Gay and Trans Pride, 183–84, 185; Mexican, 120
foreignness, 26
freedom: lack of, 113; practice of, 106n13; of sexuality, 175; unfinished project of, 174
Freire, Paulo, 106n13
funding, for undocumented student programs, 73–75, 84n8

gay panic, 176
gender, 68, 146, 172–73; dating and parenthood experience based on, 192; performativity, 215–16, 223–27; sexuality, immigration laws and, 174–77; violence and, 117
generation immigrant, 235

GEO Group, 105n5
GetEQUAL, 178
globalization, 40, 113; economic inequality and, 67; sexuality and, 151
governance, through gendered framework, 110–12
governmentality, 112
grassroots organizations, 5, 114
grassroots organizing, 10, 124–25
green card, 194, 196

health insurance, 3; access to, 141; lack of, 51, 60
heteronormativity, 173, 186n6, 213
heteropatriarchy, 71, 82, 172
heterosexuality, 147, 226–27
higher education, 9; access to, 1, 4, 5, 16; barriers to, 7; broader problems in, 67; citizenship enabling access to, 153; cost of, 11; desire for, 61; dismissal from, 56; obstacles to obtaining, 149; possibilities for, 11; pressures of, 15; pursuing, 111, 137; as safe haven, 77–78, 82–83
HIV/AIDS, 172, 186n5
homogeneity, 90–91
homophobia, 15, 71, 153, 160–61; family influenced by, 217, 221–27, 231; as fear of going home, 151; resistance to, 212
hope, 61
Hope Act, 105n2
human cognition, 27
human dignity, 123
humanization, 100
human rights: entitlement to, 99; murals representing, 100; violations of, 96

ICE (Immigration and Customs Enforcement), 16, 123, 168, 178–79
IDEAS (Improving Dreams, Equality, Access and Success), 48, 54, 60–61
identity, 67; American, 10; developing, 125; DREAMer, 15; expression of, on social media, 162; homogenous, 150; illegality, resistance and, 14; Indigenous, 90, 102; institutional values connected to, 80; intersections of, 41; national, 23; protection of, 63n1; queer immigrants formation of, 156, 163–64; social, 80; trauma, violence and, 81–83; of women, 110

identity politics, 148, 161, 164
Illegal Immigration Reform and Immigrant Responsibility Act, 1996 (IIRIRA), 175, 191
illegality, 1, 237–38; complicated web of, 4; contemporary production of, 8; through gendered framework, 110–12; identity, resistance and, 14; immigration policies and, 16–18; narrative of, 125; production and condition of, 129; prolonged experience of, 191–92
immigrant rights, 5, 143
immigrant rights movement, 14–15, 37, 102
Immigration Act, 1965, 174–75
Immigration and Customs Enforcement (ICE), 16, 82, 123, 168, 178–79
Immigration and Nationality Act, 1952, 146–47
Immigration and Nationality Act, 1965, 91, 147, 191, 194, 208n3
Immigration and Naturalization Service, 16
immigration enforcement, 3, 16, 79, 111, 117, 125, 175; anxiety associated with, 139; at the border, 17; as draconian, 87, 120; family dynamics changed from, 140–42; impact of, 132–33; increase in, 38, 87, 127–30, 135–40, 143
immigration laws: decisions shaped by, 207–8; as detrimental to families, 230; family threatened by, 218–20; gender, sexuality and, 174–77; pathways to legalization limited by, 193–94; vulnerability to, 201
immigration policies, 15; based on sexuality, 146; as draconian, 87; Executive Order 13768, 17; illegality and, 16–18; shift in, 105n1, 129, 136; of US, 2; Zero Tolerance Border Policy, 17
immigration provision, 34
immigration raids: in Postville, Iowa, 39; rumors of, 133–35
immigration reform, 23–24; challenging, 105; politics of, 25
Immigration Reform and Control Act, 1968 (IRCA), 5, 6–7, 175
immigration regime, 29
immigration relief, 139
immigration status (legal status), 3, 17; constant reminder of, 120; debate surrounding, 23; deservingness and, 99; health care access blocked by, 51; ignoring, 116; lack of, 24; mental health influenced by, 130; motivation inhibited by, 55; positions on, 8; sexuality and, 153; shame produced by, 155; as stressor, 47
Improving Dreams, Equality, Access and Success (IDEAS), 48, 54, 60–61
inclusion: citizenship, democracy and, 78, 80; initiatives for, 71, 76
Indigeneity, 90, 101–5
inequality, 5, 80; concealing, 71; experiences of, 98; exposing, 231; globalization and economic, 67
influence: on daily routine by Trump administration, 132–38; of fear on academic performance, 47; of homophobia on family, 217, 221–27, 231; on mental health, immigration status, 130
injustice, 5, 70, 237
in-state tuition, 7, 45; as benefit, 71; qualifying for, 54
internment camps, 91
intersectionality, 151, 174, 238
intervention programs, 61–62
intimacy: acceptance and, within family, 151, 156–57, 159, 220, 223; relationships and, 153, 154, 190, 204–5, 207–8; violent notions of, 156–59
IRCA (Immigration Reform and Control Act), 5, 6–7, 175
isolation: secrecy and, 118; shame and, 55–57

joy, 177, 180–86
jurisprudence of otherness, 41

knowledge producers, 6, 8, 152

labor, exploitation of, 89, 97–98, 104, 105, 225
labor-power, 112
language, 80; familiarity through, 182; metaphor and, 25
Latinx/Chicanx, 238
leadership: fostering, 74; promoting, 122
legal assistance, 137
legal consciousness framework, 196–97
legalization, 5; eligibility for, 7; immigration laws limiting pathways to, 193–94; through marriage, 191–208; mass program for, 6
legal permanent residents (LPRS), 196, 208n8

legal status, 213–14
legitimacy: of marriage, 195; perceptions of, 25; of policy proposals, 31
Lesbian, Gay, Bisexual, Transgender, and Queer (LGBTQ), 150, 239
Leticia A legal case, 1
LGBTQ (Lesbian, Gay, Bisexual, Transgender, and Queer) movement, 150, 239
love, 126, 177, 212; marriage for, compared to papers, 191–92, 197–208; trauma, fear and, 154
LPRS (legal permanent residents), 196, 208n8

marginalization, 34, 37; experiences of, 67, 89; rejection and, 102; as self-perceived, 96; of trans community, 176
marriage: legalization through, 191–208; legitimacy of, 195; for love compared to papers, 191–92, 197–208; social and cultural expectations of, 197–99
Marxism, 112
masculinity, 215, 226
master status, 148–49
McCarran-Walter Act, 1952, 174
meaning-making competitions, 30–31
MEChA (El Movimiento Estudiantil Chicano de Aztlan), 169
media, 94; presentations and misrepresentations by, 178–80
mental health, 50–51; academic counseling and services for, 57–63; immigration status influence on, 130; importance of, 129; under Trump administration, 15; of young adults, 138–42
mentoring, 60–61; of undocumented students, 1–2
meritocracy, 82, 149; beliefs surrounding, 104; claims of, 93; myth of, 10, 94; questioning, 96; rejection of, 97
meritocratic ethos, 9
Mesoamerica, 101
mestizo, 101
meta-endorsement, 36
metaphor, 41n1; cognitive structures, policy deliberation and, 27–34; conceptual, 27, 41; of "illegals," 24; language and, 25
methodological intervention, 11–14

Mexican Revolution, 106n14
Mexico-U.S. border, 96; in 2014, 118–20; families divided by, 142; militarization of, 97
middlewomen, 219–20
Migration Policy Institute, 88
militarization, of Mexico-U.S. border, 97
minority, 70
Minutemen Project, 119
mixed-status families, 51, 92, 99, 134, 137–38, 212, 214, 218, 231
morality, 34
El Movimiento Estudiantil Chicano de Aztlan (MEChA), 169
multiculturalism, 76; celebrations of, 69; diversity and, 67
murals: creation of, 105n5; human rights represented in, 100

Napolitano, Janet, 67, 71–75, 79–82
nationalism, 78, 147
National Origins Act, 1924, 90
national security, 79, 115
National Summit on Undocumented Students conference, 71–74
nativism, 87; critique of, 90; history of, 105n1
naturalization, 15, 33, 196
Naturalization Law, 1790, 90
neoliberal conditionality, 68
neoliberalism, 67, 80
New York Times, 75–79
nonprofit organizations, 9, 92
normativity: claims to, 35; perceived, 32

Obama, Barack, 10, 123
Obama administration, 16; DACA announced by, 143n1; immigration memo from, 128; protection of, 138
objectivity, 29
Office of Refugee Resettlement, 17
1.5-Generation Immigrant, 235
Operation Wetback, 143n2
oppression, 103–4, 231
Orange County Congregation Community Organization (OCCCO), 114, 122
Orange County Dream Team, 169
Orlando shooting, 157–58, 165n6

Page Law, 1875, 174
parents: coming out by, 229; deportation of, 214; experiences of, 212; queer, 214–16, 221–23; relationships between child and, 227–31
Pedagogy of the Oppressed (Freire), 106n13
People Improving Communities through Organizing (PICO), 114, 123
Plyler v. Doe, 5, 7, 91
police brutality, 124
policy change, 10
policy deliberation, metaphor, cognitive structures and, 27–34
policy recommendations, 13
political engagement, 35
positionality, 37, 42n7, 93–94, 114, 129
poverty, 76, 98
power, 80; imbalance of, 34; of nation-state, 112; privilege, capitalism and, 99; resistance and, 123; sense of, for women, 122; traditional dynamics of, 228–29; unequal dynamics of, 153
preference system, 91
presidential election, 2016 (U.S.), 67, 87, 136, 138
prison companies, 105n5
privatization, 75
privilege, power, capitalism and, 99
procedural fairness, 24–27; corruption of, 30; deliberations about, 32; push for greater, 41; as summary deportation, 31
procrastination, 46
productivity, 9
professors, lack of sensitivity from, 55
protest, 2; coming out as act of resistance and, 158; participation in, 106n6; planning of, 72; as privilege, 122; for transgender rights, 168, 177–85
public safety, 79
public transportation, 3

queer immigrants: agency and resistance of, 149; anxiety for, 158; as banned, 146–47; identity formation of, 156, 163–64; as parents, 214–16, 221–23
queer of color critique, 173–74
queer praxis, 148
queer temporality, 172–74
queer theory, 173, 239

race, 15, 37, 68, 146, 172–76; diversity, citizenship and, 82; role of, in political analysis, 38
racial hierarchy, 147
racial identification, 67
racial profiling, 113
racism, 70–71, 81–82, 153; cost of, 102; impact of, 103
Raza Studies, 103–4
recognition, humanization and, 100
reductionist identity politics, 148
reflexivity, 106n9
Refugee Act, 174
regularization, 24
relationships: between child and parents, 227–31; with counselors, 60–61; with family members, 159–60, 212; between researcher and participant, 94; solidarity and building of, 125
reorganization, engagement in, 75
research: ethics, 12–13; guidance through process of, 2; reflexive model of, 132; on undocumented life, 1–2
residency, 34; categorization of, 69–70; citizenship and, for DREAMers, 36; renewal of, 196; young adults process for permanent, 194–96
resiliency, 76, 126; academic, 45; resistance and, 112; stories of, 67; violence, trauma and, 149
resistance, 67; agency and, of queer immigrants, 149; coming out as act of protest and, 158; to DREAMer narrative, 16; forms of, 231; to homophobia and xenophobia, 212; identity, illegality and, 14; illuminating, 125; power and, 123; process of, 113; of queer community, 148; resiliency and, 112; sound and dance as forms of, 180–85; struggles of, 184
resourcefulness, 9, 80
resource shell, 82
respectability, 40, 170–71
restrictionist policy, 29
reunification, of family, 53, 147, 192–93, 197
Reyes, Zoraida, 168–70, 173–80, 186n17
rhizome, Deleuzian concept of, 148–49, 155–65
rightlessness, 170, 172–74
Roque-Ramirez, Horacio, 175

Index 251

sacrifice, 9, 16, 37, 56, 111, 185
San Diego Minutemen (SDMM), 119
scholarships, 57, 83n4
SDOP (San Diego Organizing Project), 114
secrecy, isolation and, 118
secret doors, 200–201
self-acceptance, 126
self-recognition, 148
self-worth, 114
Senate Bill 699, 91
separation: of family, 17, 29, 46, 52–54, 117–19, 124, 133, 213–14; fear of, 15
sexism, 71
sexual assault, 117, 178
sexuality, 68, 172–73, 208n1; freedom of, 175; function of, 216; gender, immigration laws and, 174–77; globalization and, 151; immigration policies based on, 146; immigration status and, 153; parent-child relationships shaped by, 230
SFOP (San Francisco Organizing Project), 114, 121–22
shame, 4, 47, 49–50, 61, 101; immigration status producing, 155; isolation and, 55–57
shootings, 157–58, 165n6, 166n8
slavery, 172, 177
smuggler (coyote), 211
social becoming, 121
social change: advocating for, 61; creating, 113, 121
social death, 172, 176
social incorporation, 95
socialization, 39
social justice, 37, 61, 83, 104, 243
social media: coverage of undocumented immigrants on, 111; identity expressed on, 162, 238; immigration raids announced on, 133–34, 142
social security number, 5, 117–18, 201
social transformation: through community engagement, 121–23; empowerment and, 124; tools needed for, 126
socioeconomic conditions, 6, 97
socioeconomic mobility, 91
solidarity, 122, 125, 184–85, 230
sonic spatial entitlement, 171–72, 181, 183–85
Southern Poverty Law Center (SPLC), 119
spatial entitlement, 181

SPLC (Southern Poverty Law Center), 119
state of emergency, 112–15, 220
status adjustment, 34, 190–96, 198–200, 203, 208n2, 208n5, 236
stereotypes, 45, 92
stigma, of academic probation, 35, 45–46, 63
storytelling, 81, 125
stress: anti-immigration policies producing, 143; anxiety, depression and, 130; within family, 51–52, 130
structural barriers, 3, 5, 9, 74, 95, 96, 104, 120, 150, 152, 153, 169, 175–77, 201, 213, 218–19, 227
suboptimization, tolerable, 68
SUCCEED Act, 105n2
Sugarman v. Dougal, 26
SUS (Services for Undocumented Students), 66, 83, 84n8

TPS (Temporary Protected Status), 17
trade, international, 40
transformational multiplicities, 163
transgender undocumented immigrants, 170–71; marginalization of, 176; recognizing humanity of, 180–85; rights for, 168, 177–85
transphobia, 71, 172, 184
trauma, 50–51, 59–60, 76; of deportation experience, 141–42; love, fear and, 154; overcoming, 116; violence, identity and, 81–83; violence, resiliency and, 149
Trump, Donald: anti-immigrant views of, 38; DACA ended by, 17, 105n3; election of, 13, 218; inauguration of, 208n9; notion of criminal by, 39
Trump administration, 127; anti-immigration policies of, 7, 128; DACA threatened by, 10; daily routine of young adults influenced by, 132–38; deportation frequency under, 141; fear cultivated by, 136–42; immigrant rights movement fractured by, 38; immigration policy and enforcement in era of, 129; mental health under, 15
truth: conception of, 41n2; regimes of, 69

UCOP (University of California Office of the President), 71–75
Undocumented Legal Service Center, 74–75
Undocumented Student Coalition, 74

Undocumented Youth Movement, 11, 16, 47, 88–89, 93, 105, 111, 150

UndocuQueer, 173; as assemblage, 161–65; political visibility through, 149–50

United States (U.S.): Department of Homeland Security, 16; discrimination by government of, 17; history of Latinos in, 103; immigration policies of, 2. *See also specific legislation*

United States Citizenship and Immigration Services (USCIS), 34, 38, 190, 208nn6–7

University of California Office of the President (UCOP), 71–75

U.S. *See* United States

USCIS (United States Citizenship and Immigration Services), 34, 38, 190, 208nn6–7

violence, 71–72, 76; of gangs, 96–97; gender and, 117; legal, 213; as legal, 111; replacing, with song, 183; sharing stories of, 184; subjection to, 77; trauma, identity and, 81–83; trauma, resiliency and, 149

visas, 24, 70, 174, 195; limit to, 34

vulnerability, 115, 212; anxiety and, 76; to deportation, 141–42; heightened, 128; to immigration law, 201; space created by, 229–30

War on Terror, 16

women: activism of, 111, 113; belonging experienced by, 124–25; economic opportunities for, 116–17; fear experienced by, 118–20; identity of, 110; political agency of, 112; sense of power for, 122

writing process: dynamics within, 2–3; emotional challenges within, 3–4

xenophobia, 39, 153–55, 172, 212, 217–18, 221–23; resistance to, 212; as threat, 227–31

Zapata, Emiliano, 104, 106n14

Zero Tolerance Border Policy, 17